Law, Science, Liberalism Way of Warfare

C000143096

Founded and rooted in Enlightenment values, the United States is caught between two conflicting imperatives when it comes to war: achieving perfect security through the annihilation of threats; and a requirement to conduct itself in a liberal and humane manner. In order to reconcile these clashing requirements, the United States has often turned to its scientists and laboratories to find strategies and weapons that are both decisive and humane. In effect, a modern faith in science and technology to overcome life's problems has been utilized to create a distinctly "American way of warfare." Carvin and Williams provide a framework to understand the successes and failures of the United States in the wars it has fought since the days of the early republic through to the War on Terror. The first book of its kind to combine a study of technology, law and liberalism in American warfare, *Law, Science, Liberalism and the American Way of Warfare: The Quest for Humanity in Conflict* makes a unique interdisciplinary contribution to the study of contemporary American security policy.

STEPHANIE CARVIN is fellow at the Centre for International Policy Studies at the Graduate School of Public and International Affairs, University of Ottawa. While a Visiting Scholar at the George Washington University Law School, Dr. Carvin served as an expert advisor to the US Department of Defense Law of War Working Group. She is the author of *Prisoners of America's Wars: From the Early Republic to Guantanamo* (2010).

MICHAEL JOHN WILLIAMS is Director of the Program in International Relations at New York University. He is the author of *The Good War: NATO and the Liberal Conscience in Afghanistan* (2011), *NATO, Security and Risk Management: From Kosovo to Kandahar* (2008), and co-editor of the critically acclaimed *Power in World Politics* (2007). He has consulted extensively on strategic aspects of international relations for policy-makers in the United States and Europe.

Law, Science, Liberalism and the American Way of Warfare

The Quest for Humanity in Conflict

STEPHANIE CARVIN AND MICHAEL
JOHN WILLIAMS

CAMBRIDGE
UNIVERSITY PRESS

CAMBRIDGE
UNIVERSITY PRESS

University Printing House, Cambridge CB2 8BS, United Kingdom

Cambridge University Press is part of the University of Cambridge.

It furthers the University's mission by disseminating knowledge in the pursuit of education, learning and research at the highest international levels of excellence.

www.cambridge.org
Information on this title: www.cambridge.org/9781107637139

© Stephanie Carvin and Michael John Williams 2015

This publication is in copyright. Subject to statutory exception and to the provisions of relevant collective licensing agreements, no reproduction of any part may take place without the written permission of Cambridge University Press.

First published 2015

Printed in the United Kingdom by Clays, St Ives plc

A catalogue record for this publication is available from the British Library

ISBN 978-1-107-06717-2 Hardback
ISBN 978-1-107-63713-9 Paperback

Cambridge University Press has no responsibility for the persistence or accuracy of URLs for external or third-party internet websites referred to in this publication, and does not guarantee that any content on such websites is, or will remain, accurate or appropriate.

Contents

Prologue

In the dark of night the vehicle bumped along the uneven ground as it sped along in the outskirts of Khasaf in Northwestern Yemen. Small rocks and debris hit the undercarriage of the truck, making for an irregular beat against the steady hum of the engine. Al-Awlaki peered out the window, surveying the dark desert landscape. He cocked his head upwards, toward the sky – it was empty.

Al-Awlaki was pushed back in his seat, bouncing up and down as the truck raced over a large rut in the road. Next to him sat the young blogger Samir Khan, the co-editor the English-language Al Qaeda web magazine, *Inspire*. Traveling at night was often the best defense against observation and al-Awlaki had good reason to avoid detection. At 40, al-Awlaki, relatively unknown outside of intelligence and specialist circles, had become a household name after President Barack Obama placed him on the CIA capture or kill list in April 2010. As the head of Al Qaeda in the Arabian Peninsula he used his flawless English to inspire global jihadism against America and her allies and now he had become a major target for the United States.

It is not clear why the men decided to travel together, rather than separately, but it would prove a costly mistake. Al-Awlaki may have thought he was safe, having recently relocated within Yemen and basing himself in the tribal region outside Sana'a where the writ of the government was nearly non-existent at the best of times. Given that the Yemeni forces were focused on battling anti-government demonstrators he may have felt that his presence would go unnoticed. Al-Awlaki was likely aware that he was being tracked – after all he had escaped an attempt against his life earlier that year. Indeed, US intelligence assets and local informants had been tracking him day in and day out since the previous September. In the days leading up to the strike, locals had seen American "planes" patrolling Marib. It was only a matter of time before al-Awlaki would walk into an American strike.

The time would be the night of Friday, September 30. Far above al-Awlaki silent killers were on the hunt for the terrorist. The whir from the propeller blades was deceivingly quiet, more reminiscent of a child's toy plane than deadly multi-million dollar weapons. These "planes" looked, in the words of Peter Singer in *Wired for War* (2009), more like a "flying meat fork" with downward-sloping tail wings and bulbous head. At 27 feet long and weighing 1,130 pounds they are by far one of the more small-scale weapons in the US arsenal, but their size and design defy a deadly predilection.

Originally intended for observation – the front of the craft houses "the ball," which shields two variable aperture TV cameras for day and night vision as well as a synthetic aperture radar to allow the drone to see through clouds, dust, haze and smoke – the Predator drone is now fitted with laser-guided Hellfire missiles. Running on a remote-split system, the drone flies out of a military base that is physically close to the target, but the pilot and sensor operator are located some 7,500 miles away in the United States. Although the precise details of the system are classified, soldiers can supposedly read a license plate from 2 miles up in the air.

Fatefully, al-Awlaki, the man who tried to inspire "lone wolf" terrorism – the ideal of individual sacrifice as a suicide bomber for the wider jihad – was killed by an unmanned weapon system. With the short press of a button by an operator sitting safe and secure in the American southwest, the Hellfire missiles rocketed away from the underside of the drone in an enormous roar of smoke and noise. The missiles hurled themselves down with precision toward the "painted" target, the laser guidance from the Predator ensuring they reached their destination with accuracy that World War II bomber pilots could only dream about. Al-Awlaki and his associates may never have known what hit them.

The Predator is the embodiment of the scientific way of war – the Western and, undoubtedly, American attempt to make war ordered and predictable. It is a synthesis of Western attempts to deliver a decided, discriminate and quick victory on the field of battle with the latest in scientific and technological developments. In the ongoing campaign against radical Islamist terrorism in South Asia, parts of the Middle East and Africa, US drones are working with astonishing results and challenging implications. In the case of al-Awlaki, the technology was used to eliminate a terrorist suspect who espoused violent rhetoric but whose material role in supporting terrorism is questionable. Additionally al-Awlaki was also a US citizen, with the rights guaranteed to all US citizens, including due process. And even if he was not an American citizen, given the self-proclaimed "universality" of American human rights, surely such acts are problematic for America's liberal conscience. The al-Awlaki case, and the use of drones, which professionals know as unmanned aerial systems (UAS) or unmanned aerial vehicles (UAV), presents a rather problematic moral dilemma for the United States: What tactics may it legitimately employ against those individuals and objects it deems a threat? In a "war on terror" are those threats all legitimate targets, or is the United States obliged to employ a criminal law framework, where suspects are to be put on trial in a court of law?

If the United States were not a liberal country, if it were a dictatorship, these questions would not be of importance. But because the United States is a country rooted in the rule of law with a belief in inviolable human rights, this issue is of paramount importance deserving careful reflection and contemplation. The complications and challenges that arise from this current state of affairs are the subject of this book – why and how did the United States develop a uniquely American way of warfare that attempts to utilize science and law to wage war within the acceptable norms of liberalism? Why does this American way of warfare work resoundingly well in some conflicts, but fails terribly to secure victory in others?

Introduction

Between annihilation and restraint

If we are to learn from the past then history must first be understood on its own terms. One general point worth emphasizing [is], namely that each society and culture tends to have a unique view of warfare which affects how they fight and as a result how they may be beaten.

Adrian Goldsworthy, *The Fall of Carthage*

Since its foundation as a republic in the eighteenth century, the United States has faced two broad imperatives: to be an example of liberty to the world and to maintain this role and protect itself by achieving absolute security. How the United States tries to balance these imperatives and the resulting tensions, particularly when it is engaged in armed conflict or perceives an immediate threat, is the purpose of this book.

We argue that the United States has often relied on science, especially applied science, to reconcile these two ends. As Auguste Comte wrote, "from science comes prevision, from prevision comes control."[1] Taking this maxim to heart, science has been seen as the key to controlling war, allowing the United States to achieve overwhelming and quick military victories, which are nevertheless relatively humane and worthy of its core liberal values. This is a reflection of America's Enlightenment roots, with its faith in rationality and science to solve complex problems through understanding the natural world.

Improving war fighting is, of course, something that many, if not most, political units have sought to do in modern times. However, there are two aspects that make the American experience unique. First, it has the manpower, resources and the capability to develop technologies

---

[1] Ian T. King, *Social Science and Complexity: The Scientific Foundations* (Huntington, NY: Nova Science Publishers, 2000), p. 20.

that have allowed it to have the most powerful and advanced army on the planet. In terms of military technology, it is unrivaled.

But second, as a liberal country, this ability to develop technology and apply it to warfare is tempered by certain political imperatives and limitations. Other attempts to perfect war in history, notably "total war" by Nazi Germany, have been done in an illiberal manner, sacrificing basic freedoms and many of the established international customs of war. The United States, however, has typically remained inside a liberal framework when it comes to the waging of war. While it cannot be denied that the United States has frequently gone to war in the name of liberal values (and that those conflicts have been waged with determination and harshness), those liberal values, and the checks and balances those values saw built into the American political process, ensure that a "total war" mindset cannot take root. It is these two factors that make the American experience unique and its prowess and engagement in the world worthy of consideration.

Yet, historically, the systematic application of science to warfare has often resulted in more brutality rather than less. Although the application of science to war was often intended as a way to find quicker, more direct paths to battle and to a decisive, humane outcome, the outcome has frequently been the opposite – and sometimes horrifically so. During World War I technology helped to prolong the conflict. The tactics employed by the generals had not kept pace with industrial achievements, and developments in technology caused the war to drag on in stalemate, rather than result in overwhelming victory. Further, the deployment of technology saw the gruesome deaths of millions on the battlefield. For example, although chemical weapons were touted as the superweapon that would quickly and easily bring an end to the bloodshed, the deaths and injuries to thousands on the battlefield quickly put this belief to rest.

Yet, in the face of what might be considered some damning evidence, the belief that scientific solutions could reconcile the demand for quick and clean wars continued throughout the twentieth century and today, especially in the United States. Why?

Achieving rapid victory is believed to be especially important in modern-day democratic systems where the will of the people can be fickle, especially in protracted conflicts. Academic scholarship has traditionally argued that a democratically elected leader must account for the fact that the public will weigh the costs of war against the benefits.[2] Yet, studies have indicated that the public tends not to make complex cost–benefit calculations. Instead, Adam Berinsky argues that when policy elites are united the public tends to give politicians leeway to war, but when elites are in conflict, public support for the war also tends to split, constraining policy options.[3] When the public is behind an elite-supported war, democracies can be very war-prone.[4] The common denominator nevertheless remains that in a pluralistic, democratic society the government is ultimately more constrained than in a dictatorship. The dictator can fight a war of duration with far less concern for public sentiment or the criticism of other elites. Democracies, when they choose to go to war, are therefore governed by an overriding logic to pursue a strategy in war that makes the most of the means available to achieve a decisive and overwhelming victory as quickly as possible.[5] The United States has been particularly influenced by this political reality.

Further, the American understanding of war falls into a Western tradition, defined most succinctly by Clausewitz, as "an act of force to compel our enemy to do our will."[6] The Dutch jurist Hugo Grotius conceived of war as "the condition of those contending by force as such" where force equates to "armed force." War, importantly for Grotius, was a condition, not a competition, striking at the heart of Cicero's concept of war as "a contending by force."[7] A little more nuance might add that war is the collective use of force by an actor to

[2] Jack Levy, "Domestic Politics and War," *The Journal of Interdisciplinary History*, Vol. 18, No. 4 (Spring 1988), 653–673; Sigmund Scott Gartner, "The Multiple Effect of Casualties on Public Support for War: An Experimental Approach," *American Political Science Review*, Vol. 102, No. 1 (January 2008), 95–106; T. Clifton Morgan and Sally Howard Campbell, "Domestic Structure, Decisional Constraints and War: So Why Kant Democracies Fight?, *Journal of Conflict Resolution*, Vol. 35, No. 2 (June 1991), 187–211.

[3] Adam J. Berinsky, "Assuming the Costs of War: Events, Elites and American Public Support," *Journal of Politics*, Vol. 69, No. 4 (November 2007), 975–997.

[4] Edward D. Mansfield and Jack Snyder, "Democratization and the Danger of War," *International Security*, Vol. 20, No. 1 (Summer 1995), 5–38.

[5] David A. Lake, "Power Pacifists: Democratic States and War," *American Political Science Review*, Vol. 86, No. 1 (March 1986), 24–37.

[6] Carl von Clausewitz, *On War* (Michael Howard and Peter Paret, trans.) (London: Random House, 1993), p. 83.

[7] Quincy Wright, *A Study of War* (Chicago: University of Chicago Press, 1942), pp. 5–6.

achieve a specific goal.[8] Quincy Wright, in his 1942 *A Study of War*, explicitly adds a legal dimension drawing on a long tradition of law in war. Wright wrote that, "war is seen to be a state of law and a form of conflict involving a high degree of legal equality, of hostility, and of violence in the relations of organized human groups, or, more simply, the legal condition which equally permits two or more hostile groups to carry on a conflict by armed force."[9] Wars can be fought between two or more states, but wars can also be fought within a state (civil war) and between a state and a non-state/sub-state group challenging the authority of the state through the use of organized violence (guerrilla war/insurgency). War is an exception from regular politics and is possessed of a singular focus.

Western warring is often an extension of the idea of state politics, rather than a mere effort to obtain territory, personal status, wealth or revenge. Western militaries put a high premium on individualism. Within open democratic societies the military is subject to criticism and civilian complaint that may improve, rather than erode, war-making ability. The idea of annihilation, of head-to-head battle that destroys the enemy, seems a particularly Western concept largely unfamiliar to the ritualistic fighting and emphasis on deception and attrition found outside Europe. Westerners, in short, long ago saw war as a method of doing what politics cannot, and thus are willing to obliterate rather than check or humiliate any who stand in their way.[10]

Although war is a continuation of politics through exceptional means, it is, for Hedley Bull, one of the accepted "institutions" of the "Anarchical Society."[11] That is to say it is an accepted activity in world politics that is defined by both norms and laws mutually agreed upon by states in the international system. Bull's conception of war is the Western model, and the anarchical society he postulates is one based on Western norms that have been imposed on the rest of the world. The sole goal of war in the Western model is to win. The pursuit of war for any other reason than victory is antithetical to the concept

---

[8] See also: Lawrence Freedman (ed.), "General Introduction," in *War* (Oxford: Oxford University Press, 1994), p. 1.

[9] Wright, *Study of War*, p. 7.

[10] Victor Davis Hanson, *Why the West has Won: Nine Landmark Battles in the Brutal History of Western Victory* (New York: Faber and Faber, 2001), p. 20.

[11] Hedley Bull, *The Anarchical Society* (New York: Columbia University Press, 1977).

of *raison d'état*, which is an essential part of the modern state.[12] War is therefore perceived as an explicitly political and conscious act, rather than a cultural expression or existential action. In the Western world, historically, the ultimate aim of war is the imposition of one's will over the will of one's opponent.

Culture and the ways of warfare

With this background, we can see that the modern military culture of the United States is directly shaped by the imperative of decisive victory and the narrative myths of the military's role in the building of the United States since the establishment of the republic in 1776. And as one might expect, American military culture is extremely important in how the United States wages war. This study is focused on the American way of warfare, which must be defined separately from "warfare." Warfare, as Christopher Coker notes, "has no battles, has no heroes, and no memorials. It is without strategic or tactical innovation."[13] War on the other hand is a political act. Recalling Clausewitz war can be understood as the implementation of force to achieve a political objective that cannot be settled by non-violent means due to a failure of normal politics and diplomacy between states. Warfare over time evolved into what today is recognized as war.

How a country wages war reflects "who" that country is and we believe that how America wages war is understood through the prism of culture. But what do we mean by "American military culture"? Although scholars often write as if a country were possessed of one, singular and unified foreign policy culture, this is not adequate to capture the complexity of modern societies. We conceptualize culture as a "tool kit" of practices. This approach is heavily influenced by sociology, rather than the positivist approaches within much international relations (IR) scholarship. Within sociology there has been less of a focus on separating culture as practice (behavior) and culture as ideas. Within the study of international relations, in particular within the US academy, there has been an effort to separate behavior

---

[12] Antoine Bousquet, *The Scientific Way of Warfare: Order and Chaos on the Battlefields of Modernity* (London: Hurst, 2009).

[13] Christopher Coker, *Warrior Geeks: How 21st Century Technology is Changing the Way we Fight and Think about War* (Oxford: Oxford University Press, 2013), p. 41.

and ideas so that culture may be conceptualized as an intervening variable to explain behavior rather than being behavior.[14] We find this approach problematic for two reasons. First, as Jeremy Black rightly points out, "model based approaches that emphasize apparently scientific analysis, and that are designed to demonstrate universal laws" are insufficient because they "focus on a limited and readily defined group of conflicts and military systems."[15] Such approaches are more about developing theory than they are about understanding reality – we are interested in reality not theory.

Studies equating culture explicitly with values fail to explain why certain cultural practices endure even when the values that promoted the development of a culture change. Take modern-day northern Europe as an example of this. Across northern Europe today religion is largely absent from life, with 48 percent of EU citizens identifying themselves as atheists.[16] Even those that identify with a religion tend not to actually "practice" their faith in the traditional fashion of church attendance. Nonetheless, the Protestant work ethic identified by Max Weber remains rooted in northern European societies. Scholars equating culture directly with values (either within IR or sociology) have

---

[14] David Elkins and Richard Simeon, "A Cause in Search of Its Effect, or What Does Political Culture Explain?" *Comparative Politics*, Vol. 11, No. 2 (1979), 127–145; Colin S. Gray, "National Style in Strategy: The American Example," *International Security*, Vol. 6, No. 2 (Fall 1981); David R. Jones, "Soviet Strategic Culture," in Carl G. Jacobsen (ed.), *Strategic Power: USA/USSR* (New York: St. Martin's Press, 1990), pp. 35–49; Bradley S. Klein, "Hegemony and Strategic Culture: American Power Projection and Alliance Defence Politics," *Review of International Studies*, Vol. 14, No. 2 (April 1988), 133–148; Andrew M. Pettigrew, "On Studying Organizational Cultures," *Administrative Science Quarterly*, Vol. 24, No. 4 (Dec. 1979); Richard Pipes, "Why the Soviet Union Thinks It Could Fight and Win a Nuclear War," *Quadrant*, Vol. 21, No. 9 (Sept. 1977); Howard Schuman and Michael Johnson, "Attitudes and Behavior," *Annual Review of Sociology*, Vol. 2 (1976), available at: www.annualreviews. org/doi/abs/10.1146/annurev.so.02.080176.001113; Jack Snyder "The Soviet Strategic Culture: Implications for Limited Nuclear Options," RAND 1977, available at: www.rand.org/content/dam/rand/pubs/reports/2005/R2154.pdf and "Anarchy and Culture: Insights from the Anthropology of War," *International Organization*, Vol. 56, No. 1 (Winter 2002), available at: http://ir. rochelleterman.com/sites/default/files/snyder%202002.pdf (all accessed July 1, 2014).

[15] Jeremy Black, *War and the Cultural Turn* (Cambridge: Polity, 2012), p. 19.

[16] Eurobarometer 225, "Social Values, Science and Technology." June 2005. Available at: http://ec.europa.eu/public_opinion/archives/ebs/ebs_225_report_en.pdf (accessed on December 31, 2012).

no way to explain this phenomenon. The example of northern Europe and the endurance of the Protestant work ethic offers clear evidence that values and culture are not directly linked to each other, and that conceiving of culture as an ideational variable that impacts behavior is as lacking in explanatory power as approaches equating behavior with culture. We therefore find the approach to culture as "practice" developed by Ann Swindler more convincing than the pseudo science of political "science" and we utilize her approach to inform our historical inquiry.

Ann Swindler's conceptualization of culture as a "tool kit" composed of "symbols, stories, rituals and world views" from which actors choose familiar pathways applied in new ways to solve new problems is a more suitable framework for analysis. From this tool kit, "strategies of action" – a persistent ordering of action over time – are constructed.[17] In this sense, culture does not define the ends of action; instead it provides the components that are used to construct strategies of action. These strategies may continue to exist, long after the values that once shaped them have withered away or evolved. As Remi Hajjar argues, this approach to culture differs from functionalist and other approaches to culture in that it "includes a contested, fragmented and coherent, and contradictory and complementary nature, which bears postmodern qualities."[18] Culture in this study is both "enabling" and "constraining."[19] Using culture as an analytical device in such a manner allows us to avoid the determinist and Orientalist approach to culture and warfare evident in other studies of warfare. This is idiographic, and, like Patrick Porter, we argue against the neo-realist idea of "strategic man" where culture has no explanatory role – but concurrently we reject the cultural determinism embodied within much of the political science scholarship on culture.[20] Most notably, practice theory allows

[17] Ann Swindler, "Culture in Action: Symbols and Strategies," *American Sociological Review*, Vol. 51, No. 2 (April 1986), 273–286.

[18] Remi M. Hajjar, "Emergent Postmodern US Military Culture," *Armed Forces & Society*, Vol. 40, No. 2 (January 2014), p. 119. See also: David Harvey, *The Condition of Postmodernity: An Enquiry into the Origins of Cultural Change* (Cambridge: Blackwell, 1989); Amy Zalmon, "Waging the First Postmodern War," *World Policy Journal*, Vol. 33, No. 3 (Winter 2006).

[19] Japonica Brown-Saracino and Amin Ghaziani, "The Constraints of Culture: Evidence from the Chicago Dyke-March," *Cultural Sociology*, Vol. 3, No. 1 (March 2009), 55.

[20] Patrick Porter, *Military Orientalism: Eastern War Through Western Eyes* (Oxford: Oxford University Press, 2013), p. 19.

us to understand how a Western tradition of warfare has endured despite substantial breaks over prolonged periods of time in Western history, and how it has come to influence the American understanding and practice of warfare.

Although we argue that military culture is an important variable in how the United States wages war, it is vital to remember that it is civilian policy-makers that set the framework within which military doctrine is composed. While these civilian policy-makers do not determine the specifics of military doctrine, they do set the parameters within which such discussion occurs, especially when it comes to limits on the military through the imposition of strategic-level policy and constraints on spending. As Elizabeth Kier argues, "the interaction between the constraints set in the domestic political arena and the military's organizational culture shapes the choice between offensive and defensive military doctrines."[21]

To understand why a military behaves in a certain fashion, one must analyze the basic assumptions, symbols, stories and formal knowledge that make up the shared collective understanding of the organization, more commonly referred to as culture. And one must look at the various ways in which the different cultures of practice embodied in different communities ultimately affect foreign policy and strategy. Therefore, to understand the contemporary American way of warfare, one must understand that the culture of the American military is not the sole determinant of how the United States fights wars. We believe that one must augment an argument that focuses only on military culture as the primary variable determining tactics and strategy on the ground in combat operations. Otherwise, such an approach is too simplifying to properly understand how the United States fights modern wars and in particular *why* it fights them in a specific manner.

Colin Kahl utilized this approach in his essay titled "In the Crossfire or the Crosshairs?" that tackled the tough question of US military conduct and civilian casualties in Iraq in the war that started in 2003.[22] Kahl argued against the belief that the US military purposefully and routinely violated the norms and laws of non-combatant immunity.

---

[21] Elizabeth Kier, *Imagining War: French and British Military Doctrine between the Wars* (Princeton: Princeton University Press, 1997), p. 21.

[22] Colin H. Kahl, "In the Crossfire or the Crosshairs? Norms, Civilian Casualties and US Conduct in Iraq," *International Security*, Vol. 32, No. 1 (Summer 2007), 7–46.

Kahl believes, like us, that the problem lies in a paradox within US military culture between annihilation and restraint and the overwhelming application of force within lawful means.[23] Kahl does not explore, however, except in the most cursory detail, the impact of America's liberal political culture on the military, nor does he examine the role that civilians play in influencing, and setting the parameters for, military action.[24]

Thus a more nuanced account of American military culture, and its interaction with the dominant political culture of liberalism and the strategic culture of American policy elites, is necessary to develop a more complete picture of the "annihilation–restraint" paradox than explicated by Kahl. To understand how America has fought wars, and especially how America fights wars today, one must view the process as an interaction between civilian and military parts of government.

Key terms

Before continuing further, it is important to explain just what we mean when we invoke some of the key terms used in this book – liberalism, annihilation, restraint and science.

Liberalism and law

For the purpose of this book, liberalism is understood to be a multi-faceted doctrine that embraces free-marketers, social egalitarians, social reformers and those who seek to spread democracy abroad. Providing a precise definition of liberalism is a challenge, particularly in the case of the United States where it may be used to identify laissez-faire economic policies or to hurl a political insult at a candidate deemed as promoting a "nanny state." However, there are certain characteristics of liberalism that are shared among its many varieties and may be discussed. First and foremost, liberals detest tyranny and embrace individual rights such as freedom of speech, freedom of movement and the right to an elected government, property rights and equality before the law. It is a doctrine that loves and cherishes life, but will endorse the resort to force in order to protect liberal values and/or particular way of existence.

[23] Kahl, "In the Crossfire or the Crosshairs?", p. 6. [24] *Ibid.*, pp. 38–39.

Liberalism lies at the foundation of the American Republic and its Enlightenment origins: the embrace of democratic values, individualism and freedom within the framework of the rule of law. As we argue in this book, this philosophical outlook has played a crucial role in the reasoning as to why Americans resort to military force, in shaping the way Americans have fought war and how they generally regard the phenomenon. Although many outside the United States regard the nation as militaristic with an oversized army, the truth is that in line with their liberal values Americans have historically mistrusted their armed forces.

Since the earliest days of the American Revolution, the United States has declared itself to be a nation of laws, including natural law, and holding "a decent respect for the opinions of mankind." If its revolution was to be legitimate, it had to be respected internationally and fought within the framework of the understood behavior of civilized states. The Founding Fathers believed that the United States must adhere to those liberal Enlightenment values through which it was claiming it had a right to exist. Naturally, this included those restraints on warfare understood as customary.

US engagement with restraints on the use of force, however, went beyond pragmatism. Consistent with liberalism is the idea that enlightened law can help improve the overall condition of humankind. As such, it is to no great surprise that the United States found itself spearheading or participating in many of the great international legal initiatives of the nineteenth century, particularly when it came to warfare. Whether it was producing the first written military manual on the laws of war in 1863 (General Orders 100, also known as the Lieber Code) or its drive to establish an international court through which disputes between states might be settled peacefully (at the 1899 Hague Conference), America has frequently and eagerly worked to develop restraints on warfare consistent with its liberal values since the mid-nineteenth century.[25]

Annihilation

In this work annihilation should be understood as the ability to force one's opponent into full, unconditional surrender, or to eliminate them

---

[25] See Stephanie Carvin, *Prisoners of America's Wars: From the Early Republic to Guantanamo* (New York: Columbia University Press, 2010), especially Chapter 2.

entirely. However, rather than an illiberal doctrine, annihilation in the American context is seen as derived from a need to achieve perfect security as a young, liberal republic established itself on the world stage: If the United States was to shine as a beacon of enlightenment and democratic values, it had to be secure from all threats. This led to an expansionist tendency, legitimated in the American mind through the concept of "Manifest Destiny," that contributed to the expulsion of all European powers from nearly all of North America, as well as the extermination of indigenous peoples. The resulting condition, American dominance of North America with largely friendly and/or weak neighbors to the north, south and (eventually) West, led to an American belief in "perfect" security and a larger trend in the American way of warfare to eliminate completely the enemy.

The United States was not accustomed to endemic war, as was the case in Europe as a result of various wars that destroyed the territories of European states prior to, and after, the establishment of the modern state system in 1648. Without the pressure to negotiate peace before achieving objectives, the United States came to see "total victory" as the only form of "victory" in what is reminiscent of the Greek way of war where conflict ultimately came down to a single, decisive battle, resulting in a clear win/loss distinction.

Restraint

Restraint, on the other hand, is the flipside of a liberal Enlightenment coin; if the American Republic truly embodied liberal values, it had to act the part. In other words, it had to be seen as conducting itself within the boundaries of civilized society. The unjustified and unrestricted slaughter of other peoples was not permissible. This was the case at least regarding conflict with other Western nations. Even if justification for harsh and brutal action was not particularly difficult to articulate in the eighteenth and nineteenth centuries (as wars with the Native Americans illustrate), the liberal love of life and the rule of law mandated that certain procedures must be followed when it came to conflict with others in the "civilized" Western world. War was allowed, but liberalism dictated that war must be rule-governed.

Thus, while the US military is driven by an overriding sense of urgency to achieve a quick, decisive victory, it finds itself restrained by the liberal values of the nation, including the rule of law. Achieving this balance is the ideal American way of war, evolved from the Western way of war. There is an innate respect for life and human rights that undeniably informs the American way of warfare. If this were not the case then in the wars most recently waged the United States could have simply razed entire villages when members of the community attacked US targets, drones would not be an issue, nor would the prison at Guantanamo Bay provoke such domestic outrage among a large sector of the electorate.

Science (and technology)

Whenever the world's most powerful military chooses to fight it is always confronted with the challenge of doing so in a way that balances its desire to vanquish its opponents with its liberal values, understandings and expectations. There is a long, recurrent struggle between annihilation and restraint within American strategic culture: a struggle between the desire for victory and the necessity of upholding the very Enlightenment values that form the crux of the American experience. For much of America's history, the solution to this dilemma has been to turn to science and technology.

With its emphasis on rationality and truth seeking, we understand "science" and the scientific tradition as an Enlightenment value that plays a key role in the way Americans have fought and continue to fight wars. For the purpose of this book, science should be understood as a systematic activity that seeks to build and organize knowledge about the natural world. Those who engage in the "scientific method" typically form hypotheses and predictions and generate explanations that are testable and may be replicated. In this sense, science should be understood as the pursuit of knowledge, and that knowledge itself. Science is about understanding, but it is also about control. If we understand how the world works through science – then it is possible to manipulate the world.

Technology is applied science – and it is understood as such here. Perhaps more than any other nation, Americans have embraced science and technology as a way to find solutions to its most challenging problems, including those posed by war. In particular, Americans have turned to technology to simultaneously develop the most lethal, most precise and often most humane weapons possible. And, as the argument in this book will suggest, the belief that technology has been able to achieve such weapons has played a key part in the willingness of Americans to use force, and in forming their perceptions of legitimacy/ illegitimacy on the battlefield.

Critical explanations

But how was this belief in law developing in an era of ever increasingly deadly weapons? Michael N. Schmitt has written on the relationship between technology and law, exploring how technology and international law influenced one another. He suggests that there are reasons to be optimistic (that there are increases in precision in weaponry that allow for more humane results, consistent with the rules of war), but he also notes that technology poses serious implications for how the laws of war are applied and developed. To compensate for their lack of high-tech weaponry (and the normative expectations that accompany them), low-tech belligerents and non-state actors are increasingly rejecting international legal norms as they try to compensate for their asymmetrical status. Schmitt is concerned that improvements in precision are creating unrealistic expectations in terms of preventing casualties in war on the part of humanitarian actors. As such these increasingly "unrealistic expectations" will be rejected by militaries as failing to balance military necessity and humanitarian concern that lie at the historical heart of the laws of war. Essentially, technology is placing two different but equally significant pressures on the laws of war.[26]

Yet others believe that attaining balance between military necessity and humanitarian principles, especially in the light of modern weapons technology, is not actually the key problem. As Chris Jochnick and Roger Normand argue, "despite noble rhetoric to the contrary, the laws of war have been formulated deliberately to privilege military necessity at the cost of humanitarian values" and "through law, violence has been legitimized."[27] In other words, the United States has strategically used law to help it wage war, not to restrain it. The idea

---

[26] Michael N. Schmitt, "War, Technology, and International Humanitarian Law," Program on Humanitarian Policy and Conflict Research, Occasional Paper Series, No. 4 (2005).

[27] Chris Jochnick and Roger Normand, "The Legitimation of Violence: A Critical History of the Laws of War," *Harvard International Law Journal*, Vol. 35, No. 1 (1994) and "The Legitimation of Violence: A Critical Analysis of the Gulf War," *Harvard International Law Journal*, Vol. 35, No. 2 (1994).

that there is difficulty achieving a balance is therefore false as both military goals and the laws of war are really two sides of the same coin. Nathaniel Berman takes a similar stance, suggesting that law has not opposed war, but helped to construct and facilitate it "through the establishment of a separate legal sphere immunizing some organized violence from normal legal sanction," privileging certain forms of violence at the expense of others.[28] Thomas W. Smith examines these concerns, paying specific attention to how technology and law have come together to confer legitimacy on military action. While technology has dramatically curbed immediate civilian casualties, "the law sanctions infrastructural campaigns that harm long-term public health and human rights."[29] Yet the massive destruction that results from Western, particularly American, warfare is legitimized through law. As he sees it:

Hi-tech states can defend hugely destructive, essentially unopposed, aerial bombardment by citing the authority of seemingly secular and universal legal standards. The growing gap between hi- and low-tech means may exacerbate the inequalities in moral capital as well, as the sheer barbarism of "pre-modern" violence committed by ethnic communities or atavistic warlords makes the methods employed by hi-tech warriors seem all the more clean and legal by contrast.[30]

These criticisms by Jochnick and Normand, Berman and Smith may be said to come from "Critical Legal Studies" (CLS), which contend, "law reflects and reproduces inequalities in national and international society." Further, rather than protecting individuals and individual rights, CLS scholars argue that international legal institutions "are molded to serve the interests of dominant states."[31] Smith notes that the law is full of biases toward high-tech nations as a "machete is more likely to be criminalized than a nuclear holocaust."[32] Smith also looks at the 1991 Gulf War, arguing that although

[28] Nathaniel Berman, "Privileging Combat? Contemporary Conflict and the Legal Construction of War," *Columbia Journal of Transnational Law*, Vol. 43 (2004–2005), 1–71.

[29] Thomas W. Smith, "The New Law of War: Legitimizing Hi-Tech and Infrastructural Violence," *International Studies Quarterly*, Vol. 46 (2002), 355–374.

[30] *Ibid.*, p. 371.   [31] *Ibid.*, p. 355, fn. 1 and p. 357.   [32] *Ibid.*, p. 359.

the Coalition hewed more or less to humanitarian law, the destruction [in Iraq] was enormous. The WHO/UNICEF mission to Iraq in March 1991 found electrical supplies cut, drinking water poisoned, environmental controls collapsed, public sanitation deteriorated. Child nutrition was dire, there were shortages of vaccines, drugs and medical supplies, and a proliferation of water-borne disease.[33]

From this view it is important to note that these activities were not excessive violence outside the norms of civilized behavior. Rather, everything the United States did was within the laws of war. In effect, high-tech states, particularly the United States, use law to sharpen their swords – not blunt them. As Smith argues, "*Bellum Americanum* is cloaked in the stylized language of the law ... it also oversimplifies and even actively obscures the moral choices involved in aerial bombing."[34]

There can be no doubt that much of what drives America's adherence to the law is that it is a tool that helps states fight better. Essentially, it is a valuable resource that provides guidance and, as CLS scholars point out, legitimacy for actions that would otherwise be considered murder. These CLS arguments, however, are made as a critique of the laws of war generally, rather than trying to understand how law and technology have historically interplayed in and helped to shape American warfare. Further, we contend that these views are overly cynical – that the desire to wage humane wars in the American tradition is genuine, and directly stems from the liberal Enlightenment origins of the nation. While there is clearly a strategic element in how the United States wages what is sometimes called "lawfare," to suggest that it only adheres to the law because it affords a distinct advantage that, in effect, hoodwinks both humanitarians and the international community, is mistaken.

A century of annihilation and restraint

Although this book will briefly review the Western way of warfare in its entirety, and the development of the American branch of Western warfare since the 1700s, it primarily focuses on recent history, that of the twentieth and twenty-first centuries. Therefore, we observe that the American inclination to utilize technology as applied science and law to wage warfare is evident in four distinct periods over the past century.

[33] *Ibid.*, p. 365.   [34] *Ibid.*, p. 369.

First, during the "Great War" America aimed at developing technology that would give the United States "superweapons" – overwhelming force that it could use to stun and defeat its enemies. Ironically, we can understand this phase as coming out of an American liberal belief that war was an aberration; war was an "evil" and when necessary it should be fought as viciously as possible in order to end the violence quickly. This desire was one of the reasons the United States experimented with chemical weapons during World War I and, ultimately, dropped two atomic bombs on Japan in 1945 to end World War II.

The Nuclear Age, however, led to new military strategies, away from overwhelming force to a more limited notion of war. Total war was seen as too dangerous – engaging was seen as inevitably leading to the use of nuclear weapons and the destruction of great swathes of the planet. Although it was an era overshadowed by "the bomb," it also became the age of guerrilla and proxy war as the superpowers found other ways to confront each other around the globe. Further, the idea of "flexible response" required conventional forces that could respond to crises in a way that did not involve a mushroom cloud. Here too, science played an important role in the quest to find new ways of fighting. Although the United States would go on to develop the hydrogen bomb during this period, McNamara and his "whiz kids" attempted to apply the scientific insights of cybernetics and "systems analysis" to guerrilla warfare in Vietnam. It was also the era that began to experiment with new weapons systems and sensors that would lay the groundwork for future conventional weapons.

The third period falls during the immediate aftermath of Vietnam, when the United States and its armed forces were shaken by the bloody and protracted conflict. It would never, and perhaps could never, again fight a war that required the mass conscription of its youth to be sent overseas. After years of fighting insurgents in the jungles of Vietnam, the armed forces desired a return to that which they considered to be "real" war – preparing for conventional conflict in Europe, even if the possibility of such a conflict was remote. Largely abandoning the lessons of counterinsurgency and guerrilla warfare, the armed forces desired to return to preparing for modes of warfare where they could use overwhelming military force in order to rapidly achieve victory on the battlefield. As such, in this third phase, emphasis was placed on developing light, high-tech weaponry and soldiers that could be rapidly deployed around the world. Developments in computer and communication technology promised a vision of the future where the US armed forces could eliminate Clausewitzian friction and achieve perfect information and, therefore, dominance on the battlefield. Armed with the latest precision-guided weapons, American soldiers would be able to fight wars, while ensuring that they were both discriminate and proportionate in their fighting. Technology promised clean, perfect wars fought entirely within the laws of war with few (if any) casualties. In short, science promised the perfect liberal war, placing the use of overwhelming forces in perfect symmetry with the laws of war. It was a promise that seemed to be fulfilled by the 1991 Gulf War.

This promise, however, was revealed to be false with the onset of the War on Terror in 2001 and the subsequent 2003 invasion of Iraq. Science and technology may have been able to deliver the fastest ground invasion in the history of warfare, but it did not, and could not, solve the difficult and complex political and cultural problems on the ground. As post-invasion Iraq descended into chaos, the low numbers of US troops sent by the George W. Bush Administration were unable to contain the chaos as a civil and ethnic war erupted. Rapid military dominance resulted in a tactical victory in the first battle, but soon after the shortcomings of the "new American way of warfare" became evident. Furthermore, in response to the spiraling security levels in Iraq the US military applied its "overwhelming force" mentality to a civil war and insurgency that saw the US armed forces lose the support of civilians as they stormed into towns, broke down doors and terrified those caught in the crossfire. Technology could also not prevent the abuses of private military companies such as Blackwater, or the shame of Abu Ghraib prison.

The election of Barack Obama in 2008 marked the beginning of a fourth period – where military technology is no longer aimed at making a faster and more effective soldier, but at taking soldiers out of the picture altogether. This is the true revolution in military affairs in the American way of warfare: war without warriors.[35] Networks and information dominance were the beginning of a revolution, but they did not, in and of themselves, constitute a revolution in warfare. It is the

---

[35] This term was coined by Christopher Coker, who has written much insightful analysis on the topic of war without warriors; see Christopher Coker, *The Future of War* (Oxford: Blackwell, 2004), *Waging War without Warriors* (Boulder, CO: Lynne Rienner, 2002), and *Warrior Geeks*.

social drivers of twenty-first-century Western societies, the risk-averse nature of the Western world that will ultimately remove the soldier from the picture of combat almost entirely. Confronted with costly and unpopular wars, and a continued need to fight the Global War on Terror (still very much in existence, but no longer labeled as such), the Obama Administration turned to science in the form of unmanned technology. Instead of sending in ground invasion forces, the United States has sent in drones, such as the one that killed al-Awlaki. Leaving a lighter footprint than a military brigade, the "promise" of unmanned aerial technology seems to once again offer the possibility of a true scientific-legal way of warfare that can deliver the best of both worlds – a decisive victory that is "clean" and supposedly responds to the demands of the laws of war.[36] In short, it seems to be a method of fighting that can meet the unique requirements of the American way of warfare.

Yet much remains unknown about this technology. Certainly, with the right intelligence, it can eliminate those deemed to be terrorists in a quick and efficient manner that does not require the use of ground troops or complex "Status of Forces Agreements" (or SOFAs). However, what will be the second and third order effects of this technology? In immediately eliminating a threat is the United States inadvertently creating problems for itself down the road? Congress and the Reagan Administration did not give much thought to the second and third order effects of arming the *mujahedeen* in Afghanistan in the 1980s, and the implications of that act have been far reaching. Is the current US government making a similar mistake, laying the groundwork for problems that will confront it in the future – or "blowback" in the parlance of US government agencies? Or is this a smart solution that will eventually win the War on Terror, as the Administration is able to extract troops deployed around the globe? Perhaps most importantly, drones that kill rather than capture raise serious moral and legal questions, especially when they are used to execute US citizens (in one case a teenage boy born in Colorado deemed a "combatant" by the Obama

---

[36] Of course not everyone agrees that drones, and the way they are being used, adhere to the laws of war. The Obama Administration's legal argument for using drones is that the United States is engaged in a worldwide "War on Terror" and that the United States has the right to use force in accordance with the right of self-defense as stated in the UN Charter. This position, however, has come under intense scrutiny for its legal and moral position. This issue will be discussed further in the Conclusion.

Administration).[37] How is guilt determined? And just who is the "enemy"? The Justice Department and Attorney General Eric Holder have argued that there are other forms of "due process" than the standard trial by jury, but many understandably remain skeptical of and unconvinced by this argument.[38] The answers to many of these questions we simply do not know.

In considering this recent history we can understand the legal-scientific way of warfare as one that seeks to balance the need to employ overwhelming force with the legal and humanitarian concerns through science and technology. It is, as we argue, a uniquely American way of warfare – one necessitated by the competing Enlightenment values of its Revolution, to protect itself as a beacon of liberty at all costs, but to do so in a way that has, in the words of the Declaration of Independence, a "decent respect for the opinions of mankind."

It remains to be seen whether a turn to unmanned technology will succeed where other approaches to balancing force and law with science have tended to fail. Thus far, history has shown that the various forms of legal-scientific warfare have frequently failed in balancing the competing imperatives that the United States faces. This seems most acute in the limited wars that the United States has engaged in, particularly where the opponent fights within a different cultural framework and understanding of warfare, such as in the Philippines, Vietnam, Iraq and Afghanistan. When an opponent fights within the Western model (such as on the European front in World War II, in Korea and in the 1991 Gulf War) the American way of war delivers decisive results that can also be precise and relatively humane. However, when America's opponents are seen as not fighting by "the rules," problems and frustration sets in within the military and political leadership in Washington, and the ability to maintain this balance often fails. Despite millions invested in

---

[37] On October 14, 2011, Abdulrahman al-Awlaki, a 16-year-old born in Colorado and the son of Anwar al-Awlaki, was killed with a group of people in a drone strike in Yemen. In 2012 the American Civil Liberties Union and the Center for Constitutional Rights (CCR) filed a lawsuit challenging the government's targeted killing of three US citizens in drone strikes far from any armed conflict zone. The suit was dismissed in April 2014. See *Al-Aulaqi v. Panetta* (aka *Al-Awlaki v. Panetta*).

[38] Conor Friedersdorf, "Eric Holder Explains when Drones Can Kill Americans Abroad," *The Atlantic* (March 8, 2012). Available at: www.theatlantic.com/politics/archive/2012/03/eric-holder-explains-when-drones-can-kill-americans-abroad/254168/ (accessed on August 1, 2012).

technology, and thousands of military lawyers employed by the US Department of Defense, the ability to achieve the liberal desire for quick, decisive and clean wars in these limited conflicts has remained elusive. The legal-scientific way of warfare still demands that opponents fight according to the rules, that combatants will carry their arms openly, distinguish themselves from the general population and adhere to the laws of war. And when this fails to happen, calamity is often not far behind.

How the United States has attempted to balance the dual imperatives of decisive victory and upholding liberal values through the use of science and the law, when and why it has, or has not, been successful are the focus of this book.

1 | *Law and science in the Western way of war*

The Greeks, I have learned, are accustomed to wage wars in the most stupid fashion due to their silliness and folly. For once they have declared war against each other, they search out the finest and most level plain and fight it out. The result is that even the victors come away with great losses; and of the defeated, I say only they are utterly annihilated.

> Mardonius explaining the Greeks to the Persian king Xerxes
> as recorded by Herodotus in *The Histories* (7.9.2)

Nevertheless, as civilization has advanced during the last centuries, so has likewise steadily advanced, especially in war on land, the distinction between the private individual belonging to a hostile country and the hostile country itself, with its men in arms. The principle has been more and more acknowledged that the unarmed citizen is to be spared in person, property, and honor as much as the exigencies of war will admit.

> US Union Army, General Orders 100, Article 22, 1863

A visitor from foreign lands to the American capital city of Washington D.C. is immediately struck by the classical design of the city and its monuments. From the ionic columns of the Jefferson Memorial set on the Tidal Basin, to the thirty-six fluted Doric columns of the Lincoln Memorial perched upon high ground overlooking the reflecting pool and the singular column of the Washington Monument, the architecture of America's capital city reflects a bygone era. The city recalls a vision of Imperial Rome, itself a copy of the magnificent Greek city-states of the fourth and fifth centuries BC. While the architecture of the US capital recalls these ancient civilizations, the very idea that Washington embodies – democracy – is a more important link to these ancient civilizations. The members of the US House and Senate, duly elected by free citizens, to create laws to order society, laws that in turn are upheld by an independent judicial system, act in a cultural fashion shaped first by the ancient Greeks and later by ancient Rome.

This form of government originates from a conceptualization of politics as consensual government, what the Greeks referred to as *politeia*. The capitalist nature of American democracy also has Hellenic roots in the individual opportunity for profit, *kerdos*, the government in this case being chosen by the *demos*, the people, who hold the *kratos* (power) to decide their own fate. It is the idea of freedom, the freedom of the citizen at the root of ancient Greek democracy, which is central to American democracy today. It is the basis for the liberal republican nature of American democracy. What makes America the country it is, is not free and fair elections, it is the rule of law, the separation of powers and the guarantee of basic individual liberties such as free speech, assembly, religion and property.[1]

War and the modern state are intimately connected. As Charles Tilly famously put it: war made the state and the state in turn makes war.[2] But states do not all wage war in the same way. How a state makes war depends on the culture of that state. Just as the liberal democratic norms of the political philosophy that inspired the American Revolution led to a particular form of government, these same liberal democratic values impact how the United States (and other liberal democracies) fights wars. Likewise, the illiberal values of an authoritarian system impact the way dictatorships wage war. The human rights abuses inflicted by German soldiers on the Eastern Front in World War II were enabled by a culture that saw their Slavic opponents as subhuman and as therefore not deserving of protection under the laws of armed conflict that the Nazis applied toward their British and American enemies. But while Nazi Germany and the United States in the 1940s waged war differently from each other as a result of their normative beliefs, they fought wars within a shared paradigm.[3] This paradigm is more or less loosely known as the "Western way of war" and it can be traced back (in a non-linear progression) to ancient Greece.

---

[1] For more on the Greeks and international relations and politics see: Richard Ned Lebow, *The Tragic Vision of Politics: Ethics, Interests and Orders* (Cambridge: Cambridge University Press, 2003).

[2] Charles Tilly, "War Making and State Making as Organized Crime," in Peter Evans, Dietrich Rueschemeyer and Theda Skocpol (eds.), *Bringing the State Back In* (Cambridge: Cambridge University Press, 1985), pp. 169–185.

[3] Wolfram Wette, *The Wehrmacht: History, Myth, Reality* (Cambridge, MA: Harvard University Press, 2006).

A review of armed conflict in human civilization yields decisively different preferences on how to wage what human beings call "war." In the Western world, war is largely fought as a decisive conflict with the use of overwhelming force to achieve victory. Technology has been critical in making the Western style or "way" of war supposedly more "effective." The result of this paradigm of war, however, was immense horror. The mechanization of war during the industrial revolutions, coupled with the mass of the nation-state, paved the way to the bloody stalemate on the Western Front in World War I and the D-Day Landings of 1944. The use of new science that led to the deployment of the atomic bomb on Hiroshima and Nagasaki came from a Western desire to win and to win decisively. Other cultures have not waged war in such a manner. This does not mean that non-Western forms of warfare were less brutal, but the cultural framework of war was different and this in turn led to different ways of waging war.

For the ancient Aztecs and their neighbors war was a ritual. The Aztecs believed that the sun was born from sacrifice and blood. Tlacaelel, who led the Aztecs at the height of their power in the 1400s, believed that the Aztecs were the chosen people of the sun god, Huitzilopochtli, and that it was their responsibility to appease him and the other gods. The Aztecs therefore felt that they needed to create war so that hearts and blood could be given to appease the sun god. This belief led to the establishment of the "flower wars" (Xochiyaoyotl) with the neighboring city of Tlaxcala. In the flower wars, warriors met in a ritual battle, the goal of which was not to kill the opponents' warriors, but to take prisoners who would then be offered as sacrifices to Huitzilopochtli. Although sometimes war led to land grabs, more often than not the goal of warfare was not to kill for the sake of expansion or political grievance as in the Western model.[4]

On the other side of the world in ancient China, the great Chinese General Sun Tzu penned *The Art of War*, outlining a distinct Chinese way of war infused with Taoist principles that saw China as embodying how heaven believed the affairs of man should be ordered.[5] China was

---

[4] Burt Bundage, *The Fifth Sun: Aztec Gods, Aztec World* (Austin: University of Texas Press, 1979); Jacques Sustelle, *The Daily Life of the Aztecs* (Palo Alto, CA: Stanford University Press, 1970).

[5] Thomas Cleary (trans.), *The Essential Tao: An Initiation into the Heart of Taoism through the Authentic Tao Te Ching and the Inner Teachings of Chuang Tzu* (New York: Castle Books, 1992).

order; outside of China, beyond the Han people, was chaos. As Christopher Coker notes, the object of war in China was "not to impose one's will but to undermine the enemy's will" through the use of asymmetry.[6] The apparent consensus was that the use of *wen* (civility) or *wu* (martial merit) was determined by the relative ability of each to preserve the state's awesomeness (*wei*), that is to say its manifest power to exert policy throughout its domain. "Contrary to later times, these elements were not evaluated in moral terms, but were merely regarded as alternatives for counteracting *luan* (chaos) along a continuum ranging from violent warfare to friendly persuasion."[7] Rather than direct conflict reaching a culminating point of victory, when the enemy's strength begins to ebb, the Chinese way of war favored formlessness, enabling the combatant to make strengths into weakness and vice versa. In today's parlance, ancient Chinese military commanders preferred strategic maneuver warfare instead of the attritional form of warfare that came to dominate Western thinking on war.[8] The pitched battles of the Western way of war are seen as inconsequential as this injunction from Sun Tzu reveals: "Those who win five victories will meet with disaster; those who win four victories will be exhausted. Those with three victories will become warlords. Those with two victories will be kings. And those with one victory will become emperors."[9]

If the Chinese preferred obfuscation and cunning to direct shock tactics, in the Levant the preference was for standoff weapons. The tradition in the Middle East is to seize ground, but then to stop and defend it rather than pressing home the advantage. Both the Persians and the Arabs favored battle plans that would be seen as reserved in the eyes of Western military strategists. The root of this, according to Ibn Khaldun, is the orientation of regional culture along kinship lines. In a closely knit group of common descent, the levels of affection for clients

---

[6] Christopher Coker, *Waging War without Warriors* (Boulder, CO: Lynne Rienner, 2002), p. 129.

[7] Ralph Sawyer, *The Seven Military Classics of Ancient China* (Boulder, CO: Westview Press, 1993), p. 33.

[8] John K. Fairbank and Frank A. Kierman (eds.), *Chinese Ways in Warfare* (Cambridge, MA: Harvard University Press, 1974); David A. Graff, *Medieval Chinese Warfare, 300–900* (London: Routledge, 2002); Mark Edward Lewis, *Sanctioned Violence in Early China* (Albany, NY: State University of New York Press, 1990).

[9] A. Graham, "The Place of Reason in China's Philosophical Traditions," in R. Dawson (ed.), *The Legacy of China* (Oxford: Oxford University Press, 1964), p. 30.

and allies resulted in a desire to avoid humiliation or loss of face, which translates into less decisive combat traditions.[10] Success was achieved in the Levantine tradition of war when a tribe was able to exploit divisions in the opposing group or when the tribe utilized "tricks and ruses" to split the opponent's group apart. As the Prophet Mohammed said, "war is trickery."[11] This form of warfare was not derived because Arabs were or are somehow less honest than Western warriors as the more Orientalist studies of warfare often argue – it was driven by logical strategic imperatives and the nature of Middle Eastern society. Shaming the enemy was unnecessary and was to be avoided – very much the opposite of prevailing Western notions of war.

Rather than achieving total victory, Native American warfare was deeply ritualistic and full of meaning. The indigenous peoples of North America fought to protect hunting grounds, take prisoners and prove merit in battle. Although it was not short of practices that would shock European colonists, such as scalping and torture, Native American warfare ultimately emphasized the preservation of life as an overriding norm. Instead of European-style tactics where soldiers were drilled to stay in formation as they faced volley attacks from their opponents in an open field, they utilized what one period observer called a "skulking [sic] way of warfare" involving ambushes, surprise attacks and the avoidance of frontal assaults. Rather than brave "last stands," if an opponent were considered too powerful, warriors and even entire villages would retreat. The lives of warriors were not to be thrown away, and mass casualties were to be avoided. Taking a prisoner was considered a greater act of bravery than killing an opponent. Although Native Americans could treat their prisoners with incredible brutality, after they had "run the gauntlet," many were subsequently warmly adopted into tribes – often as a replacement for individuals who had been lost in warfare. Further, unlike Europeans, Native American warriors did not rape women.[12]

---

[10] Malik Mufti, "Jihad as Statecraft: Ibn Khaldun on the Conduct of War and Empire," *History of Political Thought*, Vol. 30, No. 3 (2009), 385–410.

[11] Coker, *Waging War without Warriors*, p. 149; Ernest Gellner, *Muslim Society* (Cambridge: Cambridge University Press, 1981), p. 36.

[12] Thomas S. Abler, "Scalping, Torture, Cannibalism and Rape: An Ethnohistorical Analysis of Conflicting Cultural Values in War," *Anthropologica*, Vol. 34, No. 1 (1992), 3–20; Wayne E. Lee, "Early American Ways of War: A New Renaissance, 1600–1815," *The Historical Journal*, Vol. 44, No. 1 (March 2001), 269–289; Daniel K. Richter, "War and Culture: The Iroquois Experience," *The William and Mary Quarterly*, Vol. 40, No. 4 (October 1983), 528–529;

In the 366 years since the rise of the modern nation-state in Europe and increased interactions between Europe and the rest of the world, Western powers have on balance decisively defeated and eliminated most non-Western ways of war. Exceptions to the rule abound – the Western forces lost battles to many non-Western ways of war – but as the classical historian Victor David Hanson notes in his aptly named, *Why the West Has Won*, "there has been a peculiar practice of Western warfare, a common foundation and continual way of fighting, that has made Europeans the most deadly soldiers known in the history of civilization."[13] The dominance of the Western way of warfare is in no small part due to increasing technological advancement in the Western world as historian Jeremy Black convincingly argued in *European Warfare: 1660–1815*. Massive technological change and industrial development in Europe would lay the foundations for the most systematic, industrialized warfare the world had ever seen. These economic developments provided the steam, both literally and figuratively, for the West to develop a very deadly form of war as a political tool.[14]

Technology, combined with tactics and military organization that evolved within a Western political and social context, made the Western way of warfare dominant.[15] In his work, Hanson privileges the "freedom" of soldiers that fight within a "democratic" military, but this argument fails to convince. John France in *Perilous Glory* argues that rather than focusing on freedom and democracy, there are clear traits beyond these elements that are universal in warfare.[16] France believes that ways of warfare are better understood as developing from social conditions, material circumstances and technology than via the prism of democracy à la Hanson. As we argue, democracy and liberal values are critical to understanding how the Western way of warfare has evolved, but from this we do not come to share Hanson's conclusion that the Western way

Armstrong Starkey, *European and Native American Warfare 1675–1815* (London: UCL Press, 1998).

[13] Victor Davis Hanson, *Why the West Has Won: Nine Landmark Battles in the Brutal History of Western Victory* (New York: Faber and Faber, 2001), p. 5.

[14] For more on the international economy of Europe see: David S. Landes, *The Unbound Prometheus: Technological Change and Industrial Development in Western Europe from 1750 to the Present* (Cambridge: Cambridge University Press, 1972).

[15] Jeremy Black, *European Warfare: 1660–1815* (New Haven, CT: Yale University Press, 1994).

[16] John France, *Perilous Glory: The Rise of Western Military Power* (New Haven, CT: Yale University Press, 2011).

of warfare is necessarily superior and indomitable because of democracy. Our approach is similar to that of France, in that we hold culture to be more than just political values. Culture may have value-based roots, but values may change while culture stays the same. This is the essence of the practice theory approach to culture in this work. It is also worth noting here, as France does too, that there is nothing inevitable about continued Western victories as a result of the Western way of warfare. As Japan demonstrated in the Russo-Japanese War of 1905 the "Western" way of warfare is not just fought by Western nations. When Japan abandoned traditional Japanese approaches to war that forsook modern technology, and adopted a Western way of warfare, it handily defeated a major Western military power. Furthermore, we must stress that we do not believe that the Western way of warfare is dictated by freedom and democracy. Such liberal values influence the United States and other liberal nations, but not all Western nations. As already stated, Nazi Germany as well as Stalin's Russia both fought in the Western tradition, but they did so in an illiberal fashion that led to total, unrestrained war against the enemy rather than the more restrained American way of warfare that at the very least argues with itself over the best way to balance the tendency toward annihilation with liberal restraint (even if it does not always succeed).[17]

One must also recognize that there is a fair bit of cross-fertilization between different ways of warfare. Although the Western way of warfare managed to impose itself on other cultures, gradually extinguishing other cultural types of warfare, it also utilized indigenous styles of warfare, particularly in the colonial era to police colonies, and it at times adapted non-Western aspects of warfare into the Western model. Furthermore, as Peter Lorge convincingly illustrates, numerous non-Western developments in warfare had a major impact on Western warfare – one of the most notable being the importation of gunpowder from China.[18] Ancient China possessed numerous structural and political institutions, which saw the use of gunpowder in warfare (with similar characteristics to Western war). The Greeks also used trickery, subterfuge

---

[17] We view Germany and Russia as Western nations, especially because when it comes to the use of force and military tactics and strategy both subscribe and have contributed greatly to the Western canon of literature on warfare.

[18] Peter A. Lorge, *The Asian Military Revolution: From Gunpowder to the Bomb* (Cambridge: Cambridge University Press, 2008).

and indirect methods in warfare; such tactics were not limited to non-Western actors.[19]

As we have seen, different regions of the world evolved different norms of warfare based primarily on social conditions, conceptions of politics, material conditions and technology. Non-Western ways of warfare, however, no longer exist in the modern world and, as the following case studies illustrate, the problem today is not that the opponents of the United States fight in a different cultural model, instead they have adapted the concept of irregular warfare (a form utilized extensively in the West and written about by Western military historians) as a weapon of the weak to use against US forces, making America's strength in conventional warfare a weakness. We agree with Patrick Porter that the reason for the American military's inability to "win" in Iraq and Afghanistan is not because the opponent utilizes some special cultural form of warfare that must be mapped.[20] It *does* matter, however, that the combatants have shared norms about how war is waged – which it is clear they often do not. This is not so much because of a different culture (i.e. "Asia" or "Middle Eastern") but simply because to win they must not play by the same rulebook as their Western opponent – they have to rewrite the rulebook to suit them. This is not unique to non-Western combatants. A weak opponent within the Western world would do the same; the Irish Republican Army (IRA) tactics against the United Kingdom during "The Troubles" is evidence of this concept. The same goes for the strategy and tactics used by Dutch and French resistance fighters against occupying German forces in World War II.

The Western way of war annihilated other cultural forms of warfare, reducing the experience of war today to one that is largely universal – at least in terms of how the military, public and scholars understand war. The Western way of warfare has proven lethal and no soldiers of the European tradition are more deadly than those of the present-day United States of America. From Iraq to Afghanistan and from Osaka

---

[19] Everett L. Wheeler, *Stratagem and the Vocabulary of Military Trickery* (Leiden: E. J. Brill, 1988); Adrienne Mayor, *Greek Fire, Poison Arrows and Scorpion Bombs: Biological and Chemical Warfare in the Ancient World* (New York: Overlook, 2003); Barry Strauss, *Salamis: The Naval Battle that Saved Ancient Greece* (New York: Simon & Schuster, 2005).

[20] Patrick Porter, *Military Orientalism: Eastern War through Western Eyes* (New York: Columbia University Press, 2009).

to Darwin the American military colossus bestrides the globe. Across the seven seas the ships of the US Navy, once a provincial force created to eliminate the Barbary pirates, ply the waves with absolute conventional superiority. Among them eleven supercarrier battle groups, each one containing all of the firepower expended in World War II multiple times over, are ready to be dispatched wherever the American President believes they are needed to uphold US interests and maintain international stability. According to the US Department of Defense there are 662 American overseas bases and US personnel are on the ground in 148 countries.[21] Day and night America watches the world through a vast network of satellites and unmanned aerial vehicles; the latter have moved away from simply observing to actually engaging in combat, or, better put, engaging in missions to assassinate individuals deemed hostile to the United States of America, such as in the case of al-Awlaki and his conspirators. Today even America's allies, some of the most powerful states in the world, need American assistance to accomplish successful military missions using the latest technology as was most evident in the 2011 NATO campaign against Libya.[22]

This global footprint and the ability to project force around the world is partly the product of the Western way of war that the United States uses in combat. No other nation on earth, in the West or beyond, has taken the use of war as a rational tool of statecraft and applied science and technology to such an astounding level in an attempt to achieve decisive and overwhelming victory in the shortest time frame possible. But the US way of war is driven by a second imperative rooted in its liberal nature. The Greeks fought decisive wars in order to return their soldiers, landed citizens, to their fields and farms as soon as possible. Today, the United States has not only the imperative of time to worry about, but also the very real dilemma that as a liberal state it holds human life to be sacred. As a liberal state the United States, theoretically, abhors war. As Thomas

---

[21] US Department of Defense, "Base Structure Report: Fiscal Year 2010 Baseline – A Summary of the DoD's Real Property Inventory" (Washington D.C.: Department of Defense, 2010).

[22] M. J. Williams, "Implications for British Defense Dependency on Foreign and Security Policy," in *Operations in Libya*, Ninth Report of Session 2011–2012, UK Defence Select Committee, UK House of Commons, pp. Ev W4–Ev W7. Available at: www.publications.parliament.uk/pa/cm201012/cmselect/cmdfence/950/950vw.pdf (accessed on August 1, 2012).

Paine wrote in *The Rights of Man*: "Government on the old system is an assumption of power, for the aggrandizement of itself; on the new [republican system], a delegation of power for the common benefit of society. The former supports itself by keeping up a system of war; the latter promotes a system of peace, as the true means of enriching a nation."[23] This does not mean that liberal states do not go to war – they do. Despite Paine's belief that the republican state promotes a system of peace as the true means of enriching a nation, the United States has resorted to force numerous times in just the last decade. In doing so it seemingly contradicts the Enlightenment belief, typified in the writings of Abbé Saint-Pierre and Immanuel Kant, that republican states are inherently more peaceful. At the same time, however, the way the United States conducts war is very interesting. There is an intense struggle between the deep-rooted cultural tendencies of the Western way of war for a fast decisive victory, against the liberal imperative to protect not only the lives of American soldiers, but also those caught up in the fog of war in theaters of combat. The struggle between restraint and annihilation lies at the heart of the American way of war, and the impulse toward annihilation runs deep.

The classical roots of the Western way of war

It may seem odd to think that America's most recent wars in Iraq and Afghanistan are informed by a way of warfare going back to ancient Greece, but just as the American political system is influenced by Greece, so too is the way America wages war. The ancient Greeks approached war as a problem, one that they could solve rationally and one whereby they could utilize logic to win. "War" for the Greeks, writes Coker, was not "a matter of blood vendetta, revenge, or honour, as it is for the tribe or clan; it is a collective interest embodied in the state."[24] War, Aristotle tells us, is an acquisitive activity, and the main purpose of war in ancient Greece was to acquire slaves, which in turn allowed for more production and greater societal wealth. "The Greeks extended their understanding of the instrumentality of war by treating it as a

[23] Thomas Paine, *The Rights of Man, Common Sense and Other Political Writings*, ed. Mark Philp. (Oxford: Oxford University Press, 2008).
[24] Coker, *Waging War without Warriors*, p. 27.

technical problem that could be solved by better tactics (larger armies) or technology (more destructive weapons)."[25]

In waging war there were several factors that influenced how the Greeks came to think of war.[26] First, the average Greek soldier, often referred to as a *hoplite* in reference to the type of shield he carried, was a citizen. Usually a farmer, this man would own enough land to support himself and his kin. He was a free man and he fought not for a king or emperor, but for himself – for his land. This made the *hoplites* formidable fighters, for a man who fights for his home fights to the death in a way far more sacrificial than the mercenary paid to keep guard. Because the armed forces of Greek city-states were composed of farmers, men with responsibilities to tend to other than war, it was necessary for war in Greece to be waged quickly. The people voted for war and were committed to it, but this needed to be balanced against other requirements. This balance is where one finds the roots of the decisive battle tradition that dominates Western thinking on war to this day. In the course of an afternoon a war could be decided – one side would win, one side would lose and an agreement would be reached. It was a highly instrumental form of war, not based on ritual, religion or even ethics. It was all about winning the battle, settling the score and moving on. War was a tool to achieve what could not otherwise be reached through diplomacy, and was therefore highly instrumental; it was the means to an end. As such, it was imperative to make war more efficient and effective, not least because an army of farmers and citizens, rather than professionals or mercenaries, had other things to do. The exception to this rule was Sparta. Having enslaved the Helots to perform agricultural labor, the Spartans were free to develop a "professional" and well-trained military force rather than employ a citizen militia.

The need to achieve settlement of the conflict as quickly as possible led to the idea of the decisive battle, which in turn lent itself to the

---

[25] *Ibid.*

[26] For more information on Greek warfare see: P. A. L. Greenhalgh, *Early Greek Warfare: Horsemen and Chariots in the Homeric and Archaic Ages* (Cambridge: Cambridge University Press, 2011); Victor Davis Hanson, *Wars of the Ancient Greeks* (New York: Harper, 2006) and *Hoplites: The Classic Greek Battle Experience* (London: Routledge, 1993); Mayor, *Greek Fire*; Philip Souza, *The Greeks at War: From Athens to Alexander* (Oxford: Osprey Publishing, 2004); Hans van Wees, *Greek Warfare: Myths and Reality* (Bristol: Bristol Classical Press, 2004).

concept of mass. The Greeks would locate a large, flat plain upon which their forces would meet. Because a war could in theory be settled in the course of an afternoon, it became imperative to field the largest force possible. Numbers alone, however, were not the sole focus of the campaign. The Greeks also applied technology and strategy to help them wage war. They created the *phalanx* formation. The *phalanx* was a rectangular arrangement of *hoplites*. These foot soldiers were equipped with both shields and spears. The type of spears ranged from standard 7- to 9-foot-long *doru* to the 21-foot *sarissa* favored by Alexander the Great's Macedonian troops. The shields they carried were large, bronze discs that provided ample cover from assault.

The troops were lined up in a rectangular formation so that the spears of the first group would protrude from their shields and the second row could have their shields raised up to provide cover from arrows and javelins with their spears pointed up and out ready for assault. The outside wings of the *phalanx* put their shields to the sides to provide lateral protection for the group. The result is that the *phalanx* resembled a massive turtle with spikes. The Greek *phalanx* was a much more heavily armored unit than the non-Greek combatants they would fight. Combat was in close contact – spearing and hacking away at the enemy just feet, sometimes only inches, away. The carnage was immense and the goal was to annihilate the enemy so that he could fight no more, the war could be won and the victor could take his spoils and return to his toil in the fields. The probability of victory in this type of conflict depended on mass to win the pitched battle. At sea a similar correlate of war emerged, but such conflict was based around triremes, the Greek oar-warships, rather than the *phalanx*. There was little mercy for enemies on land or at sea, especially for those who were not Greek and were therefore not seen as "fully" human.

The Greeks also favored and agreed upon the ideal of the decisive battle because as Barry Strauss put it, "The Greeks preferred pitched battle not only because their farmer-soldiers wanted to end wars quickly and get back to their fields or because they wanted to spare human life but because they wanted recognition. With the possible exception of a siege that ended in assaulting the walls, pitched battle was the main military arena for winning kudos."[27] There was a central, humanistic

[27] Barry Strauss, "The Queen at Salamis: Or Cunning and the Culture of Ancient Greek Warfare," paper presented at the January 2004 meeting of the

element to the Greek way of warfare. Greek warfare was not humane in the sense of how they behaved toward others, but rather their humanity stemmed from "the indispensability of man."[28] War for the Greeks was a test of the "vitality" of the individual and their people.[29]

Up until the Peloponnesian War limited and localized conflict was the norm. War would become more encompassing beginning with the Spartan attacks against Attica. The Peloponnesian War would be a much wider and more protracted struggle that would destroy whole cities, and because it was so all-encompassing it would mark the beginning of the end of Greek civilization. Because war was instrumental for the Greeks, rather than ritualistic, they also problematized challenges that fell outside of the norm of the pitched battle. The Greeks would develop an upper hand against many of the people they fought because of the way they reasoned about war. The Greeks were the first ancient peoples in the West to create long-term analysis. For example, consider the conundrum that Athens faced at the start of the Peloponnesian War. Athens was a sea power, but its archenemy in the Peloponnesian War, Sparta and the Peloponnesian League, were land based. Pericles had to determine how a sea power could defeat a land power given that the latter was inaccessible to attack by sea. The answer was for Pericles to alter the existing rules. Rather than going on the offensive, Athens would pursue a defensive strategy on land. When the Peloponnesian League invaded Attica, the Athenians chose to remain barricaded in the city rather than engaging in a pitched battle that they knew they could not win. The result was to check the Spartan strategy that was traditional, rather than innovative. Pericles' decision was revolutionary in that it threw the Greek rulebook on war out the window. Pericles calculated the military, financial, political and psychological forces that constitute "grand strategy" and therefore decided to maintain a defensive posture on land, an offensive pattern at sea and regular foreign trade to feed the war effort.

As Greek civilization receded, the Greek way of warfare would continue to live on, being adopted by the "barbarians" of Rome. As such the Greek way of warfare ceased to be just Greek, becoming instead what we now call "Western." The Romans were an even more instrumental people than the Greeks. The Romans were actively

American Historical Association cited in John A. Lynn, *Battle: A History of Combat and Culture* (New York: Basic Books, 2004), p. 4.
[28] Coker, *Waging War without Warriors*, p. 19.   [29] *Ibid.*, p. 21.

building an empire that needed access to resources, and while citizens would continue to form a core of the military, war was professionalized in ancient Rome. No longer was war simply a civic duty. The Romans created a bureaucracy to manage the military. Each legion functioned faultlessly because of the regular drilling of the troops and a semi-professional officer corps (the centurions) that managed the legions. But the root of their success was the drill. The Roman legions drilled, drilled and then drilled some more. As Josephus wrote of the Romans, they "are sure of victory ... for their exercises are battles without bloodshed and their battles bloody exercises."[30]

The Romans fought in close order waves of very thin lines avoiding a heavier arrangement such as the *phalanx*.[31] The Roman system of fighting was more fluid than that of the ancient Greeks. The Romans more easily focused manpower along the line, and the continuous drill meant the army was used to maneuvering warfare in close quarters. The front line would first cast their *pila*, a javelin-like weapon, before drawing their swords and then charging their enemy at speed head on. The heritage of the *phalanx* is seen in the formation of attack, but the heaviness of the formation is cast aside. The Romans were also able to combine the benefits of missiles (javelins) with the versatility of the sword.

The results of the systematization of warfare in ancient Rome were ruthless battle with appalling results for the enemies of Rome. Whereas war in ancient Greece reached its apotheosis in the Peloponnesian Wars that began the decline of Greek civilization, the Romans engaged in such total war on occasion after occasion to build the empire. In Gaul (modern-day France), Caesar killed over a million people in battle or in a retributive massacre. Another million people were taken as slaves – and all of this in just eight years. Even when the Romans suffered

---

[30] *Ancient History Sourcebook: Josephus (37–after 93 CE): The Roman Army in the First Century CE.* Available at: www.fordham.edu/halsall/ancient/josephus-warb.asp (accessed June 30, 2014).

[31] For additional reading on warfare in ancient Rome see: M. C. Bishop and J. C. N. Coulston, *Roman Military Equipment* (Oxford: Oxbow Books, 2011); Ross Cowan, *Roman Battle Tactics* (Oxford: Osprey Publishing, 2007); Adrian Goldsworthy, *The Complete Roman Army* (London: Thames & Hudson, 2003) and *Roman Warfare* (New York: Smithsonian Books, 2005); *The Conquest of Gaul*, S. A. Handford (trans.) revised with a new introduction by Jane P. Gardner (New York: Penguin, 1982); Pat Southern and Karen R. Dixon, *The Late Roman Army* (New Haven: Yale University Press, 1996).

a resounding defeat, such as they did on the battlefields of Cannae on August 2, 216 BC at the hands of Hannibal's forces, they would have the last laugh. Roughly a year after the defeat Rome was on the offensive attacking Sicily, and the forces lost at Cannae had already been replenished. This pattern was repeated numerous times. When a Roman legion would lose for whatever reason, the Romans would eventually come back to finish the job. This was because the enemies of Rome, writes Victor Davis Hanson, were "fighting a frightening system and an idea, not a mere army."[32]

The system of Rome would eventually collapse, however, and it would do so partially as a result of abandonment of drill and discipline. In the third century the Roman Empire was recruiting more and more legionnaires from the tribes it had conquered. Romans, who were increasingly unwilling to do the fighting themselves, welcomed this development. The military was only able to recruit 1 percent of the home population to serve and Roman cities preferred to pay for the military than to meet their quotas for military service.[33] As a result the Roman Army was Germanicized and the fate of the two peoples – the Romans and the Germanic peoples of Europe that Rome had conquered – became so intertwined that by the time the central authority of Rome collapsed there was little left of the Roman military tradition. The Roman military had been "barbarized" to the point that the close order drill and training that dominated Rome at the pinnacle of its power were all but lost. As Europe descended into the dark ages, the Western tradition would recede into the background as war became less instrumental.

The Middle Ages would see the rise of feudal warfare, not linked to the affairs or interests of the state. During this period there is a clear break with the Western tradition, which scholars preoccupied with a focus on a constant Western tradition overlook. The Middle Ages, however, are important because they too contributed to the cultural repertoire of Western warfare as we understand it today. In particular, the Middle Ages with their focus on siege warfare laid the foundations for the advancement of "scientific" approaches to war that would emerge in the Enlightenment. "Clausewitz argued that medieval wars were waged relatively quickly: not much time was wasted in the field;

---

[32] Hanson, *Why the West Has Won*, p. 128.
[33] Coker, *Waging War without Warriors*, p. 41.

their aim was to punish the enemy, not subdue him. When his cattle had been driven off and his castles burned, one would go home."[34] The reality was a bit more complex. The trend in the Middle Ages was to avoid pitched battle in favor of siege warfare. Roger Boyle, First Earl of Orrey, summed up this approach noting "We make war more like foxes, than like lyons; and you will have twenty sieges for one battell."[35] Medieval warfare was far less systematic and far wider ranging than ancient Greek or Roman warfare. War in this period was based on the concept of the *chevauchée*, meaning "ride." During the Hundred Years' War the English undertook eleven *chevauchées* across France devastating the country. In 1355 alone the English overran 675 miles destroying 18,000 square miles of land, burning, pillaging and raping their way.[36]

The *chevauchée* was brutal for at least three reasons. First, sustaining a military force in the Middle Ages, before the advent of logistical support systems for the military, meant that the soldiers (and their mounts) lived off the occupied land and surrounding communities. If one considers that a medieval military force with 5,000 horses consumed 875 tons of green forage, or 437.5 tons of dry forage, per week it is easy to understand the scale to which the military stripped the countryside of resources.[37] Second, purposely laying waste to the land also removed the ability of the opposing force to sustain itself. As Count Philip of Flanders advised, "Thus should war be begun: such is my advice. First law was to the land [so that] nothing is left [for the enemy] of which they could have a meal."[38] Since the aim of the sovereign was to protect his people the devastation also served to undermine the legitimacy of the opposing sovereign making it more difficult for him to raise the funds and manpower required to launch a counter campaign. Finally, warriors expected financial gain

[34] Carl von Clausewitz, *On War* (Michael Howard and Peter Paret, trans.) (London: Everyman, 1993), p. 710.

[35] Cited in Geoffrey Parker, *The Military Revolution: Military Innovation and the Rise of the West, 1500–1800* (Cambridge: Cambridge University Press, 1988), p. 16.

[36] Clifford J. Rogers, "By Fire and Sword: Bellum Hostile and 'Civilians' in the Hundred Years' War," in Mark Grimsley and Clifford J. Rogers (eds.), *Civilians in the Path of War* (Lincoln, NE: University of Nebraska Press, 2002), p. 37.

[37] Lynn, *Battle*, p. 86.

[38] Cited in *ibid.* See also: John Gillingham and J. C. Holt (eds.), *War and Government in the Middle Ages* (Cambridge: Cambridge University Press, 1984), p. 84.

from their adventures. Plunder was a standard military custom across Europe, with explicitly outlined guidelines as to the division of spoils accumulated in war.[39] This expectation of gain worked well with the ravages of the *chevauchée*. Attackers expected (and demanded) ransom for prisoners and payments from town and villages that wanted to be spared the horror of war.

A modern-day traveler around Europe can easily observe in many cities the remnants and, in some cases, entire original medieval city walls. These walls varied in height and were normally between 8 and 20 feet thick. Earlier walls were made of wood, but those that endure today were constructed of stone often carted from quarries miles away from the city. These walls were often ringed by moats – a wall of water – ideally an engineered strip of water outside the walls filled from a natural source that prevented draining. The presence of the moat made it exceedingly difficult to attack the wall directly and made undermining the wall impossible. In the absence of a moat some cities relied on a double wall, in between which was the "killing field" – a space where once having breached the first wall invading soldiers would be trapped as they attempted to scale the second wall, making them easy targets for the defending force to pick off. The development of these walls was a direct result of medieval siege-based warfare. The *chevauchée* led to a reliance on fortifications and a defensive architecture. Instead of being wide open to the ravages of an attacking force, the defenders could find refuge behind the great walls of the city.

The rebirth of the "Western" tradition

Decades of war, culminating in the Thirty Years' War, devastated Europe and turned a prosperous continent into a land racked by endemic violence and famine.[40] The result of the Thirty Years' War would be the birth of the European nation-state as European polities assigned control of territories to sovereign leaders, seeking, among other things, to reduce the influence of religion in statecraft. With the creation of the state, the re-enchantment of war occurred as states

[39] Robert Stacey, "The Age of Chivalry," in Michael Howard, George J. Andreopoulos and Mark R. Schuman (eds.), *The Laws of War: Constraints on Warfare in the Western World* (New Haven, CT: Yale University Press, 1994), pp. 34–35.

[40] Geoffrey Parker, *The Thirty Years' War* (London: Routledge, 1997).

sought to secure their "national interest." The instrumental logic of warfare, so critical to the concept of war in Greece and Rome, returned. With the return of instrumental logic of warfare so too returned the need to create military forces that were effective on the field of battle. The result was that military forces returned to drill and order. Such regimentation came at a time when mechanization was on the rise and the idea of science to improve war captured the imagination. As the military historian Azar Gat noted, "the ideal of Newtonian science excited the military thinkers of the Enlightenment and gave rise to an ever-present yearning to infuse the study of war with the maximum mathematical precision and certainty possible."[41]

During the Renaissance the rise of science encountered a general re-engagement with the past. The ancient philosophical debates of the Greeks were of great interest to Renaissance thinkers and while the conditions may have changed, the ideas of the ancients were seen as worthy of study, engagement and indeed application. One of the most noted to do this was Niccolò Machiavelli, author of, among other works, *The Prince* and *The Art of War*. The latter, as Thomas Arnold argued in *The Renaissance at War*, is a striking example of how Renaissance thinkers synthesized ancient and modern thought into one work popularizing the subject.[42] It was this kind of writing that "transformed a Greco-Roman experience into a style that become distinctively 'Western.'"[43] The Renaissance would repair the rupture that occurred in the development of warfare during the Middle Ages. Machiavelli's work lamented the mercenary style of warfare that dominated the feudal system. He felt that an army of citizens, as in the ancient worlds, would be inherently stronger than one hired by a prince. Machiavelli believed that Rome's downfall started after the end of the Punic Wars when the Roman Republic shifted away from a citizen-based army toward a more professional one. For Machiavelli, the strengths of the Greek and Roman systems were the social and political institutions based in republican democracy. This is a theme that modern writers, such as Victor Davis Hanson, agree with and have sought to reinforce through their writings. For Hanson the critical component in

[41] Azar Gat, *A History of Military Thought: From the Enlightenment to the Cold War* (Oxford: Oxford University Press, 2001), p. 30.
[42] Thomas Arnold, *The Renaissance at War* (London: Cassell, 2001), p. 60.
[43] Coker, *Waging War without Warriors*, p. 47.

the Western way of war is the "freedom" of the Western soldier, which is manifested as a result of the political institutions of Western states, namely liberal democracy. Free men, who fight for their land, for their rights, for their state or nation have higher morale argued Machiavelli. They are also more likely to innovate, as Hanson notes, because they are free men and they understand that initiative is rewarded, and not punished as is characteristic in an authoritarian system. Such innovation can make the difference between success and defeat in battle as seen in the examples of the greatly outnumbered Western naval forces at Lepanto defeating the Ottomans in October 1571 or the devastation of the Aztecs at the hands of the Spanish in 1521. Although the rise of republics would not occur for some time, Machiavelli's argument would find realization in the creation of the United States and other Western democracies in the centuries to come.

The modern era transformed the Greco-Roman way of war into the cultural form we recognize today. The Greeks may have applied logic to war, but it was Enlightenment thinkers that utilized science in a systematic way to provide empirical answers to the "art" of war. Humanity became obsessed with measuring the world as it decoded the science of mass, force, momentum, time and space. Newton's *Principia Mathematica* of 1687 embodied the soul of the Enlightenment, arguing that the function of the universe could be understood in a rational and predictable way through the use of mathematics and geometry. As Bousquet argues in *The Scientific Way of Warfare*,

a further implication of Newton's findings was that, equipped with the knowledge of the fundamental laws governing it, it was possible (at least theoretically) to predict completely the future and past of all physical systems. Indeed, if a system's state at any given moment is known with precision, then the past and future of the system can be predicted with absolute certainty.[44]

Newtonian methods would become the basis for understanding the world and for the behavior of elements within it. This was just as true in the study and pursuit of war as it was in the natural and physical sciences.

---

[44] Antoine Bousquet, *The Scientific Way of Warfare: Order and Chaos on the Battlefields of Modernity* (London: Hurst, 2009), p. 46.

Following on the Middle Ages, the period of the Enlightenment and the corresponding Military Enlightenment was dominated by a conception of battle as "universally bloody but only rarely decisive."[45] Conflicts were settled by exhaustion during a siege; rarely was it battle in the Greco-Roman mold that decided the outcome. Soldiers were generally considered the personal property of the sovereign or military commander, who was loath to sacrifice them in battle. In his recounting of the development of the Prussian state Christopher Clark concludes that "Pitched battles were thus relatively rare and armies spent most of the war years engaged in marches, manoeuvres and occupations. It was an arrangement that spared the troops, but weighed heavily on the host populations."[46] Military strategists at this time were weary of open-field battles because they were unpredictable. The siege, however, was another matter. "The geometric character of military practice in the siege could yield results on schedule, provided that attackers followed the proper procedure."[47] Defense in these circumstances was also considerably more calculated. The application of science to war in the Enlightenment period evolved out of the medieval emphasis on defensive fortifications. In the sixteenth century the design of the fortress and walls evolved away from high walls toward low, thick construction designed to repel artillery attack and to serve as a platform for defensive artillery. High medieval walls might have defended against archers and soldiers with pikes and swords, but they were more susceptible to gunpowder-fueled artillery. The introduction of new weapons technology would prompt further evolution in defensive strategies – it was at this time that the "star fortress" was designed with angled and countered walls placed to offer defenders countless geometric possibilities for the use of artillery.[48] "The geometric patterns of fortifications and the methodical practices of siege warfare so attracted the Europe eye," contends John Lynn, "that they were proposed as models for armies on the battlefield."[49] As Frederick the Great put it, "we should draw our dispositions for battle from the rules of besieging

---

[45] Lynn, *Battle*, p. 129.
[46] Christopher Clark, *Iron Kingdom: The Rise and Downfall of Prussia, 1600–1947* (New York: Penguin, 2006), pp. 30–31.
[47] Lynn, *Battle*, p. 131.   [48] Parker, *The Military Revolution*.
[49] Lynn, *Battle*, p. 119.

positions."[50] "The principles which serve for the conducting of a siege," argued Turpin de Crisse, "may become rules for forming the plan ... of campaign."[51]

Scientific advances impacted warfare it at least two ways. First, the forward march of technology would lead to the creation of new weapons and new weapons would lead to new tactics. The introduction of gunpowder from China, for example, rendered thin fortress walls useless. As the gun improved, it quickly eclipsed other weapons systems, such as the longbow, in effectiveness. These weapons also forced a change in how wars were fought – the science of warfare would advance greatly as warfare made use of geometry and the new science of ballistics to improve bombardment, and consequently fortifications, of cities and military installations. War was becoming scientific: as Louis Pierre de Chastenet argued, military tactics could "easily reduce to sure rules, because [they are] entirely geometrical like fortifications."[52] Some, such as General Guibert, were unsatisfied with the lack of advancement of what became known as military science as compared to other sciences. For Guibert, writes Azar Gat, tactics should:

Constitute a science at every period of time, in every place and among every species of arms; that is to say, if ever by some revolution among the nature of arms which it is not possible to foresee, the order of depth should again be adapted, there would be no necessity in putting the same [tactics] in practice to change either manoeuvre or constitution.[53]

All of this advancement occurred within a highly mechanistic framework, a "clockwork universe" where science and the drill could make war ever more effective and deadly. The introduction of drill in this period can be traced to the army of Maurice of Nassau, Prince of Orange, and was improved upon by subsequent generations of military commanders such as Gustavus Adolphus of Sweden and Frederick the Great of Prussia. In the sixty-plus years that the Dutch Republic fought

[50] R. R. Palmer, "Frederick the Great, Guibert, von Bulow: From Dynastic to National War," in Peter Paret (ed.), *Makers of Modern Strategy* (Princeton, NJ: Princeton University Press, 1986), p. 103.

[51] Turpin de Crisse, *The Art of War* (London, 1761) cited in Azar Gat, *The Origins of Military Thought: From the Enlightenment to Clausewitz* (Oxford: Oxford University Press, 1989), p. 37.

[52] John A. Lynn, *Battle: A History of Combat and Culture* (New York: Basic Books, 2004), p. 126.

[53] Gat, *A History of Military Thought*, p. 50.

against the considerable military forces of Spain's Catholic monarchy the small northern European country "developed a robust fiscal regime and a distinctive military culture with recognizably modern features: the regular and systemic drilling of troops in battleground manoeuvres, a high level of functional differentiation and a disciplined professional officer corps."[54] By the time Frederick's army marched across Europe, the efficiency of gunfire improved so much through drill, training and of course technology that the number of ranks required for sustained volleys against enemy forces fell from ten to three.[55] The tradition of drill was alive and well:

Commanders were expected to execute minutely the general rules of the war game in detail and into which the common soldiers would be integrated as if they were parts of a neatly composed machine. The machine was regarded as a well-organised man-made assembly of smoothly cohering parts, whose order was perfectly in line with the principles of organization followed by "nature."[56]

As in Rome the drills became battles without blood and battles became bloody drills. Like the Romans before, Enlightenment thinkers attempted to make war more effective, thereby improving the instrumentality of conflict through the use of science and technology applied through drill.

Warfare ordered like a clockwork machine, however, would not stand up against societal change in Europe. While technological development continued apace in the nineteenth century, the more dynamic changes to armed conflict would occur within the organization of the military. National revolutions would create a wider polity from which to draw forces and to animate the population to war. The introduction of the *levée en masse* in Napoleonic France brought a size and scale to warfare unseen in the modern era. Napoleon also delimited control in his military, preferring instead to create units capable of more autonomy on the battlefield. The *corps d'armée* reordered the military. Prior to the development of the corps concept, militaries used infantry, cavalry and artillery in units such as regiments,

---

[54] Clark, *Iron Kingdom*, p. 40.
[55] Bousquet, *The Scientific Way of Warfare*, p. 59.
[56] Harald Kleinschmidt, "'Using the Gun': Manual Drill and the Proliferation of Portable Firearms," *The Journal of Military History*, Vol. 63, No. 3 (July 1999), 612.

battalions and divisions making up one large force. Napoleon broke his army into pieces, composed of these constituent units commanded by a sub-commander. As such they were flexible, but still able to mass when needed.[57] He moved drastically away from the controlled, mechanical nature of Frederick the Great's army toward a much more fluid and dynamic system. Napoleon sought out battle, he did not try to avoid it.[58] As Van Creveld notes, "whereas Napoleon's opponents sought to maintain control and minimise uncertainty by keeping their forces closely concentrated, Napoleon chose the opposite way, reorganizing and decentralising his army in such a way as to enable its parts to operate independently for a limited period of time and consequently tolerate a higher degree of uncertainty."[59] Prussian military theorist Carl von Clausewitz offered perhaps the most damning critique of his own nation's approach to war in the Napoleonic age. Whereas Napoleon embraced, and therefore utilized, uncertainty to his advantage, the Prussian military remained entrenched in the clockwork army of Frederick the Great's time during the Napoleonic Wars, consequently losing terribly to more fluid French forces.

The absolute, the mathematical as it is called, nowhere finds any sure basis in the calculations in the art of war ... from the outset there is a play of possibilities, probabilities, good and back luck, which spreads about with all the coarse and fine threads of its web, and makes war of all branches of human activity the most like a gambling game.[60]

Clausewitz reintroduced the idea of the "art" of war into the nineteenth-century debate in military studies contrary to the endeavors of some of his contemporaries, such as Jomini, who still sought to control battle and reduce war to rules and science. Clausewitz, as Beatrice Heuser notes, "wanted to get away from the simple, mechanistic rules. His purpose was to teach his reader how to think about war, rather than give prescriptions for set battle pieces."[61] Despite Clausewitz's appeal for more understanding that no plan survives first contact with the

---

[57] M. J. Williams, *The Good War: NATO and the Liberal Conscience in Afghanistan* (Basingstoke: Palgrave, 2011), p. 66.

[58] Lynn, *Battle*, p. 199.

[59] Martin van Creveld, *Command in War* (Cambridge, MA: Harvard University Press, 1987), p. 61.

[60] Carl von Clausewitz, *On War*, p. 86.

[61] Beatrice Heuser, *Reading Clausewitz* (London: Pimlico, 2002), p. 122.

enemy and that thus the "science" of war was limited, the industrializa-
tion of war continued to reinforce the Western tradition toward decisive
conflict predicated on increasing mass with the rise of the European
nation-state. The Industrial Revolution and the creation of the steam
engine would allow nineteenth-century military forces to move great
distances, capturing territory at previously unknown speed. New communications such as the telegraph, and later the telephone, would
allow commanders to communicate with units at great distances. All of
these developments necessitated supply lines, and logistics would come
to be a critical component of the Western way of war. The military
machine – men and material – both needed to be fed. Without food-
stuffs, ammunitions, etc. it was impossible to wage modern war. Thus
began the logistical legacy from which Western militaries still benefit
today. The horrific result of technology combined with mass and the
traditional Western canon of the decisive battle led to the bloodiest
conflicts of the modern age. The first attempt at mass, mechanized
war was the US Civil War, about half a century in advance of World
War I. World War I resulted in both a tactical and strategic stalemate as
the combatants focused their efforts in concentrated locales. In the Battle
of Verdun alone, over a quarter of a million men were killed and another
half a million were injured. The total number of military deaths eclipsed
10 million. Seven million civilians were killed during the war. Another 15
million soldiers and civilians were injured. No wonder that veteran Ernst
Junger wrote that, in World War I, the soldier was "just like charcoal,
which is hurled under the glowing cauldron of war so as to keep the work
going."[62] The horror of World War I, however, would do little to change
the way countries in Europe waged war. In the matter of a few short
decades the world would once again be plunged into war by an
imbalance of power in Europe.

World Wars I and II altered the global landscape in numerous ways.
Not insignificantly the two wars accelerated the rise and development
of the United States as a world power, while reducing the power of
European states. Although the United States was destined for great-
ness, possessing a large, fertile continent with a healthy population
multiplying year after year, its rise benefited from the destruction
of major powers in Europe during the course of the two world wars.

[62] Ernst Junger, *Der Kampf als Inneres Erlebnis* (Berlin: E. S. Mittler & Son,
1926), p. 14.

The wars prevented any one continental power from being overwhelmingly large and thus challenging the United States. The two wars also drained the coffers of the British, who after World War II found themselves bankrupt and unable to maintain an empire that was becoming increasingly susceptible to American rhetoric of "self-determination." The rest of Europe was likewise devastated, allowing the United States to assume both economic and military hegemony within the "West." The rise of the United States thus occurred on the heels of war, and its hegemony would be cemented in a very real Cold War. It is during this period that a distinctly American interpretation of the Western way of war emerges.

The legal tradition in the Western way of war

Throughout the history described above, it is clear that war, fought for whatever reason, has brought about immeasurable death and suffering. As armies have marched through cities, towns, farms and villages they have often indiscriminately killed, robbed, raped and pillaged in the name of nationalism, empire, religion, progress or, quite simply, for their own pleasure and profit. Reflecting back on this sad history of human warfare, it is not surprising to find that Cicero's phrase *inter arma enim silent leges* (in times of war the law falls silent) is still quoted approvingly today; the history of war is indisputably a history of violence. Whether it is marauding hordes or nuclear weapons, the idea that law can place restraints on war can seem laughable to some. What good can an agreement between states do in a struggle against plundering mercenaries or nuclear weapons? As Clausewitz notes in *On War*: "Attached to force are certain self-imposed, imperceptible limitations hardly worth mentioning, known as international law and custom, but they scarcely weaken it. Force – that is, physical force, for moral force has no existence save as expressed in the state and the law – is thus the means of war; to impose our will on the enemy is its object."[63] In other words, like physics, the only thing that can stop the use of force is force. If anything, armies who have engaged in the Western way of warfare have continuously improved their lethality throughout the ages. Time, money and dedication have been aimed at creating a better and more efficient killing machine. What room could there possibly be for restraint?

---

[63] Carl von Clausewitz, *On War*.

And yet, indisputably, restraint exists. While our mental images of war might be of violence, death and despair, there are at least two ways we can see that war has always been subject to control. First, since ancient times, warriors engaged in armed conflict have fought by certain rules, or codes of honor that dictate whom they may attack, when and how. While not laws, per se, combatants have followed codes of conduct or rituals, reflecting various cultures and social norms that governed their behavior on and off the battlefield. Whether it was the European chivalric code, or the complex rites of Native American warfare, these are the rules that allowed societies to differentiate between that which was "war" and that which was simply murder and pillaging. As Van Creveld eloquently argues regarding the "need for the law of war":

War consists of killing, deliberately shedding the blood of one's fellow-creatures. Now no society can tolerate the shedding of blood and killing unless they are carefully circumscribed by rules that define what is, and is not, allowed. Always and everywhere, only killing done by certain authorized persons, under certain specified circumstances, and in accordance with certain prescribed rules is saved from blame and is regarded as praiseworthy. Conversely, bloodshed which ignores the rules or transgresses them will attract punishment or, in some societies both past and present, atonement. Different societies at different times and places have differed greatly as to where they draw the line between war and murder; however, the line itself is indispensable. Some combatants deserve to be decorated, others hanged. Where the distinction is obliterated, society falls to pieces and war, as opposed to indiscriminate violence, becomes impossible.[64]

We can find these rules in historical records and works of art, culture and literature. Homer's *Iliad* is full of examples of such rituals – the desecration of Hector's body by Achilles after battle would have been understood to be a shocking act that fell outside the understanding of civilized conduct; the violence shown to the corpse falls outside the known rules, norms and limits of warfare. Shakespeare takes pains to justify the killing of French prisoners of war at the battle of Agincourt – a post facto rationalization aimed at explaining what was clearly understood to be a war crime at the time.

---

[64] Martin van Creveld, "The Clausewitzian Universe and the Law of War," *Journal of Contemporary History*, Vol. 26, No. 3/4 (1991), 422.

While it is clear that these rituals, codes and rules may not have always led to results that we would consider humanitarian today, it is clear they have historically played a role in placing limits on warfare. Even Clausewitz, who dismissed international law and argued that the essence of war is violence, recognized in his *On War* that war was, and would forever remain, a social activity. Perhaps more importantly for Clausewitz, although war required much energy and force, it needed to be controlled. If, to use Clausewitzian language, victory was succeeding in compelling the enemy to do our will, anything that took away from achieving this ultimate objective was wasteful. War was not and could not be random bursts of chaos. It might be deadly violent, but for an activity to be war, and for it to be successful, it had to be subject to direction and order. Forces that did not concentrate and conserve their energy wasted precious resources. By this logic, when troops lacked discipline, left the camp or battlefield to attack and pillage civilians and towns, they took force and resources away from the main objective – decisive victory – that the armed forces were trying to achieve.

Second, beyond ritual and tradition, it is clear that some societies did explicitly draw moral and legal codes for regulating, if not moderating, warfare. Dating back to some of the earliest known legal codes, such as the Code of Hammurabi (circa 1750 BC), societies made laws for the purpose of regulating their militaries and civilians in times of war. In early Christian writings, particularly those of Augustine, rules on warfare were deemed necessary to preserve and protect the souls of soldiers who engaged in violence. As such, effort is given to establishing those circumstances in which war is just; it may only be fought to right a wrong, as a last resort, and in such a way as to avoid the.sin of bloodlust. Further, as will be discussed below, the idea that "natural law" (that is to say unwritten law, derived and determined by rational thought) placed constraints on certain actions and behaviors in warfare was well established by writers in the medieval and Enlightenment periods.

Together, these socio-cultural norms and rules and legal codes have helped societies distinguish between legitimate and illegitimate violence, and regulate the conduct of hostilities. And while it might be tempting to view the "laws of war" as an oxymoron, or to quote Cicero's dictum, "silent," it is clear that warfare has always been subject to some control and regulation, regardless of time, place and culture. When considered through this historical view, the idea of placing greater legal restraints on the waging of war becomes a more understandable and reasonable proposition.

As such, while it might be tempting to view Western military might as unstoppable and directed toward ever increasing levels of brutality and lethality, understanding the history of war without consideration of the forces that have at least attempted to control and define it is to miss a significant part of this violent, social phenomenon. This is especially important in the case of liberal countries, particularly the United States, that have felt compelled to use whatever means necessary to defend themselves and their values, but also bound to act in accordance with these same liberal values in times of war. In other words, while the United States sees itself as the guardian of liberal values in the world, it must perform this task in a way that is regarded as civilized and with a view to acting within the boundaries of international norms and laws.

The laws of war and the early American Republic

Although the early American Republic saw itself as a new and egalitarian nation, the Continental Army under the leadership of George Washington immediately adopted the British Articles of War (which, in turn, were based on Roman law).[65] On the face of it, this was something of a strange choice – the British military was known for its drill and discipline as well as harsh punishments. Fully rooted in a class-based system, it was not a perfect fit for a nation that would eschew such hierarchy. However, the decision makes more sense in light of the fact that the new army was in immediate need of a code of military conduct and discipline – it made sense to stick with what they knew. After all, Washington himself had been a military leader in the British Army and fought in the Seven Years' War (also known as the French and Indian War) under these rules.

Although there were certainly aspects of irregular warfare carried out throughout the conflict (such as Nathanael Greene's tactics), Washington was aware that if his army and new country were to be seen as valid by the international community of states (upon whom the United States would depend for legitimacy as it separated from Britain), they would

---

[65] Edmund M. Morgan, "The Background of the Uniform Code of Military Justice," *Military Law Review*, Vol. 28 (April 1965), 17–35.

have to fight and win in conventional battles that followed the understood rules of warfare.[66] Further, military professionals from France
who had arrived to assist the Continental Army to defeat the British
would also help to entrench European norms of warfare. As such, this
cultural knowledge of warfare established the overriding understanding
of warfare for the US armed forces that continues to this day: proper
"war" is conventional war and follows the conventional rules. Irregular
tactics, skirmishes abroad and conflict with Native American peoples,
though bloody, were appreciated as something different from the normal
business of warfare – and as such the normal rules were sometimes
deemed not to apply.

Although they may not have used the language of modern humanitarians, it is clear that the leaders of the young republic were concerned
with issues related to the laws of war. This is easily understandable
given the fact that the British looked upon those within the Continental
Army as rebels, and therefore not deserving the rights, honors and
privileges of "proper" prisoners of war. As such, those captured could
find themselves in poor conditions, on half-rations, with no chance of
parole. Some of the first international treaties that the United States
signed with Prussia (1785) and Morocco (1786) had clauses aimed at
preventing similar treatment of its soldiers in the future, providing good
treatment of prisoners captured in case of war. America was placing
faith in the power of law and treaties to protect itself in the future.

There were limits, however, as to how, where and to whom the law
applied. While the law was applied to British soldiers in the American
Revolution (Washington believed this was key in demonstrating the
moral worthiness of the revolution) and the War of 1812, such policies
did not apply to conflicts with Native Americans throughout the nineteenth century. Although some form of racism was no doubt a factor,
there were at least three other reasons why this was the case. First,
Native Americans were viewed as having consistently backed America's
enemies; they had largely stayed neutral during the revolution and sided
with the British during the War of 1812. Second, they were viewed as
occupying land that had been deemed by providence to belong to the
young republic under the doctrine of "Manifest Destiny." Third, Native
American warriors were seen as engaging in a way of warfare that was

[66] Don Higgenbotham, "The Early American Way of Warfare," *The William
and Mary Quarterly*, 3rd Ser., Vol. 44, No. 2 (April 1987), 230–273, p. 254.

"uncivilized." And where neither side recognized the other's cultural understanding of warfare, there was limited room for restraint – only those who fought by the rules deserved their protection.

This cultural factor, specifically the cultural recognition of warfare, is key to understanding how the United States applied the laws of war in the nineteenth century. Although the law did not apply to the Native Americans, it was, by and large, applied to the Mexican–American War.[67] As the United States confronted two armies during the 1860s – the Confederate Army and the Native Americans in the West – it applied the law to the former but not the latter, even though neither technically qualified for protection.[68] However, there is no question that the fact that Native Americans did not fight according to Western notions of the laws of war lent legitimacy to a policy that denied them protections. For the laws of war to apply to the conflict, the activity being engaged in needed to be recognized as proper war. In the case of Native American warfare, that was simply never going to happen. While there is no question that this was also a convenient argument for US forces to make, it is also clear that cultural recognition has played an important role in how and why the United States applies the laws of war up to the present day – a topic to which we will return in a moment.

The first humanitarian treaties

The laws and customs of war at this time, a gentlemanly code of conduct, enforced by military leaders who were nobles or gentlemen and had the luxury to read and understand works on the subject, were not suited to an age of mass warfare. This was a significant problem for the United States during its Civil War where the Union Army was in need of a simple doctrine it could disseminate to its commanders in the field, who were not such highly educated noblemen. Major General Henry Halleck, who would spend much of the war as the General-in-Chief of the Union Armies in the field, realized that he required simple guidance that he could provide to his men that would clarify their rights

[67] Flory, *Prisoners of War: A Study in the Development of International Law* (Washington D.C.: American Council on Public Affairs, 1942), p. 18.

[68] The Confederate Army would not have qualified, as it was a rebelling republic and not a true state belligerent. The Native Americans did not qualify for similar reasons (despite being recognized by Thomas Jefferson as a "Dependent Domestic Nation").

and obligations. Although he had written his own treatise on the laws of war,[69] for this he turned to Dr. Francis Lieber, a professor at Columbia University who had been delivering a series of lectures on the laws of war. Lieber was a Prussian who fought in the Napoleonic Wars and for Greeks against the Turks. Immigrating to the United States after being persecuted for his democratic ideas, he had lived in both the North and the South of the country. Further, the laws of war were more than just an academic exercise for Lieber: his three sons were fighting in the conflict, two for the Union and one for the Confederacy (who was eventually killed). Lieber agreed to Halleck's request, and wrote the basis of what would become General Orders 100 (aka "the Lieber Code"), consisting of 157 articles, in plain language, which described the rights and obligations of belligerents in time of war. Halleck oversaw the distribution of the pamphlet to the troops, and it became the first modern military manual of an army.

While the Lieber Code was a matter of practicality for the United States, it met well with developments elsewhere. At the same time the Code was being distributed among Union military commanders, Clara Barton was helping to pioneer the humanitarian movement with her "Sanitary Commission," a neutral organization that sought to aid injured soldiers during the war. Both of these ideas – formally codifying the laws of war, and neutral humanitarian aid agencies – were also simultaneously taking root in Europe. Like Barton, Florence Nightingale had worked to improve conditions for wounded and sick British soldiers during the Crimean War. And Henry Dunant, a Swiss businessman who was appalled by the condition of survivors in the aftermath of the 1859 Battle of Solferino, had begun to campaign for an international convention on the rules of war. The Lieber Code and the actions of Barton would contribute to a burgeoning movement to formalize an international humanitarian code. Although it was still caught up in its Civil War, the United States participated in the international conference that led to the drafting of the 1864 Geneva Convention (although it did not ratify this agreement until 1882). This was the first of several treaties that the United States would sign and ratify over the next fifty years, including the 1899 and 1907 Conventions (which helped to codify the law of land warfare) and the 1906 Geneva Convention.

[69] H. W. Halleck, *International Law, or, Rules Regulating the Intercourse of States in Peace and War* (New York: D. Van Nostrand, 1861).

But even by the end of the nineteenth century, the United States had not greatly changed the way it applied the laws of war. At the same time that it was negotiating the laws of land warfare, the United States was engaged in a ruthless irregular war in the Philippines. After having routed the Spanish in a quick conventional campaign, the United States found itself bogged down in a several-year irregular war campaign that featured ambushes, mutilation of corpses and massacres of civilians as US troops grew frustrated at the native insurgency and Filipino fighters struggled for independence. In December 1900, the US Commander in the Philippines, Arthur MacArthur, declared that Filipino guerrillas would be considered war rebels, traitors and would be punished accordingly. In one particularly tragic case following the massacre and mutilation of forty-eight American troops, Brigadier General Jacob H. Smith ordered his officers to turn the island of Samar (where it was suspected the rebels were hiding) into "a howling wilderness" and to shoot any males over the age of 10.

News of the massacre prompted outrage back home in the United States, with newspapers and politicians demanding accountability for the actions at Samar. Smith was eventually charged with "conduct to the prejudice of good order and discipline" (but not murder).[70] However, during his court-martial, Smith based his defense on the Lieber Code's rules that stated in Article 24:

The almost universal rule in remote times was, and continues to be with barbarous armies, that the private individual of the hostile country is destined to suffer every privation of liberty and protection and every disruption of family ties. Protection was, and still is with uncivilized people, the exception.

In other words, the Filipino fighters and population did not deserve protections under the laws of war because their method of fighting was not "proper" war; there was no need to apply restraints to uncivilized warfare.[71] This was also the logic of MacArthur when he denied protection to guerrilla fighters; the laws of war could be used to deny rights as well as grant them. Such a selective application of the laws of war was not, of course, merely a US policy; such attitudes pervaded European

---

[70] David L. Fritz, "'Before the Howling Wilderness': The Military Career of Jacob Hurd Smith, 1862–1902," *Military Affairs*, Vol. 43, No. 4 (December 1979), 186–190.

[71] Peter Maguire, *Law and War: An American Story* (New York: Columbia University Press, 2001), p. 63.

powers, especially as they fought for colonies in Asia and Africa. The British did not feel any obligation to hold back as they fought the Mahdi Army in Sudan, nor did the Belgians, French, Germans, Italians or Dutch restrain their armies when they needed to establish, exert or emphasize their control over colonies. In this sense, we can see US behavior as firmly rooted in this European understanding of proper warfare and its rules and customs.

Yet what is interesting is that the United States continued to see itself as different from European countries – that it was a country with virtues and values that made it separate from the Old World. Unfortunately for those who did not engage in the Western way of warfare, in this important regard, the United States was not exceptional. However, where it may have been different from other Western nations was in its apparent willingness to at least give its enemies the opportunity to adhere to the laws of war and engage in a conventional mode of conflict, even if it meant certain defeat for them. (The Filipinos tried to engage the Americans in conventional battle before they resorted to irregular tactics – but met with disaster each time.) For example, as he set out to engage Pancho Villa during the "Punitive Expedition" in 1916, General John J. Pershing sent the Mexican a copy of the Hague Conventions, apparently as a way of indicating the rules he expected his foe to abide by.[72] Non-Western nations were at least given the opportunity to behave like "civilized" peoples – even if that opportunity was remote. But when that opportunity was turned down, the results were often bloody.

The rise of the American way of war

The Western way of war developed over centuries and was initially unique to the West – it was not a universal condition until forced on others through Western conquest. The focus within Western warfare, unlike in other forms of warfare, is on the decisive battle where the enemy is defeated through the destruction of his forces. War is waged between like units – infantry against infantry, navy against navy; conflict was therefore symmetrical. In the era of the modern nation-state,

[72] Geoffrey Best, "Restraints on War by Land before 1945," in Michael Howard (ed.), *Restraints on War: Studies in the Limitation of Armed Conflict* (Oxford: Oxford University Press, 1979), pp. 17–37.

the mobilization of the population too created ever larger military forces and became the hallmark of Western militaries from the Napoleonic Wars up through World War II. War was conceptualized in the Western tradition as an extension of politics, to break an impasse that could not be solved through dialogue and diplomacy. War was thus instrumental and rational. The application of science to warfare helped to make it more effective, but also to make it more deadly. At the same time war was regulated. Whether it was the informal norms and customs of the ancient Greeks or Romans or the more formal development of the laws of war in Europe from the fifteenth century onward, war was anything but a free-for-all. What made war war, rather than just violence, was the acceptance of common norms and later a legal framework. Although the Western way of war evolved out of European conflicts, it would be an offspring of Europe, the United States of America, that would do the most to advance a combination of science and law to wage war in a manner it believed to be compatible with its political ideals.

2 | *The American way of war*

What is war? War embraces much more than politics ... it is always an expression of culture, often a determinate of cultural forces, in some societies the culture itself.

John Keegan, *A History of Warfare*

The Americans, as a race, are the foremost mechanics in the world. America, as a nation, has the greatest ability for mass production of machines. It therefore behooves us to devise methods of war which exploit our inherent superiority.

General George S. Patton, *War As I Knew It*

Although the early American officer corps drew on the common canon of writings of great European military leaders when the country fought for independence against the British Crown, and the US military continued to engage with the development of military science in Europe post-independence from Great Britain, the American experience in war in the New World of the North American continent differed from that of the Old World. The American historical experience beyond continental Manifest Destiny reinforced a uniquely American approach to Western warfare. To understand how Americans fight war, it is necessary to understand how Americans view war. This is because how a country conceptualizes and understands war directly impacts how that country instrumentalizes war as a tool of policy.

The particular American preference for decisive, overwhelming conflict becomes apparent when one takes into consideration three factors. First, historically the Western way of war is driven to decisive victory by economic constraints that go back in history to the Greek city-states discussed in the previous chapter. Second, the United States, as a contemporary liberal power, considers war an aberration – thus it views conflict as the suspension of civilized politics to engage in a dirty task that should be accomplished as quickly as possible. Finally, and again historically in line with the Western way of warfare, the democratic nature of the contemporary United States necessitates that wars are fought in a timely matter. Just like in ancient Greece, the public will only fight for a certain amount of time before domestic affairs and political infighting consume attention that was hitherto directed, in a somewhat unified manner, on a common war effort.

The desire for overwhelming force and speedy victory is not without restraint. Despite a chemical and biological weapons capability that had developed by the end of World War I, the United States was one of the first countries to spearhead a movement to ban them. Further, it is clear that the deployment of these first weapons of mass destruction necessarily followed certain rules. Given its understanding of its role in the world, the United States could not bring itself to engage in the first use of chemical weapons on the battlefield – although it indicated that it was more than happy to retaliate in kind should the need arise.

This chapter explains how law, science, the Western tradition and technology combined with the American historical experience up to World War II to create a unique form of warfare that sought to annihilate all opposition, but one that did so in such a way that it was still seen as legitimate domestically and internationally.

"Free security" and the strategic culture of the United States

The two most decisive factors in creating the American strategic mindset are the geographic location of the United States and the liberal, democratic nature of the nation's constitution. The two are mutually reinforcing. The United States is a product of the Enlightenment and therefore, as a nation, is strongly rooted in the Enlightenment belief that the world ought to be other than it is. The United States, as a liberal state, abhors war. Liberals, according to Sir Michael Howard in his landmark *War and the Liberal Conscience*, are "all those thinkers who believe the world to be profoundly other than it should be, and who have faith in the power of human reason and human action to change it, so that the inner potential of all human beings can be more fully realized."[1] Liberal states are democratic in nature, democracy being, according to Lipset, "a political system which supplies regular

---

[1] Michael Howard, *War and the Liberal Conscience* (London: Hurst, 2008), p. 3.

constitutional opportunities for changing the governing officials, and a social mechanism which permits the largest possible part of the population to influence major decisions by choosing among contenders for political office."[2] The common denominator of a liberal democracy is a shared value system that allows the peaceful "play" of power along predetermined, socially accepted norms.[3]

Liberal democratic states believe, as Thomas Paine wrote, that war is not due to human nature, but rather "a false system of government" that predisposes man to war.[4] If authoritarian governments were replaced by ones elected by the people, then war would not occur as no man would choose to bring down upon himself the chaos and disorder of war. This is the argument made famous by Immanuel Kant, and from this the modern-day "democratic peace theory" (democracies do not go to war with other democracies) emerged. If a democracy went to war, the logic went, it would be for a just cause.

If the consent of the citizen is required to decide whether or not war is to be declared, it is very natural that they will have great hesitation in embarking on so dangerous an enterprise. For this would mean calling down on themselves all the miseries of war, such as doing the fighting themselves, supplying the costs of the war from their own resources, painfully making good on the ensuing devastation.[5]

For the young American Republic, the causes of war rested on injustice in government. As a liberal democratic republic, war was seen as an aberration, not the norm. The result is that the United States came to see war as a failure of politics, rather than as a continuation of politics in the Clausewitizian sense dominant in European strategic thought. Samuel Huntington sums up this conundrum best:

The American tends to be an extremist on the subject of war: he either embraces war wholeheartedly or rejects it completely. This extremism is required by the nature of liberal ideology. Since liberalism deprecated the moral validity of the interests of the state in security, war must be either condemned as incompatible with liberal goals or justified as an ideological

---

[2] Seymour Martin Lipset, *Political Man* (London: Mercury Books, 1966), p. 45.
[3] *Ibid.* [4] Thomas Paine, *Collected Writings*, Vol. I (London, 1894), p. 388.
[5] Immanuel Kant, "Towards Perpetual Peace," in Pauline Keingeld (ed.), *Toward Perpetual Peace and Other Writings on Politics, Peace and History* (New Haven, CT: Yale University Press, 2006), p. 74.

movement in support of those goals. American thought has not viewed war in the conservative-military sense as an instrument of national policy.[6]

Early Americans viewed war as the result of a monarchical system of government that bent humankind to the will of an illegitimate institution. The United States, argued John Adams, should only fight defensive wars since as a republic she could not and would not seek out war.[7] This was possible, as George Washington noted, because of the "detached and distant situation" of the United States from Europe. Washington stipulated in his Farewell Address to the nation in 1796:

The great rule of conduct for us in regard to foreign nations is in extending our commercial relations, to have with them as little political connection as possible. So far as we have already formed engagements, let them be fulfilled with perfect good faith. Here let us stop. Europe has a set of primary interests, which to us have none; or a very remote relation. Hence she must be engaged in frequent controversies, the causes of which are essentially foreign to our concerns. Hence, therefore, it must be unwise in us to implicate ourselves by artificial ties in the ordinary vicissitudes of her politics, or the ordinary combinations and collisions of her friendships or enmities.[8]

Washington went on to question the logic of involvement in European affairs; "Why forego the advantages of so peculiar a situation? Why quit our own to stand upon foreign ground? Why, by interweaving our destiny with that of any part of Europe, entangle our peace and prosperity in the toils of European ambition, rivalship, interest, humor or caprice?"[9] The United States had the ability to pursue a different project, a republican project based upon equality under the law, self-rule and mercantilism. To engage with Europe would be to cast aside the benefits of this unique enterprise. The geographic location of the United States thus helped to form American strategic culture. The isolated location of the young republic, free from the endemic conflicts of Europe, allowed Americans to view war as the exception, rather than the rule of international politics. Location

---

[6] Samuel Huntington, *The Soldier and the State: The Theory of Politics and Civil–Military Relations* (Cambridge, MA: Belknap Press, 1957) p. 151.
[7] Reginald Stuart, *War and American Thought: From the Revolution to the Monroe Doctrine* (Kent, OH: Kent State University Press, 1982).
[8] Cited in: Felix Gilbert, *To the Farewell Address: Ideas of Early American Foreign Policy* (Princeton, NJ: Princeton University Press, 1970).
[9] *Ibid.*

legitimated (perhaps not recognized as such) the liberal American belief that war was the result of dictatorial monarchies. This was made all the more possible given the self-perception that America was indeed exceptional among nations.

The American Revolution was a clear attempt to break with the tyrannies, despotism and monarchies of the Old World that, in true Enlightenment fashion, were seen as the root of conflict and injustice. As Felix Gilbert notes, "Americans believed that in taking up arms they were defining the true rights of Englishmen and they acted as the legitimate heirs of the proud English tradition of freedom, handed on in unbroken succession from the days of the Magna Carta."[10] The resulting understanding of war as an aberration meant that war, when it did arise, was viewed as absolute endeavor; a task that often required some sort of "moral crusade" to justify the act. Inevitably, this gave rise to certain dilemmas. "A war fought in the name of high moral principle," wrote the American diplomat George Kennan, "finds no early end short of some form of total domination."[11] The extension of this argument is the idea that war should always end in unconditional surrender, what historian Russell Weigley labeled a "characteristically American war aim."[12] As Dominic Tierney notes, "in modern history it's very unusual to insist that the enemy submit entirely to one's demands."[13] The absolute victory favored by Americans was not common in Europe where conflict was concluded as part of a mutually agreed negotiation by warring parties.

One must appreciate how these differences eventually significantly impacted the establishment of the American way of warfare, and the understanding of war within an American mindset, as separate from that of Europe. As Huntington argues, each culture develops a slightly different view of war, although this view is situated within a larger, shared Western framework:

The military institutions of any society are shaped by two forces: a functional imperative stemming from the threats to the society's security and a societal

---

[10] *Ibid.*, p. 19.

[11] George Kennan, *American Diplomacy: Expanded Edition* (Chicago: University of Chicago Press, 1984), p. 100.

[12] Russell Weigley, *The American Way of War* (Bloomington: University of Indiana Press, 1973), p. 281.

[13] Dominic Tierney, *How We Fight: Crusades, Quagmires and the American Way of War* (New York: Little, Brown & Company, 2010), p. 19.

imperative arising from the social forces, ideologies, and institutions dominant within the society. Military institutions, which reflect only social values,
may be incapable of performing their military function. On the other hand, it
may be impossible to contain within society military institutions shaped
purely by functional imperatives. The interaction of these two forces is the
nub of the problem of civil–military relations. The degree to which they
conflict depends upon the intensity of the security needs and the nature and
strength of the value pattern of society.[14]

For most of American history, the US public and civilian institutions
were incredibly distrustful of the military. The US Congress worried
about militarism in the new country from the outbreak of war in 1776
going forward. The pattern for the United States was to raise an army in
times of need and then, following the conflict, to disband the army,
greatly reducing its size and diverting finances to other, more worthwhile domestic endeavors. The one exception to this rule was the
development of the US Navy, which was created not to wage war, but
to protect US shipping from piracy in waters around North Africa.
Where the Navy was seen as a necessary requirement for a mercantile
nation like the United States, the Army was viewed as a threat to
American republicanism. The worry over a standing military has
roots stretching back to the American Republic's English heritage. As
one English anti-army pamphlet of 1675 argued, "the power of Peerage
and a Standing Army are like two Buckets, the proportion that one goes
down, the other exactly goes up."[15] The basis for English concerns was
the quartering of soldiers among civilian populations and the subsequent hardship that civilians thus bore. Early attempts to regulate this
behavior can be traced back to Henry I's London Charter of 1130 that
contained the passage "let no one be billeted within the walls of the city,
either of my household, or by force of anyone else."[16] The Magna Carta
upheld the "ancient liberties and free customs" including the rules
against quartering in London and other cities. A right to arms and the
English citizen militia concept was by the fifteenth century seen as
essential to the development of "government under law" and a way to

---

[14] Huntington, *The Soldier and the State*, p. 2.
[15] Anon, pamphlet of 1675 entitled "Letter from a Person of Quality," cited in
J. G. A. Pocock, "Machiavelli, Harrington and English Political Ideologies in the
18th Century," *William and Mary Quarterly*, Vol. 22, No. 4 (1965), 560.
[16] D. Douglas and G. Greenway (eds.), *English Historical Documents 1042–1189*
(Oxford: Oxford University Press, 1961), p. 945.

check absolutist royal tendencies.[17] Similar sentiment prevailed among Prussian noblemen in the seventeenth century that saw the expansion of state power and a standing military as a challenge to "liberty."[18] The American Founding Fathers, deeply impacted by the quartering of standing British forces in the homes of American colonials, came to see a standing military as a threat to liberty. This polices made such an impact that President Madison subsequently included in the Bill of Rights a provision against the quartering of soldiers in homes. Although the government created under the new constitution was stable enough to govern a standing force, the public and many policy-makers remained skeptical of the need for a large standing military.

The result over the next century was an American military that was improbably small for such a growing nation. Prior to the US Civil War the regular size of the Army was in the range of 6,000 to 15,000 soldiers who manned permanent fortifications, dealt with the "Indian menace" and managed other emergencies. After the Civil War this number was closer to 25,000 – but it was still incredibly small for a nation that had just fought the most deadly war in its history and remained internally conflicted. The American Army was a footnote in American history as Colonel Arthur L. Wagner wrote:

It is clear that our military future will not be shaped by theories based on military principles alone. The military policy of the United States will be strongly affected by the popular predilection for economic expenditures in times of peace; by a jealousy of standing armies; by reliance upon volunteers in time of war, and by a more or less active influence of popular armies in the direction of armies in the field.[19]

A small peacetime force was the norm until the establishment of a prolonged peacetime military mobilization was seen as required by the challenges of the early Cold War period. Prior to the Cold War the military was raised from among the population and consequently

---

[17] Max Beloff, *The Age of Absolutism 1660–1815* (New York: Harper Torchbooks, 1962).

[18] Christopher Clark, *Iron Kingdom: The Rise and Downfall of Prussia, 1600–1947* (New York: Penguin, 2006), p. 56.

[19] Carol Reardon, *Soldiers and Scholars: The US Army and the Uses of Military History* (Lawrence: University of Kansas Press, 1990), pp. 26–27.

citizens took a direct interest in the wars of the nation. This also created a strong upward pressure on policy-makers and politicians to keep conflict within certain boundaries, which in turn limited the scope of the military and political leadership in conducting war. Americans were by and large isolationist when it came to wars among the Great Powers. Citizens were willing to man an armed force so long as it was necessary to fight a war, but they were not keen on wars of choice beyond the expansion of the United States in achievement of Manifest Destiny. The conditions of the Cold War, however, forced the United States to rethink its previous strategy and require a professional military to become a permanent fixture of national life, rather than an episodic actor in times of conflict.

At this time, the didactic of war or peace created a steadfast belief within the United States military and the wider public that total, unconditional victory in warfare was the norm. Because war is seen as an aberration there is a desire to end it as quickly and decisively as possible. When coupled with the domestic political pressure of public support for war this mindset is further amplified. In the United States the conflict needs support of the public, just as President Woodrow Wilson discovered in the run-up to involvement in World War I. Wilson wanted to enter the war because he was worried about the European powers pushing a "victor's peace" on Germany and the Austro-Hungarian Empire. But once mobilized, he failed to realize that the American people would not settle for an armistice. They wanted complete and total victory over their opponent.[20] In the American mind, their opponent had forced their country to war and thus the horrors of war were the fault of the enemy – it was the role of the US armed forces to complete the job. As President Franklin D. Roosevelt later argued, "we must face the fact that modern warfare as conducted in the Nazi manner is a dirty business. We don't like it – we didn't want to get in it – but we are in it and we're going to fight with everything we've got."[21] Contrarily, General Douglas MacArthur rather more forcefully put it, "the concept of

[20] Michael Pearlman, *Warmaking and American Democracy: The Struggle over Military Strategy 1700–Present* (Lawrence: University of Kansas Press, 1999), p. 188.
[21] George E. Hopkins, "Bombing and the American Conscience during World War II," *The Historian*, Vol. 28, No. 3 (May 1966), 463.

appeasement, the concept that when you use force you can limit that force ... to me that would have continued an indefinite extension of bloodshed."[22]

These examples help to explain the rise of the "annihilation" tendency in the American way of warfare. Recall George Kennan's assertion, cited earlier, that a war of moral principle has no end short of total domination. The United States actively cultivated a crusader mentality to justify involvement in wars.[23] As such, when engaged in a war, there is a strong tendency to execute the most decisive and, consequently, brutal war possible. The Americans have been able to develop the idea of unconditional surrender in part because of their nation's geographic position – free from the constantly shifting borders of Europe, the nation become accustomed to perfect security rather than war as a regular feature of life. These two variables combined to form part of an equation within the American strategic mindset that war was an aberration and that it must end with total victory, rather than compromise.

On the other hand, for European states it has proven historically impossible to avoid war. Indeed, the modern idea of the state was born out of the ashes of the Eighty Years' War of Dutch Independence and then the Thirty Years' War. Because of the tight proximity of states on the European continent, it became difficult for states to avoid becoming embroiled in conflict when it broke out. This was made even more difficult by the rise of alliance systems in the centuries following the Thirty Years' War. Although the intention of alliances was to avoid war through the appearance of looking stronger, alliances frequently had the effect of bringing more states into a conflict once it had started. The result was almost always total, endemic war on the continent, and European culture developed in such a way that conflict was not seen as an aberration – even within an increasingly politically liberal continent. War was a regular occurrence and familiarity with war led to acceptance of it as a tool

---

[22] Christopher M. Gacek, *The Logic of Force: The Dilemma of Limited War in American Foreign Policy* (New York: Columbia University Press, 1994), p. 64.

[23] For more on the role of identity in the creation of foreign policy see: David Campbell, *Writing Security: United States Foreign Policy and the Politics of Identity* (Minneapolis: University of Minnesota Press, 1998).

of policy (as Clausewitz famously argued). Wars were therefore not conceptualized as absolutist. There was no requirement for "total victory" – rather the aim was more often a negotiated settlement and the end of the conversation of war until the next conflict. There was therefore a desire to keep wars limited in nature – war was a critical component upholding international order, it was in itself not disorder. The desire for limited war, however, became more and more difficult to achieve. Advances in munitions technology coupled with the social forces of nationalism increased the scale and devastation of war in Europe, eventually leading to the near total destruction of most of Europe in World War II.

America's "detached and distant situation" enabled the United States to develop a strategic culture predicated on the twin ideas of war as an aberration and decisive victory as the sole goal of warfare. Had the young, weak American Republic been surrounded by bellicose European powers pursuing wars of national interest, the nation would have most likely developed very different notions on the use of force and the goals of warfare. This is not to say that the United States was never involved in war. But exposure to large-scale war with another state was limited – aside from the War of 1812, the Japanese bombing of Pearl Harbor and the attacks on New York City in 2001, Americans have been spared direct attacks on the US homeland. Although the United States engaged in a series of smaller conflicts, such as the Mexican–American War and the various wars against indigenous tribes in North America, Washington policy-makers enjoyed the upper hand in these conflicts and the country was not ravaged at will by neighbors – a decidedly different state of affairs than in continental Europe during the same period. It is not clear if the average American realizes how exceptional this war-free history has been, but one of America's most noble statesmen noted the nation's good fortune. As President Lincoln argued, "Shall we expect some transatlantic military giant to step the Ocean, and crush us at a blow? Never! . . . If destruction be our lot, we must ourselves be its author and finisher."[24] This sublime isolation allowed the United States to develop free from foreign involvement and to pursue the pacification

---

[24] David Mayers, *Wars and Peace: The Future Americans Envisioned, 1861–1991* (New York: St. Martin's Press, 1999), p. 5.

of the continent uninterrupted. In *Diplomacy*, Kissinger notes this, writing:

America's most significant military experiences had been its own Civil War, which had been fought to the finish, and the First World War. Both of which had ended in total victory. In American thinking foreign policy and strategy were compartmentalized into successive phases of national policy. In the ideal American universe, diplomats stayed out of strategy and military personnel completed their task by the time the diplomacy started ...[25]

Eliot Cohen traced this trend back even further than Kissinger, placing it before the American Civil War experience. For Cohen, it was the hybrid nature of war in the American colonies that started on the "Great Warpath" that influenced the early roots of the American way of warfare. In an environment where European norms of warfare clashed with Native American approaches and an emerging colonial (American) approach to war, even the professional European soldiers posted in the New World found themselves accepting acts that would have been considered savage in Europe – and to some extent contradictory. For Cohen this set a pattern that would be repeated throughout American history.

It was never the American way to take artistic satisfaction in the elegant rituals of surrender in the European manner. Honor mattered, but victory mattered more. American military culture thus became a self-contradictory hybrid of form, restraint and etiquette, on the one hand, improvisation, raw energy and unwillingness to accept limits on the other. The story of Fort William Henry [where after surrender the English and American units were slaughtered by France's native allies supposedly under French protection] is part of the explanation why.[26]

The result was a cycle throughout the nineteenth century that led to the ruthless expansion of the United States westward, ultimately facilitating the growth of the nation and the strengthening of the economy. The westward expansion through native lands and the eventual eradication of European powers in the central portion of the North American continent, in line with the Monroe Doctrine of 1823, provided the United States with a secure footing for Great Power status in the

---

[25] Henry Kissinger, *Diplomacy* (New York: Simon & Schuster, 1994) p. 402.
[26] Eliot A. Cohen, *Conquered into Liberty* (New York: Free Press, 2011), p. 70.

twentieth century. The geographic position of the United States rein-forcing the belief inherent in American liberal values that war was exceptional rather than routine led to an American way of war that decouples war from the peace following war.

As the British strategist Colin Gray notes, "Americans wage war as a largely autonomous activity, leaving worry about peace and its politics to some later day."[27]

This American view of war is distant from that which developed in Europe during the nineteenth century. As Clausewitz wrote in Book VIII of *On War*:

It is, of course, well known that the only source of war is politics – the intercourse of governments and peoples; but it is apt to be assumed that war suspends that intercourse and replaces it by a wholly different condition, ruled by no law but its own.

We maintain, on the contrary, that war is simply a continuation of political intercourse, with the addition of other means ...

How could it be otherwise? Do political relations between peoples and between their governments stop when diplomatic notes are no longer exchanged? Is war not just another expression of their thoughts, another form of speech or writing? Its grammar, indeed, may be its own, but not its logic.[28]

This is a decidedly different view of war from that dominating American strategic thought. As Benjamin Buley highlights, "a distinction may be introduced for the purpose of analysis between the three concepts that for Clausewitz were no doubt intertwined: the sovereignty of politics in war, the political utility of force, and war as a continuation of politics."[29] For Clausewitz the logic of war was the logic of politics – they were one and the same. War, like politics, was a process to realize a political goal. The grammar of the process was, however, different. The sovereignty of the political objective sets the course for war, even if war is a unique enterprise. In the United States the view of war as an aberration led to the creation of a mentality that war was a breakdown or failure of politics, rather than a logical extension of that enterprise.

[27] Colin S. Gray, "The American Way of War: Critique and Implications," in Anthony D. McIvor (ed.), *Rethinking the Principles of War* (Annapolis, MD: Naval Institute Press, 2005), p. 28.
[28] Carl von Clausewitz, *On War* (Michael Howard and Peter Paret, trans.) (London: Random House, 1993), p. 605.
[29] Benjamin Buley, *The New American Way of War: Military Culture and the Political Utility of Force* (London: Routledge, 2008), p. 10.

This is the traditional way of warfare that led to the American belief in the effectiveness of force as an overwhelming and total enterprise, rather than as a limited political one. This view would dominate the American strategic mindset through World War II. Only in the Nuclear Age, when the presence of nuclear weapons made the idea of total war an anathema, did the idea of more limited war creep into the American lexicon.

Americans would prove throughout the course of the nineteenth and early twentieth centuries that they were more than willing to use force when their interests were at stake. However, a contradiction arising from their Enlightenment beliefs was emerging; the need for absolute victory, but also to be seen as legitimate domestically and internationally. Even if the American people expected and demanded nothing short of overwhelming victory, there were also expectations that the use of force was undertaken in a restrained manner acceptable to America's liberal Enlightenment values. When the need to use force arose, it was clear that not every weapon would be or could be on the table. For all of its exceptionalism, it is not clear that the United States felt that it could go beyond European nations when it came to fighting well – especially when it came to fighting other Western nations. As noted in the previous chapter, by the 1860s, the United States began to participate in most, if not all, international conferences on developing treaties such as the 1864 Geneva Convention, and the 1899 and 1907 Hague Treaties.[30]

As technology improved and developed, however, particularly those inventions that made industrialized slaughter ever easier, it was clear that balancing these competing tendencies of annihilation and restraint would often become harder – even where the new technology promised ever more humane methods of fighting and killing.

Systematizing war and the technological imagination of America

The desire and necessity for overwhelming victory led to a high level of systematization in the American way of war. To be sure, the broader

---

[30] However, as indicated above, the (professed) preference for the United States was to avoid war altogether. This was a major reason the United States put great effort into establishing an international Permanent Court of Arbitration – an institution where states could solve their disputes peacefully, reflecting perfectly the Enlightenment values of respecting the rule of law and rationality rather than the irrational use of force.

Western way of war has always been systematic. Like the Romans before them, the Americans took the basics of Western warfare and turned war into a machine – to date the most high-tech war machine in the history of humankind. The United States was not the first country to conceptualize and implement war as a machine. In the 1930s and early 1940s the National Socialists and the *Wehrmacht* in Germany reconstructed war out of the ashes of the stalemate that was the Great War. Germany, a highly industrialized country, also utilized technology to wage war in a revolutionary fashion – which German technology and strategic thinking did indeed enable.

The most recent military-technological revolutions – two in this century and two in the last – demonstrate that the advantage in warfare goes to those nation-states that can most effectively utilize new technologies. Perhaps the best example in this century was the Nazi blitzkrieg, made possible by advances in internal combustion engines, aircraft design, radio and radar, and other technologies in the two decades following World War I. Although all major military organizations had access to these technologies, only the Germans used them to initiate new operational concepts and innovate organizationally.[31]

The Germans utilized the power and scale afforded by ethnic nationalism with modern, often cutting-edge technologies, to launch blitzkrieg – essentially the template for maneuver war as it is practiced to this day. But while Nazi Germany developed blitzkrieg, but the United States has practiced maneuver warfare since the 1940s in a more systematic fashion. This systemization of warfare by the United States should not be surprising as America is, like Germany, what could fairly be described as a "machine nation." The United States is a country compelled to efficiency almost since birth. Even today one finds on US government forms a "public burden" specification at the top of the sheet detailing the estimated time burden of completing the form. The American desire for efficiency spans the gamut from tax forms to warfare. The use of machines to improve efficiency dates back to the early years of the republic when the young America lacked the manpower to compete globally and needed to compensate for its still small populace. By the eve of the Civil War in 1860, the United States, in the span of roughly

---

[31] Andrew F. Krepinevich Jr., "Keeping Pace with the Military-Technological Revolution," *Issues in Science and Technology*, Vol. 19, No. 4 (1994), p. 24.

half a century, had transformed itself from a colonial backwater into the second largest industrial power in the world after Great Britain. As John Ellis argued, the United States in the nineteenth century "far outstripped any other country in the development of machines to do jobs previously undertaken by skilled workers."[32] The problem facing the United States was a shortage of skilled workers. A lack of skilled workers meant that laborers had to be paid high wages, reducing the competitiveness of American producers. "Thus machines were rationalized, centralized production units were introduced to multiply the productivity of the individual worker."[33] As the Industrial Revolution proceeded apace, it began to impact other sectors of life beyond the economy, including warfare. The Industrial Revolution of the nineteenth century would have a tremendous impact on the conduct of war. The invention of the combustion engine gave war mechanical power. Railway lines allowed large amounts of men and material to be transported great distances, enlarging the scale of warfare. Because the United States was short of skilled labor it lacked the craftsmen to produce a range of technologies and remained dependent, particularly on Britain, for large amounts of finished goods especially heavy machinery. This shortage of skilled labor also affected the ability of the United States to produce guns. As John Ellis notes, "there were simply not enough gunsmiths to satisfy the demands of the Army."[34]

The United States depended on weapons that were old and unreliable, principally imports from Europe that were past their prime. The country was in effect largely unarmed compared to countries in Europe. America's geographic position enabled this luxury – in Europe such a shortage would have been an invitation to invasion. Given the labor situation in the United States, the country was forced to compensate for the lack of skilled labor with machines. This in turn led to a dependency on machines – so much so that the nation would come to believe in the unlimited potential of what machines could accomplish. Automation could be applied to any process. It should be no surprise then that the machine gun was created in the United States. The US Civil War further necessitated the need for automation in warfare in what would prove a great, protracted struggle between countrymen. It would become the first war of the industrial era, perhaps best captured by Walter Mills, who argues that once the US had entered into the Civil War:

---

[32] Ellis, *The Social History of the Machine Gun*, p. 21.   [33] *Ibid.*   [34] *Ibid.*, p. 22.

technology was to intensify the scope, deadliness, and universality of the struggle with a speed that would previously have been impossible. The railroad and the river steamboat enabled both sides to mobilize, supply and deploy armies of unprecedented size with an unprecedented promptness ... In 1861 the Confederate Congress began by voting, two days after Lincoln's inauguration, an army of 100,000 volunteers. It is said to have had one third of them organized and under arms in little over a month ... Lincoln, who had started by calling for 75,000 militia in mid-April, is said to have had something like 250,000 men under arms by July ... When in the immediately following days after Bull Run both sides took serious measure of the struggle laying before them, the Northern Congress voted an army of 500,000 men and the Southerners one of 400,000 ...

Begun on this scale the war was to be waged with a mounting intensity for which, again, the new ... technology was in large part responsible. It is estimated that from first to last about 900,000 individuals served in the Confederate armies and about 1,500,000 in those of the North. In providing these hosts with weapons, accouterments and clothing, as well as with transportation and supply, industry on both sides was to perform remarkable feats.[35]

What is perhaps most surprising about this war that killed more Americans than any other conflict in US history to date is the motivation for the creation of some of the technologies that would make the fighting so deadly. Many of these weapons were not intended to kill millions of men – they were actually motivated by humanitarian reasons stemming from US liberal values. Consider for instance this excerpt from a letter that Richard Jordan Gatling, one of the early machine gun pioneers, wrote on developing what would become known as the "Gatling gun":

It may be interesting to you to know how I came to invent the gun that bears my name ... In 1861, during the opening events of the war ... I witnessed almost daily the departure of troops to the front and the return of the wounded, sick and dead. The most of the latter lost their lives, not in battle, but by sickness and sickness incident to the service. It occurred to me that if I could invent a machine – a gun – that would by its rapidity of fire enable one man to do as much battle duty as a hundred, that it would to a great extent supersede the necessity of large armies, and consequently exposure to battle and disease would be greatly diminished.[36]

---

[35] Walter Mills, *Arms and Men* (New York: New American Library, 1963), pp. 102–103.

[36] P. Whal and D. R. Toppel, *The Gatling Gun* (London: Herbert Jenkins, 1966), p. 18. See also: C. J. Chivers, *The Gun* (New York: Simon & Schuster, 2010), especially Chapter 1.

Gatling's belief that his invention would make war more humane, rather than more inhumane, was typical of the society in which he lived. "Technical utopianism" was increasingly evident within American culture; as Howard Segal noted, "a growing number, even majority, of Americans were ... coming to take for granted: the belief in the inevitability of progress and in progress precisely as technological progress."[37]

The synthesis of war and industry in the United States was well underway by the end of the Civil War. This Zeitgeist would graft itself onto the culture of war making in an unprecedented fashion. Systematization was the way of the future, as Frederick Winslow Taylor argued, and the country was disadvantaged because of the great loss of productivity due to "inefficiency in almost all our daily acts." The idea behind what would become known as "Taylorism" was the study of work processes to reduce inefficiency and to inject machine-like precision into production methods in an effort to reduce waste. The perfection of mechanization, the systematization of life, was the goal. The hallmark of such an approach is evident on roads around the world in the blue and silver badge of the Ford Motor Company – the first in the world to introduce assembly lines that improved productivity 1,000 percent. Before long "Fordism" would become a globally embraced American ideal.[38] The Industrial Revolution would transform the way all Western nations fought, but no nation would apply technology to the pursuit of war like the United States.

In a 1915 interview with the *New York Times*, American inventor Thomas Edison stated that:

The war of the future, that is, if the United States engages in it, will be a war in which machines, not soldiers, fight ... machines should be invented to save the waste in men. America is the greatest machine country in the world, and its people are the greatest machinists ... They can, moreover, invent machinery faster and have it more efficient than any other two countries. It is a machine nation; its battle preparation should be with machinery.[39]

[37] Howard P. Segal, *Technological Utopianism in American Culture* (Chicago: University of Chicago Press, 1985), p. 1.
[38] Carroll Pursell, *The Machine in America: A Social History of Technology* (Baltimore, MD: Johns Hopkins University Press, 1995), pp. 210–211.
[39] H. Bruce Franklin, *War Stars: The Superweapon and the American Imagination* (Oxford: Oxford University Press, 1988), p. 72.

The Americans, of course, were not the only ones looking to apply technology to "improve" war, although they excelled at it. This is a trend within the Western way of warfare more generally, and as trench warfare took hold on the fields of Europe, scientists began to research even more efficient and effective ways to break the stalemate between the Great Powers. The first science fiction novels promised a future where scientists worked to discover weapons that were so terrible that there would simply be no choice but to end war forever. Life mirrored art as scientists worked with their governments to develop just such a weapon that would bring victory to their side and end the war. As P.D. Smith argues, it was the dawn of "the age of the superweapon."[40]

By this time both Europe and America held an almost unshakeable faith in science to bring about a better world – a belief that had been reinforced by popular science magazines and science fiction of such writers as Jules Verne and H. G. Wells.[41] Yet the American approach to the "future" differed from that of Europe. Recall once more the liberal republican nature of the United States and consider that in many ways America was a country without a past – society was hers to create. This reality was also evident in the military. In Europe an exclusive officer corps, drawn from the upper echelons of society, continued to dominate the armed forces. The militaries of European Great Powers – Britain, Germany and France – were effectively controlled by an upper-class officer corps, and distant from technological and social developments in their societies. European officers were, according to Vagts, "romantics in an industrial age." In Europe, there was a "decided hardening" within the general staffs:

Evidenced in their reluctance to consider technological innovations; how utterly averse they were to changes in material was discovered to their great chagrin by industrialists like Colt, Krupp and Whitworth, and the military

---

[40] P. D. Smith, *Doomsday Men: The Real Dr. Strangelove and the Dream of the Superweapon* (London: Allen Lane, 2007), p. 97

[41] Perhaps the only exception to this was the British, who were deeply skeptical about the value of superweapons. Instead, a belief in old-fashioned soldiering seems to have dominated strategic thinking. Indeed, this was a belief so strong that the military leadership failed to comprehend the strategic advantage of the first tank when it was delivered to them on the battlefields. Smith argues that, "surprising the enemy with a fiendish new invention offended the British sense of fair play." Smith, *Doomsday Men*, p. 107.

inventor and officer Werner Siemens grew so disgusted with the Prussian officer service that he gave it up to go into industry.[42]

Contrary to an increasingly automated mentality that the United States was applying to war, in Europe war was still an act of will. To be a warrior was to be a unique individual in society, as Clausewitz wrote, "For as long as they practice [war] soldiers will think of themselves as a guild in which regulations, laws and customs, the spirit of war [are] given pride of place."[43] For the officer corps of Europe, war was still about man and his ability to master the battlefield. "War," according to Christopher Coker, "separates into two those human beings who will risk all and those who fear for their lives. Both may be the same genetically, but their behavior is different, and it is socially produced."[44] For European military leaders the technology that was embraced in egalitarian America represented a very real threat to the social fabric not only of their military establishment, but also of the wider nation as a whole.

It is not coincidental then that of all the great European strategists the American military could reify, they chose not Clausewitz and his writings on the "fog of war," favoring instead Jomini. Antoine-Henri, Baron de Jomini systematized the approach to war embodied by Frederick the Great and Napoleon.[45] Jomini was driven to do so because his intellectual roots were in the eighteenth-century Enlightenment. Jomini was fond of logic and order, and was thus driven to define war as an ordered system – very much the opposite of the approach Clausewitz applied to war. According to Weigley, Jomini was "repelled when he found elements of the chaotic and demoniacal in Napoleon's character and methods of war. He abhorred indiscriminate bloodshed."[46] Whereas Clausewitz viewed war as an extension of politics,

---

[42] A. Vagts, *A History of Militarism* (New York: The Free Press, 1967), p. 224.

[43] Clausewitz cited in Christopher Coker, *Waging War without Warriors* (Boulder, CO: Lynne Rienner, 2002), p. 54.

[44] Coker, *Waging War without Warriors*, p. 55.

[45] This is not to say that Clausewitz was not widely taught within the US military establishment. As Heuser notes, after Vietnam Clausewitz was made mandatory reading in a number of US military academies. Beatrice Heuser, *Reading Clausewitz* (London: Pimlico, 2002), p. 18. But in the early republic, and one can even argue today, it is the spirit of Jomini that inspires the technological mindset of the US military, rather than Clausewitz.

[46] Weigley, *The American Way of War*, p. 82.

Jomini conceptualized war as the suspension of politics – it was a series of battles to be won, after which the political would reassert itself into the equation.[47] This fit the American mindset decidedly well; as Major General John Schofield informed a group of American officers in 1877, "It is the Science of War in the broadest sense, not simply the Art of War, that we are to study." It is therefore not surprising when historian Azar Gat notes that:

All the translations of Jomini's major works into English were done in America. Indeed, and this has not been fully recognized, in no other country was Jomini translated so extensively ... The Civil War was conducted by West Pointers, and it has been justly said that the generals on both sides went into the war with a sword in one hand and Jomini's *Summary of the Art of War* in the other.[48]

The result of technological progress with increasingly systematized warfare would reach three new plateaus in the twentieth century. In the Great War of 1914–1918, where the machine gun would finally come into its own, the last remnants of war as a human-centric, gallant and heroic enterprise died in the trenches of France. The response to the innovation of the machine gun was the development of the tank, a weapon that rendered irrelevant the defensive tactics of World War I. The next plateau would be World War II, a conflict that would see improvements in existing technology – airplanes, tanks, missiles, submarines – combined in neo-Napoleonic strategies by the Germans and then the Americans, which made war faster, more mobile and utterly more destructive than ever before. Although the Germans are often credited with technological advancement in the warfare of the mid-twentieth century, it was the Americans that truly mechanized and systematized warfare. The Germans may have instituted blitzkrieg against their less powerful European neighbors, but the German army was more dependent on horses and walking infantry than the more mechanized American Army.[49] German tanks may have been superior

---

[47] Gray, "The American Way of War"; John A. Nagl, *Learning to Eat Soup with a Knife: Counterinsurgency Lessons from Malaya and Vietnam* (Chicago: University of Chicago Press, 2005), Chapter 3; and Weigley, *The American Way of War*.

[48] Azar Gat, *A History of Military Thought: From the Enlightenment to the Cold War* (Oxford: Oxford University Press, 2001), pp. 288–289.

[49] George F. Hoffman, *Through Mobility We Conquer: The Mechanization of the US Cavalry* (Lexington: University of Kentucky Press, 2006); George F. Hoffman and Donn A. Starry (eds.), *Camp Colt to Desert Storm: The History of US Armored Forces* (Lexington: University of Kentucky Press, 1999).

to American tanks, but the Americans produced more tanks and then implemented them in an analytical fashion aimed at the most effective use of existing capabilities. The Americans were entirely focused on the war effort; the German government meanwhile sacrificed military logic to use resources to pursue a genocidal purge. President Franklin Roosevelt understood the inherent industrial advantage the United States held over Nazi Germany, calling for a "crushing superiority of equipment" to overcome the enemy that observers note was "a shrewd calculation of America's comparative advantage in modern warfare and of the political dangers and economic opportunities that American belligerency posed on the home front."[50] The Americans, as Martin van Creveld indicates, pursued a "managerial approach" to warfare.[51] As a British officer observed in World War II:

The Americans were analytic. They approached warfare as they approached any other large enterprise; breaking it down to its essentials, cutting out what was superfluous, defining tasks and roles and training each man as if he was about to take an individual part in some complicated industrial process. Indeed, the American system for basic training resembled a conveyor belt, with soldiers instead of motor-cars coming off the end.[52]

Americans systematized war to the point that it became an industrial process mirroring industrial society. American military leaders attempted to remove uncertainty, using science as a way to advance American war, making it an attempt to win wars decisively and as quickly as possible. As General Albert Cody Wedermeyer, Chief of Staff to the Supreme Allied Command South East Asia Command in World War II noted, the US forces "counted on our advanced weapons systems – technical prowess and stupendous production capabilities – to enable us to win the war."[53]

The United States was now fully on the path that would eventually take war into the Nuclear Age – the third plateau. But the development of the bomb was not the first time the liberal ethos of the United States was challenged by the development of a "superweapon." The

[50] David M. Kennedy, *Freedom from Fear: The American People in the Depression and War* (Oxford: Oxford University Press, 1999), p. 469.
[51] Martin van Creveld, *The Culture of War* (New York: Presidio, 2009).
[52] Eliot A. Cohen, "The Strategy of Innocence? The United States, 1920–1945," in Williamson Murray, MacGregor Knox and Alvin Bernstein (eds.), *The Making of Strategy: Rulers, States and War* (Cambridge: Cambridge University Press, 1994), p. 464.
[53] Kennedy, *Freedom from Fear*, p. 361.

challenge to balance overwhelming force with an enlightened form of warfare is perhaps most evident in one of the most feared aspects of World War I: chemical weapons – a weapons system that remains taboo to this day.

Law, science and the Great War

Although science promised devices that would help nations dominate the battlefield, oftentimes states would come to see these weapons as so deadly that they seemed to defy even the tenuous moral standards of war. In the early twentieth century, one of the "superweapons" that supposedly promised to make war "better" was poison gas. But gas weapons would only serve to make matters on the ground worse for nations and their armies rather than providing any real scientific solution: "For real soldiers fighting on the Western Front in cratered moon-like landscapes, having to face clouds of suffocating gas, flame-throwers (first used in 1914) and attacks from above by aircraft, it must have seemed as if they entered an alien world, dreamt up by the crazed imagination of a fiction writer."[54] This was the reality that the United States entered when it sided with the Allies in the war dubbed "the war to end all wars" by President Woodrow Wilson. Indeed, the reaction of the Allied nations to the use of gas on the battlefields was shock and revulsion. The dastardly effects of the weapons instantly became a major reference point for anti-German propaganda. However, despite the protest and denunciations, the Allies were quick to realize the potential of the gas weapons – and the need to catch up rapidly. Although German prowess in chemistry had given the nation a head start, Great Britain, France and the United States did not take long to develop and deploy their own chemical weapons. By November 1918, the French alone had produced nearly 3 million shells filled with mustard gas. Additionally, according to Smith, "In the event that war should last into 1919, the Allies had prepared for a massive assault using gas cylinders mounted on tanks which would have advanced during an artillery barrage, saturating the ground and air with poison."[55]

[54] Smith, *Doomsday Men*, p. 106.
[55] *Ibid.*, pp. 117–118. Among the German soldiers gassed on the fields of World War I was Adolf Hitler. His experience is often cited as one of the reasons that Nazi Germany never resorted to gas or chemical warfare during World War II.

By the end of the "Great War," the Allies had over 75,000 scientists and service personnel engaged in chemical weapons development alone. Both Britain and the United States had harnessed their scientific might and developed their own specialist scientific-military facilities "dedicated to the new scientific form of warfare."[56] In fact, it was an American who discovered an even more deadly weapon than mustard gas – although it was too late to be deployed in World War I: Lewisite. Named for its discoverer, W. Lee Lewis, Lewisite shared many of the same characteristics as mustard gas, including destroying skin tissues, and was fatal if inhaled. However, Lewisite is a systemic poison that can cause death merely by being deposited on a person's skin, causing excruciating pain in the eyes and skin followed by vomiting. It was a chemical so strong that it could kill a man in a minute, after exposure to a concentration of only fifty parts per million. Although never deployed by the United States, Smith argues that Lewisite marks America's rise to world dominance in the field of scientific superweapons.[57] For its creator, however, the terrifying gas represented "the most efficient, most economical, and most humane, single weapon known to military service."[58]

Lewis was not alone in believing that gas weapons were humane. In fact, the debate about the use and regulation of gas weapons largely centered around three arguments: that the weapons were repugnant (not only cruel, but also not chivalrous) and should be banned; that the weapons might be repugnant, but they were efficient and effective (which, as discussed below, was the position taken by elements of the US military and chemicals industry); and those (many who were inventors, such as the German Fritz Haber) who argued that they were a genuinely humane alternative to the other technologies of death that existed at the time. After all, many traditional weapons that left men dying for hours, if not days, from terrible wounds, may have been seen as an honorable military death, but not truly a painless one.

But the argument for the United States to employ gas weapons largely rested on the second standpoint – that the weapons might be terrible, but they were effective. The weapons also offered the possibility of

---

[56] Smith, *Doomsday Men*, p. 118.   [57] *Ibid.*, p. 119.

[58] *Ibid.*, fn. 66. Smith cites W. Lee Lewis, "Is Prohibition of Gas Warfare Feasible?", *Atlantic Monthly* (June 1922), 840, quoted in Gilbert F. Whittemore, Jr., "World War I, Poison Gas Research, and the Ideals of American Chemists," *Social Studies of Science*, No. 5 (May 1975), 135–163, p. 158.

being a deterrent. Of course, there was also the argument that the Germans, who used the weapons first, actually deserved it. Those who worked on the weapons, particularly the American commander of Edgewood Arsenal (the first scientific military weapons lab in the United States), William Walker, expressed a strong desire to drop the one-ton mustard gas bombs on German cities where "not one living thing, not even a rat, would live through it."[59]

It was not clear, however, that the American public or civilian leaders felt the same way. Indeed, public opinion during the war seems to have been strongly against such weapons. Newspaper reports of the effects of the weapons increased anti-gas weapon sentiment among significant sections of the American public, a trend that reflected an ever growing chorus of outrage in Europe against their use on the battlefields in France and Belgium. The questions for policy-makers, however, were could this public outrage be channeled into regulation? And should it be?

The record of implementation of the laws of war in World War I on all sides was mixed. Some of this was, no doubt, due to the very newness of the codified laws of war (the 1899 and 1907 Conventions on the Law of Land Warfare as well as the 1906 revised Geneva Convention had yet to be truly tested in warfare) and the skepticism of certain military commanders. However, as Geoffrey Best argues, it was also due to the "novelties of scale and science"[60] – the sheer length of the war combined with deployment of new military technologies – horses and airplanes, cavalry and tanks, swords and gas weapons. Clearly, the battlefields of World War I were destined to be testing grounds not only for new weapons and strategies, but also notions as to how force should be restrained on the battlefield.

For example, as Best argues, up until World War I, "The laws of war had historically been developed on the assumption that the man trying to injure or kill an enemy could see what he was doing." But with the invention of submarines, airplanes and long-range shelling, this was no longer the case, posing at least two major changes for the way belligerents conducted war and the laws of war. First, there were problems related to targeting over great distances. Although a military target being fired upon might be perfectly legitimate under the laws of war,

---

[59] Smith, *Doomsday Men*, p. 119.

[60] Geoffrey Best, *Humanity in Warfare: The Modern History of International Law of Armed Conflicts* (London: Methuen & Co. Ltd., 1980), p. 48.

relatively primitive shelling (by today's standards) meant that non-military targets were frequently hit. Thus, there was the problem of double effect – a commander may have had perfectly good intentions, but the effects of that intention could go awry, landing a shell on a hospital or town rather than a military stronghold. But how could you tell if this was a legitimate error or a "convenient" mistake? And what could be done about it? Second, a change occurred where for the first time in history an entire fighting force may not engage at close quarters with their enemies. As Best suggests, "It may be difficult to experience feelings of common humanity with people fifteen miles beyond or five miles beneath."[61] Science had replaced the very messy hand-to-hand combat, and even the firing lines. But what was taking their place? It was not yet entirely clear.

Still, for humanitarians and the laws of war, all was not lost in the chaos and trauma of World War I. Best contends:

The fundamental humanitarian principles of protecting the sick and wounded, and of treating prisoners decently, survived the war intact, strengthened, indeed, by so many millions of people's becoming acquainted, in the course of so prolonged a war, with the work of ambulances and hospitals on the one hand, the predicaments of POWs and their families on the other.[62]

As such, rather than abandoning the project, humanitarians turned to renewing and strengthening the laws of war – and a major priority was gas weapons. A significant push for international reform and legislation was an effort that the United States spearheaded in the immediate aftermath of World War I. After all, the "Great War" had resulted in 1.3 million casualties from gas, including 91,000 deaths,[63] and newspapers and popular science and science fiction magazines in the United States were full of stories of coming wars where entire cities would be wiped out by planes carrying bombs laden with asphyxiating gases.

During the war, the International Committee of the Red Cross (ICRC) issued a plea for all belligerents to abandon "barbaric" gas weapons and appealed to a "spirit of humanity" to preserve some

---

[61] *Ibid.*, p. 53.
[62] *Ibid.*, p. 52. As Best notes, "Not until the later 1930s did the fundamentally anti-human tendencies of these new ideologies, already evident in domestic policy pursued in time of peace, begin to make a characteristic mark on the conduct of war" p. 52.
[63] Schmitt, *War, Technology and International Humanitarian Law*, fn. 6.

semblance of civilization on the battlefield. Three months later, the Allies (including the United States) issued a formal reply, indicating that they agreed that gas was barbaric, but asked what could they do in light of Germany's use of the weapon? Germany, in turn, blamed the use of gas on the British, but in September 1918 suggested that it had, in fact, acted with great moderation during the course of the war. It was, however, happy to discuss a ban even though Germany mistrusted the word of the Allies.[64] For its part, Germany had argued that by the strictest literal reading of Convention II in the 1899 Hague Convention and the 1907 Hague Convention (IV) concerning Asphyxiating Gases their gas weapons were not illegal.[65] A shell or a bomb could, after all, have the primary purpose of being disruptive, and then have the "incidental" effect of being gravely poisonous.[66] As such, efforts to ban the weapons in the 1920s were aimed at closing this loophole.

The first attempt to specifically ban gas weapons to take place after World War I was the 1922 Washington Naval Conference (also known as the Washington Arms Conference) where there was a discussion on "the Use of Submarines and Noxious Gases in Warfare."[67] Despite their development of gas weapons during World War I, and enthusiasm for them from certain quarters, the Americans took the lead in trying to eliminate the weapons. The relevant text of the Treaty was based on an American proposal by Secretary of State Charles Evans Hughes and declared:

The use in war of asphyxiating, poisonous or other gases, and all analogous liquids, materials or devices, having been justly condemned by the general opinion of the civilized world and a prohibition of such use having been declared in treaties to which a majority of the civilized Powers are parties.

In order to achieve the required consent of the Senate, the Harding Administration took pains to involve prominent senators in the negotiations as well as developing a committee of prominent Americans to

---

[64] Caroline Moorehead, *Dunant's Dream: War, Switzerland and the History of the Red Cross* (London: HarperCollins, 1999), p. 255.

[65] Best, *Humanity in Warfare*, p. 49.

[66] William H. Boothby, *Weapons and the Law of Armed Conflict* (Oxford: Oxford University Press, 2009), p. 123.

[67] The Treaty of Versailles banned the use, manufacture and importation of asphyxiating and poisonous gases by Germany, but it was neither applicable to the United States, nor did the United States ratify the Treaty (over the issue of the United Nations).

mobilize public opinion. Although a report by the technical subcommittee of the Committee on Limitation of Armaments questioned whether it was really possible to limit the use of gas against the armed forces of the enemy, the Advisory Committee of the United States Delegation and the General Board of the Navy argued that regardless of expert opinion, the "conscience" of the American public demanded the total prohibition of chemical warfare.[68] As a result, the Senate gave its consent to the Treaty without any dissent.[69] However, although an agreement was reached between the British Empire, France, Italy, Japan and the United States, the failure of France to ratify the Treaty (over concerns related to submarine warfare) meant the Treaty never entered into force.[70]

The next major attempt was the 1925 Geneva Gas Protocol, which used language similar to the 1922 Washington Treaty, adding "bacteriological methods of warfare" to the banned weapons of war. Again, the US government (under President Coolidge) was a major supporter of the Protocol. However, where the Harding Administration placed considerable effort on involving the Senate in the process of negotiation and gaining their support, the Coolidge Administration did not. Rather than sending a Senator as a representative to a conference that could subsequently help ensure support for ratification, the Administration sent a Congressman, Theodore E. Burton. Perhaps assuming that a great effort to gain support was not necessary given the strong support for banning chemical weapons three years previously, developing momentum for ratification was largely ignored – allowing those opposed to the Protocol to mobilize.

Opposed to the Treaty was the Army's Chemical Warfare Service. They did not want to lose their weapons nor the funding that had been made available to them since World War I. To support their argument they enlisted the backing of the American Legion, the Veterans of Foreign Wars, the American Chemical Society and the chemical

---

[68] Linda C. Fentiman, "When Smoke Gets in Your Eyes: Proposed Ratification by the United States of the Geneva Protocol on Chemical-Biological Warfare," *Buffalo Law Review*, Vol. 24 (1974–1975), 159–188, p. 166. Fentiman cites Conference on the Limitation of Armament, S. Doc. No. 126, 67th Cong., 2d Sess. 384–85 (1922).

[69] George Bunn, "Banning Poison Gas and Germ Warfare: Should the United States Agree?", *Wisconsin Law Review*, No. 2 (1969), 375–420, p. 377.

[70] Boothby, *Weapons and the Law of Armed Conflict*, p. 123.

industry generally. Senator James Wolcott Wadsworth, Chairman of
the Military Affairs Committee, led the Senate opponents of the
Protocol, arguing that it would likely be torn up in time of war and
that poison gas was actually more humane than many other weapons.
Additionally, the ambiguities as to whether the Gas Protocol banned
the use of tear gas (which by this time was widely used by police forces
in the United States) were another major argument held up against
ratification. In light of the major opposition that had gathered, a
growing tendency toward isolationism and neutrality on the world
stage, coupled with the failure of the Coolidge Administration to
garner the support and votes needed in the upper chamber, the
Protocol was withdrawn back to committee, and formally withdrawn
by President Truman in 1947.[71] Regardless of the failure of the United
States to ratify, the Gas Protocol came into effect through the ratification of other signatories and was upheld among European nations
in World War II.

And yet, this did not mark the end of US concern over gas weapons.
The Roosevelt Administration, noting that the Japanese had not signed
the Gas Protocol (amid allegations that Japanese forces had used chemical weapons in China), threatened massive retaliation if the Japanese
used chemical weapons against America or its allies in 1942. In 1943,
Roosevelt went further and declared that the United States condemned
gas weapons as "outlawed by the general opinion of civilized mankind"
(although Roosevelt did not mention the Gas Protocol in his denunci-
ation).[72] He also went so far as to declare that the United States would
not be the first to use such weapons, although it would retaliate in kind
if such an attack were carried out against it. The Japanese, replying
through a neutral channel, indicated that they would refrain from the
use of gas if the Americans and Allies did as well.[73]

In this sense, by World War II, the US legal position on gas weapons should be understood as dualistic, combining a literal/positivist

---

[71] Bunn, "Banning Poison Gas and Germ Warfare: Should the United States
     Agree?", p. 378. See also Bunn, "The Banning of Poison Gas and Germ Warfare:
     The U.N. Role," *American Society of International Law Proceedings*, Vol. 64
     (1970), 194–199; R. R. Baxter and Thomas Buergenthal, "Legal Aspects of the
     Geneva Protocol of 1925," *American Journal of International Law*, Vol. 64
     (1970), 853–879, p. 855, fn. 11; Fentiman, "When Smoke Gets in Your Eyes."
[72] Fentiman, "When Smoke Gets in Your Eyes," p. 176.
[73] Bunn, "The Banning of Poison Gas: The U.N. Role," p. 197.

understanding of international law with a sentimentally driven belief that chemical/gas weapons clearly violated civilized principles. In the case of the former, it is clear that various US administrations did not wish to adhere to any law that could potentially prohibit tear gas (something seen as very different than the mustard gas of World War I). Furthermore, the United States would continue to maintain, up until the 1970s, that any treaty prohibiting the use of chemical weapons did not bind it.[74] This is in keeping with the need to protect and preserve America's ability to fight and defend itself in times of war, using scientific innovation and overwhelming force. However, arguments resting on the idea that the use of such weapons violated the very foundations of international law and order, as well as the principles of all decent peoples, reflect the liberal sensibilities in line with the Enlightenment values upon which the country was founded.

This was not the first time that the United States had taken such a stance on an issue arising out of World War I. After the United States entered the conflict, it declared that it did not consider the Geneva Conventions or the Hague Conventions to apply because all belligerents in the conflict (specifically, Serbia) were not ratified signatories to these treaties. This was an incredibly literal reading of the humanitarian law applicable to the conflict and one that the ICRC found astonishing. Yet this does not mean that the United States believed that the conflict was beyond regulation; even though the most recent humanitarian treaties did not apply, the United States frequently made formal complaints to Germany over its treatment of American prisoners of war, demanding that "the German Government immediately take such steps as will effectively guarantee to American prisoners in its hands, both in letter and in spirit, that humane treatment which by all the principles of humanitarian law and usages is to be expected from the Government of a civilized state and its officials."[75] To enforce this humane treatment, the United States threatened retaliation against German prisoners of war in its

---

[74] The United States would eventually ratify the 1925 Gas Protocol in 1975, after President Nixon had resubmitted the Treaty to the Senate in 1970. Nixon had done so in light of heavy criticism of the United States using herbicides in Vietnam, which some countries argued violated international law.

[75] The Americans relayed their concern in a letter to the German government sent via the US Ambassador in Spain. Telegram from Secretary of State

hands, relying upon the legal principle of reciprocity. Additionally, they argued that the treaties they had signed with Prussia in 1799 and 1828 (both with provisions for treatment of prisoners of war) applied to the conflict. However, in addition to these formal legal strategies, it is clear that the United States was also relying on customary international law to enhance its arguments, suggesting that although the Hague Rules might not formally apply, they did represent a bare minimum standard to which any "civilized" nation would adhere regardless of formal legal obligation. But, ultimately, a major aspect of the US legal strategy was to proceed to negotiate a separate prisoner of war agreement with Germany for the purpose of the conflict. Starting in September 1918, the two sides negotiated a treaty with 184 articles, going into such specific detail as to how high off the floor a prisoner's bed should be. While the resulting treaty was very progressive for its time, it suffered from the drawback of coming into force on November 11, 1918 – the day of the Armistice.[76]

This story is both puzzling and revealing – if the United States was truly so concerned about the humane treatment of its prisoners, why did it not just use the international treaties that were already in existence? Why did it insist upon such a literal stance if it put its own soldiers at risk and without modern protection? There can be no question that the United States had adopted (and not for the first nor last time) a strategic legal position to defend a stance that advanced its own interests. After all, it is not clear that the United States would have adopted or continued to hold such a complicated stance if it had not been on the side that clearly had the upper hand in 1918.

This tale, and the American approach to gas weapons, reveals that the US attitude toward law in war generally must be understood as trying to reconcile a tricky position between a strict positivist reading of international law and a concern for the standards of civilized behavior as recognized by the international community. Whether a positivist or a

---

Robert Lansing to Joseph E. Wilard, January 28, 1918 [850], *United States Department of State Papers Relating to Foreign Relations of the United States, 1918, Supplement 2, The World War* (Washington D.C.: US Government Printing Office, 1918), pp. 19–21.

[76] For information on the discussions leading to the decision to create an agreement and its outcome see Stephanie Carvin, *Prisoners of America's Wars: From the Early Republic to Guantanamo* (New York: Columbia University Press, 2010), pp. 85–88.

principled stance, there is a pressing concern to respect the rule of law. But how could this be done in a war with superweapons – where fighting seems to require not just a rebalancing of the competing imperatives of "annihilation" and "restraint," but perhaps a reconceptualization of this balance entirely?

This was a dilemma that grew more complicated as science developed more and more destructive weapons. Even if these weapons were intended to make war more efficient and to save lives, they ultimately ended up making a conflict more destructive and had little impact on shortening the length of a war. For example, as the war in the Pacific was coming to an end, the use of poison gas was urged by some members of the military as a way to reduce American casualties in the island campaigns. Ultimately, however, Admiral Nimitz argued, "the United States should not be the first to violate the Geneva Convention."[77] In saying so, Nimitz recognized that the United States as a liberal power needed to stay within the boundaries of international law and the values the Allies were fighting for when confronting the Axis powers, even if they were not formal members of the Treaty.

This stance of balancing positivist and natural interpretations of international law is also clear in the pronouncement of General Myron Cramer, the Judge Advocate General of the Army who argued during the war:

The United States is not bound by any treaty which specifically excludes or restricts the use of chemicals, whether toxic or non-toxic in time of war ... An exhaustive study of the source materials, however, warrants the conclusion that a customary rule of international law had developed by which *poisonous gases and those causing unnecessary sufferings* are prohibited ... The United States has officially announced that it will observe this principle ...[78]

Clearly, for the United States there were limits to expediency. We can understand the arguments of these military men through the recognition that as well as using overwhelming force and technological innovation America had a need to be seen as fighting in a way that is legitimate,

---

[77] Fentiman, "When Smoke Gets in Your Eyes," p. 176. Fentiman cites John Norton Moore, "Ratification of the Geneva Protocol on Gas and Bacteriological Warfare: A Legal and Political Analysis," *Virginia Law Review*, Vol. 58, No. 3 (March 1972), 419–509, p. 436.

[78] Cited from Fentiman, "When Smoke Gets in Your Eyes," pp. 176–177.

even if it sometimes had to take an odd or complicated legal stance to do so. In other words, when it comes to the American way of warfare, legitimacy often came from a very strict reading of the legal rules – but not so strict that it could be seen as inconsistent with American and Western values (significantly, in that order).

Certainly, there is a temptation here to argue that such a stance is more indicative of hypocrisy than a concern for law or values. And yet, it is clear that the United States did not always adopt legal arguments that were in its national interest – or were strategically prudent. The support of the Harding Administration or Office of the Navy was clearly based on the idea that gas weapons were beyond the pale. Nor could necessity ever justify a first use of gas weapons against Japan, even if it would have been strategically useful. There can be no question that this need to be seen as legitimate, and following international law, had a major impact on how the United States chose to fight. However, in absence of a nuclear treaty, the United States clearly felt that it was freer to act.

Conclusion

Because the American mindset is one that demands total victory when confronted with war, and it suspends politics until after the war is complete, the country is willing to use whatever means possible to reach a victorious end state as quickly as possible. This is why, despite the examples of humanitarian restraint discussed above, it is undeniable that the United States is the only country in the history of the world to have used atomic weapons in warfare. But the usage of atomic weapons is understandable within the American way of war. Somewhat ironically, the United States systematized war and applied science to such an extreme that, by the 1950s, war between the Great Powers was untenable. The use of such terrible weapons was justified by US leaders because the war was seen as forced on the United States by aggressor nations like Japan and Germany and because the use of these terrible weapons, while horrific, would shorten the war, thereby in the end reducing deaths if the conflict were of a more protracted nature. "We have used [the bomb] against those who attacked us without warning at Pearl Harbor, against those who have starved and beaten and executed American prisoners of war, against those who have abandoned all pretense of obeying international laws of warfare. We have used it in order to shorten the agony of war."[79] This logic is similar to the arguments in favor of using chemical weapons during World War I (or even earlier arguments about the need to use harsh tactics against the "uncivilized" warfare of Native Americans and Filipinos) but this time the United States was willing to overcome what had been a reluctance to be the first to use a new and terrible superweapon. Despite the knowledge that the bomb would cause massive amounts of suffering, science had provided the promise of a weapon that could win the war.

While one may not agree with the decision to use nuclear weapons against Japan, it is possible to track the development of these competing imperatives that led to the decision to do so: to overwhelm and annihilate, the need to act within the boundaries of civilized force as represented by humanitarian values and an affinity for scientific solutions to solve the problems of war through mass production and superweapons. These elements, we have seen, are present at the foundation of the American Republic, through the nineteenth century and on to World War II. The nuclear era, however, put new pressure on these conflicting tendencies given that the advent of nuclear weapons meant that full-scale war among the Great Powers was essentially suicide. Yet, these tendencies, rooted in the fabric and foundation of the United States, remained. The United States would again find itself turning to science to find a solution to overcome the nuclear dilemma facing Cold War American strategists.

---

[79] Michael Walzer, *Just and Unjust Wars: A Moral Argument with Historical Illustrations* (New York: Basic Books, 2000), p. 264.

3 | Vietnam and the "science" of war

All wars and military development should have taught us that ... a war, small or large, does not follow a prescribed "scenario" laid out in advance. If we could predict the sequence of events more accurately, we could probably have avoided war in the first place.

Vice Admiral Rickover, 1966, cited in Gibson, *The Perfect War*

When the Nixon Administration took over in 1969 all data on North Vietnam and the United States was fed into a Pentagon computer – populations, gross national product, manufacturing capability, number of tanks, ships, and aircraft, size of the armed forces, and the like. The computer was then asked, "When will we win?" It took only moments to give the answer: "You won in 1964!"

Colonel Harry Summers, "Lessons: A Soldier's View"

America's war in Vietnam was almost without historical precedent. Aside from the insurgency in the Philippines, the United States had not ever fought a war without any fronts. Although the American military had engaged in several "small wars" over the course of American history, nothing matched the challenge and scope of what was then known as the Vietnam "conflict." Unlike Britain, the United States had little experience in colonial policing, as these irregular wars were often known. Coming on the heels of Korea, the United States was reluctant to get fully involved in a traditional ground war in Asia. The atomic bomb was briefly considered as a possibility to stop communist expansion in Vietnam, but the Eisenhower Administration ruled out this option since it thought that it would ultimately be counterproductive. This left the United States with limited options. Yet, the Americans felt that something had to be done as the "domino theory," which held great sway in Washington, argued that the expansion of communism could not be left unchecked.

Before America's engagement in Vietnam, American military thought was dominated by a binary view of war and peace. War as we illustrated in the last chapter was, for the American mind, essentially the suspension of politics and the implementation of total war. Total war in the nuclear age, however, was not a feasible option for US civilian policy-makers – the risks of escalation and annihilation were too great. Policy analysts believed that there had to be a way to make use of large-scale conventional military force without triggering a wider war. Korea demonstrated that there were still adversaries willing to fight conventional wars without resorting to nuclear weapons since the Soviets did not use them to support the North Koreans. The subsequent development of operations research and systems analysis that began in World War II, and developed throughout the 1950s, led to the belief among civilian policy-makers that war could still function as an instrument of policy if it were limited and constrained. This idea, which first emerged in the Korean conflict, would be applied in practice to America's subsequent engagement in Vietnam.

Rethinking war and strategy

Through the 1950s and into the 1960s the United States continued to view war as an aberration rather than a standard occurrence in international affairs, with an absolutist conception of war that rested on the traditional Western idea of the decisive victory resulting in the imposition of peace terms by the victor. The dawn of the nuclear age, however, made this approach to war largely untenable. How could anyone win a nuclear war that could wipe out large swathes of the planet? Despite this reality, in the 1950s there had been a push in Washington to develop ever more potent nuclear weapons and to stockpile them as strategic reserves.

A number of theoretical physicists and scientists involved in the invention of the atomic bomb and who had subsequently become influential figures in Washington advocated for these stockpiling efforts. Many of these scientists were Hungarian émigrés who had first fled the Nazis and later the Soviet Union as it consolidated its control over Eastern Europe. These scientists, men such as John von Neumann, Edward Teller and Eugene Wigner, described themselves as radical anti-communists and advocated taking an aggressive posture against the Soviet Bloc. They believed it imperative that the United States develop more powerful weapons to win the inevitable nuclear war against the USSR. In particular, Edward Teller, who played an important role in convincing President Harry Truman that the new atomic bombs were weapons through which the United States could win the Cold War, lobbied hard for the funding to develop hydrogen-based weapons, commonly known as "H-bombs." Teller (who relished his reputation as "Mr. H-Bomb") and former Nazi rocket scientist Wernher von Braun successfully petitioned Congress to support their research, by exaggerating the Soviet threat – a strategy that may have been somewhat dishonest, but very effective after the explosion of the first Soviet atom bomb in 1949. Teller would go on to advocate using nuclear bombs to blast out a harbor in North Alaska, rejecting the health risks posed by the deadly fallout that would follow as the "necessary price to pay for military readiness."[1]

John von Neumann, a groundbreaking mathematician influential in the development of the modern computer, assisted with Teller's effort to create the H-bomb with his number-crunching supercomputer named MANIAC (Mathematical Analyzer, Numerical Integrator, and Computer or Mathematical Analyzer, Numerator, Integrator, and Computer). Yet, despite his knowledge of the direct and indirect destructive power of the weapons he was creating, von Neumann advocated a pre-emptive atomic strike against the Soviet Union given his belief that the human race faced an inevitable doomsday war. In his view, war with the Communist Bloc was unavoidable, and von Neumann (who clearly had a knack for acronyms rooted in dark humor) is also attributed with naming the strategy that would eventually emerge by the 1950s: Mutually Assured Destruction or MAD.

Appointed to the Atomic Energy Commission, by President Dwight Eisenhower, von Neumann helped to oversee the building of the US nuclear arsenal. He also worked to silence critics, such as the famous nuclear scientist Robert Oppenheimer, who argued against building H-bombs. In 1954 he made a significant recommendation to the US government when he advised that research should be started immediately into creating a force of intercontinental ballistic missiles (ICBMs) that could be launched to attack the Soviet Union at a touch of a button.[2] Truly, the very American dream of turning to science to help decisively win wars was rapidly descending into a nightmare.

But there were those who continued to believe that a nuclear war could be "won." When President Kennedy sought to stop the Soviet placement

---

[1] P. D. Smith, *Doomsday Men: The Real Dr. Strangelove and the Dream of the Superweapon* (London: Allen Lane, 2007), pp. 356–358.

[2] Smith, *Doomsday Men*, pp. 361–362.

of missiles in Cuba in 1962 he was appalled by the suggestion of his generals that the use of nuclear weapons was an option. But in many cases, conventional weaponry had already been given up for nuclear capabilities. As Bernard and Fawn Brodie note, this turn to nuclear weapons had actually weakened the US ability to defend its interests:

The United States Air Force essentially deprived itself of a conventional capability, removing from its bombers the bomb shackles for carrying conventional bombs. During the Matsu–Quemoy crisis of 1958 the U.S. Joint Chiefs informed the President that the United States had no ability to intervene effectively for the defense of Taiwan unless he granted permission to use nuclear weapons.[3]

It seemed apparent that conventional forces were still needed by nuclear powers or else they would be unable to respond to small crises throughout the globe or, worse, they would actually be forced to use nuclear weapons. The all or nothing mentality of the US military was poorly suited to the new strategic realities of a nuclear era Cold War. As early as 1950, Paul Nitze's NSC-68 recognized the imperatives of devising a new approach.

If war comes, what is the role of force? ... In the words of the Federalist (No. 28) "The means to be employed must be proportioned to the extent of the mischief." The mischief may be a global war or it may be a Soviet campaign for limited objectives. In either case we should take no avoidable initiative that would cause it to become a war of annihilation, and if we have the forces to defeat a Soviet drive for limited objectives it may well be to our interest not to let it become a global war. Our aim in applying force must be to compel the acceptance of terms consistent with our objectives, and our capabilities for the application of force should, therefore, within the limits of what we can sustain over the long pull, be congruent to the range of tasks which we may encounter.[4]

The need to match the "mischief" of the Soviet Union proportionately was incongruent with the American conception of war. Policy-makers

---

[3] Bernard and Fawn M. Brodie, *From Crossbow to H-Bomb: The Evolution of the Weapons and Tactics of Warfare* (Bloomington: Indiana University Press, 1973), pp. 282–283.

[4] NSC 68: United States Objectives and Programs for National Security (April 14, 1950), *A Report to the President Pursuant to the President's Directive of January 31, 1950*. Available at: www.fas.org/irp/offdocs/nsc-hst/nsc-68-4.htm (accessed June 30, 2014).

in the nuclear age became increasingly frustrated by the black and white view of conflict held by the military that rendered the use of force irrelevant in all cases except major war. George Kennan, one of the most influential American foreign affairs experts, argued in 1961 that the situation was the logical conclusion of attempts to use technology to escape the horrors of war.

The atom has simply served to make unavoidably clear what has been true all along since the day of the introduction of the machine gun and the internal combustion engine into the techniques of warfare ... that modern warfare in the grand manner, pursued by all available means and aimed at the total destruction of the enemy's capacity to resist is ... of such general destructiveness that it ceases to be useful as an instrument for the achievement of any coherent political purpose.[5]

Civilian strategists were not content with the military mindset of total war, and as the Cold War wore on into the 1950s and 1960s, the civilian side of the defense establishment began to become more influential on US strategic thinking. They confronted the same problems that their forebears had, but now under a nuclear shadow. Following World War II the American public were loath to get involved in another conflict, and the Korean War justified the concerns of men like Paul Nitze that technology would need to serve as an alternative to national will.[6] Additionally, because war was now so dangerous, the imperative became, in the words of Bernard Brodie, to avert war – "It [war] can have almost no other useful purpose."[7] The use of unrestricted nuclear war meant "the end of strategy as we have known it."[8]

   The response to these challenges was to turn to science, technology and systematization – albeit this time to pursue limited, rather than total, war. Inspired by retired general Maxwell Taylor's book *The Uncertain Trumpet* – which restated the case for enlarging conventional capabilities – and the disastrous Bay of Pigs Invasion, the Kennedy Administration moved away from the Eisenhower Administration's

---

[5] Chris Hables Gray, *Postmodern War: The New Politics of Conflict* (London: Routledge, 1997), p. 138.
[6] Gregg Herken, *Counsels of War* (Oxford: Oxford University Press, 1987), p. 51.
[7] Bernard Brodie, "War in the Atomic Age," in Brodie (ed.), *The Absolute Weapon: Atomic Power and World Order* (New York: Harcourt, Brace & Co., 1946), p. 76.
[8] Herken, *Counsels of War*, p. 38.

doctrine of "Massive Retaliation" and toward a new doctrine of "Flexible Response."[9] This move had already been considered by the Eisenhower team, as an April 7, 1958 memorandum of a meeting between US Secretary of State John Foster Dulles and US Secretary of Defense Neil McElroy documents.[10] Secretary Dulles concluded that the proliferation of nuclear weapons and the increased destructive power meant that the possibility of using such weapons was too danger-ous. The Kennedy Administration concurred with this logic and con-sequently pursued a substantial buildup of conventional forces and new weaponry to fill in a conventional deterrence component otherwise missing from the US arsenal.[11] Around the same time, advances in computing further reinforced the belief among civilian strategists that war could be conducted in a limited fashion.

The computer at its most basic is a calculator. Antoine Bousquet in his excellent book on war and computing provides an interesting sum-mary of the roots of the word, noting that, in English, the term "com-puter" was originally ascribed to a group of individuals who do arithmetic calculations. Other languages help to place the purpose of the machine more accurately. In French, computer is *ordinateur* – "a machine that puts things in order" – whereas in Finnish the term is *tietkokone* or "knowledge machine." Icelandic perhaps has one of the most insightful and "poetic" terms, as Bousquet puts it, with *tolva*, which translates as "number prophetess."[12] What Bousquet is getting at is that the essence of the computer lies in being a machine that provides an analytical capacity beyond what is humanly possible. When applied to warfare, such a machine was believed to make war relevant again to strategy. This machine promised to enable civilians to sever the dominance of the total war mentality within the American military

---

[9] General Maxwell Taylor, *The Uncertain Trumpet* (New York: Harper, 1980).

[10] "John Foster Dulles's Changing Thought on Nuclear War and Weapons Effects," Memorandum of Conversation, April 7, 1958, with June 20, 1969 cover letter from Gerard C. Smith, Top Secret. Available at: www2.gwu.edu/%7Ensarchiv/nukevault/special/doc07.pdf (accessed July 1, 2014).

[11] Brodie and Brodie, *From Crossbow to H-Bomb*, p. 284. However, Martin van Creveld notes that attempts to develop a limited war doctrine for nuclear weapons was the focus of much thought in the 1960s and 1970s. However, these waves of nuclear war fighting doctrines soon fell out of favor after "choking on one's absurdities." *The Transformation of War* (New York: The Free Press, 1991), p. 9.

[12] Antoine Bousquet, *The Scientific Way of Warfare* (London: Hurst, 2009), p. 96.

establishment. As Martin van Creveld argues, computers possessed a certain attraction:

Computers with their binary on–off logic seem to appeal to the military mind. This is because the military, in order to counter the inherent confusion and danger of war, is forever seeking ways to make communications as terse and unambiguous as humanly possible. Computers by their very nature do just that. Had they only been able to stand at attention and salute, in many ways they would have made ideal soldiers.[13]

Computers enabled the defense establishment to process large amounts of information to help create a better picture of war through what is known as operations research (OR) and systems analysis (SA). The British originally implemented operations research in the 1930s, which the Americans subsequently adapted in World War II. During the war, operations research focused on issues such as bombing accuracy, weapons effectiveness and target damage. It also examined how to prevent the loss of aircraft and how to defend bases.[14] Strategic bombing in the war between two symmetrical, technological forces became one large system in and of itself, which evolved into a battle of attrition between two similar technological systems.[15] Because strategic bombing was repetitive, it lent itself to continual statistical evaluation with the aim of improving the next operation. By the end of World War II and the dawn of the Cold War, this approach to conflict viewed war as a mathematical problem that could be manipulated by analysts to provide a scientific approach to war that was manageable. Fred Kaplan in *The Wizards of Armageddon* illustrates the depth and complexity that systems analysts went through to figure out the equation of war. In this passage Kaplan refers to the planning of Ed Paxson, a RAND researcher engaged in planning for the next war:

His [Paxson's] dream was to quantify every single factor of a strategic bombing campaign – the cost, weight, and payload of each bomber, its distance from the target, how it should fly in formation with the other bombers and their fighting escorts, their exact routing patterns, the refueling procedures,

[13] Martin van Creveld, *Technology and War* (New York: Touchstone, 1991), p. 239.
[14] Clayton J. Thomas and Robert S. Sheldon, "Air Force Operations Analysis," in Carl Harris and Saul Gass (eds.), *Encyclopaedia of Operations Research and Management Science* (Norwell: Kluwer Academic Publishers, 2000), p. 8.
[15] Van Creveld, *Technology and War*, p. 194.

the rate of attrition, the probability that something might go wrong in each step along the way, the weight and inaccuracy of the bomb, the vulnerability of the target, the bomb's "kill probability," the routing of the planes back to their bases, the fuel consumed, and all extraneous phenomena such as the weather – and put them all into a single mathematical equation.[16]

This approach to war rose to prominence in 1961 with the naming of Robert McNamara as John F. Kennedy's Secretary of Defense. McNamara was previously an analyst in the Statistical Control Office of the War Department where he studied Air Force operations using the new computing power of early computers. McNamara was involved in planning the bombing raids on mainland Japan during World War II and he advocated the firebombing and low-altitude bombing that General Curtis LeMay adopted in the American campaign against the Japanese. Following the war McNamara went to the Ford Motor Corporation where he would apply the same scientific approach to automobile manufacture and the management of the company. Under McNamara the Pentagon defense establishment would be dominated by computerized statistical logic, much to the chagrin of many in the armed forces.

Although Russia experts such as George Kennan argued that the Soviet Union should be contained using non-military means, as the Cold War wore on America's strategy of containment became increasingly militarized. The focus within the US defense establishment, including at the think-tank RAND, was on capabilities rather than intentions.[17] As the 1957 Gaither Report on "Deterrence and Survival in the Nuclear Age" argued it was not so much what intentions they had at the moment, but rather what the Soviet Union could do with the capabilities they possessed.[18] This reductionist strategy led to the view of the Cold War as a zero-sum conflict between the superpowers. For Paul Nitze, one of the

---

[16] Fred Kaplan, *The Wizards of Armageddon* (New York: Simon & Schuster, 1984), p. 87. RAND stands for Research and Development Corporation. It was set up in 1948 by the Douglas Aircraft Company as a "think-tank" to advise the US government.

[17] John Lewis Gaddis, "Implementing Flexible Response: Vietnam as a Test Case," in Robert J. Art and Kenneth N. Waltz (eds.), *The Use of Force: Military Power and International Politics* (Oxford: Rowman & Littlefield, 2004), p. 222.

[18] "Deterrence and Survival in the Nuclear Age," Washington D.C.: Executive Office of the President, November 7, 1957. Available at: www.gwu.edu/~nsarchiv/NSAEBB/NSAEBB139/nitze02.pdf (accessed on July 18, 2012).

influences behind NSC-68, every Soviet advance was a de facto American loss. As Buley puts it, "Rather like Newton's Third Law, every Soviet action would require an equal and opposite American Reaction. Scientific strategists took the Manichean interpretation of the Cold War enshrined in NSC-68 and translated it into mathematical terms, in the process stripping it of any embarrassing ideological or political content that could not be stated scientifically."[19] The goal was to remove the constraints placed upon the use of force so that it could be suited once more to the national interest. In this sense, the new civilian strategists professed adherence to Clausewitz in a way that American military leaders of the nineteenth and early twentieth centuries had not. But there is an irony here that should not be overlooked: "the best and the brightest" saw themselves as following in the footsteps of Clausewitz, viewing war as a continuation of politics through other means, but, in reality, the approach taken was much closer to systematizing Jomini. They wanted to use war as a tool of policy, but they thought, contra Clausewitz, that they could calculate and control war.

In her book *Reading Clausewitz*, Beatrice Heuser cites Anatol Rapoport's critique of these rational-choice strategists who "attempted to reduce nuclear war and deterrence to a matter of calculable rationality, susceptible to such mathematical technique as game theory ... It was precisely to this intellectualization of war, this reduction of bloody tragedy to a mathematical problem, this elimination of all moral and political content from the complex equation, that Clausewitz himself was objecting."[20] The Kennedy Administration and the scientists at RAND missed this irony. But the idea of making war "safer" or limiting and controlling it through systems analysis was not immediately accepted by the military. At a lecture by RAND nuclear strategist William Kaufman at Strategic Air Command on nuclear counterforce strategy, General Thomas Power let loose on a civilian, arguing with ferocity against the logic the theoretical physicist put forward in the 1950s: "Why do you want us to restrain ourselves? Restraint! Why are you so concerned with saving their lives? The whole idea is to kill the bastards! Look, at the end of the war if there are two Americans and one Russian, we win!"[21]

[19] Benjamin Buley, *The New American Way of War: Military Culture and the Political Utility of Force* (London: Routledge, 2008), p. 56.
[20] Cited in Beatrice Heuser, *Reading Clausewitz* (London: Pimlico, 2002), p. 159.
[21] Kaplan, *The Wizards of Armageddon*, p. 246.

General Power typified the classic American military view of war as an all or nothing struggle, a suspension of politics while the enemy is destroyed and forced to succumb to a unilateral peace. What the General missed is the fact that this new generation of civilian strategic thinkers was far removed from General William Sherman's maxim that "war is hell" and could not be otherwise. As liberals, the young guns of the Kennedy team valued human life and they believed the world could, and should, be different than it was. The Administration therefore sought to create a new approach to warfare that implemented science as a way to "bend an opponent's will" with the most efficient use of force as part of a graduated scale.[22] This would save both US lives as well as the lives of the enemy, while also being most cost-effective. After all, McNamara had been senior executive at the Ford Motor Company and was a stalwart Fordist bent on efficiency. Strategists of the likes of Thomas Schelling and Herman Kahn praised the US war effort in Vietnam in the mid-1960s as an "exemplary" way to "communicate with the enemy."[23] "By adapting macroeconomics, game theory, systems analysis, and other managerial techniques, the Kennedy administration advanced 'limited war' to greater specificity, making it seem much more controllable, manageable, and therefore desirable as foreign policy."[24]

What is perhaps most frightening for students of this period is how much the strategists tried to control what was in many ways not a controllable system. Kaplan, writing on Albert Wohlstetter's *Foreign Affairs* article "The Delicate Balance of Terror," decries the "almost mechanical concept of a very delicate balanced set of scales that once tipped even slightly off kilter, wiped out the deterrent power of America's nuclear weapons and slid the world toward the precipice of a calamitously destructive war that the Soviet Union would almost certainly win."[25] The problem was, that in injecting American rationality into their analysis, American policy-makers by and large failed to consider what the opponent might actually be thinking. Their models assumed that the Soviets, Chinese and Vietnamese were thinking the same way as the Americans. This is not surprising given that the systems research performed by the likes of Herman Kahn and his contemporaries at RAND placed no value on understanding the opponent. As Edwards

---

[22] James Gibson, *The Perfect War* (New York: Atlantic Monthly, 2000), p. ix.
[23] Herken, *Counsels of War*, p. 156.   [24] Gibson, *The Perfect War*, p. 80.
[25] Kaplan, *The Wizards of Armageddon*, pp. 109, 172.

points out, systems analysis "discourages the study of one's opponents, his language, politics, culture, tactics and leadership."[26] The focus was on using mathematics to determine strategy, not just advance tactics in warfare.[27]

The result would ultimately be failure in Vietnam, but this was something that the strategists just could not grasp. Later in the war, when McNamara was criticized about the conduct of the conflict and its impending failure, he shot back, "Where is your data?' Give me something that I can put in a computer. Don't give me your poetry."[28] Ultimately, even Robert McNamara himself decried that Americans were possessed of an "almost ineradicable tendency to think of our security problem as being exclusively a military problem ... We are haunted by this concept of military hardware."[29]

Stumbling into Vietnam

By the time the United States left Vietnam in 1973 defeated, it was the logical conclusion of an enterprise that was heavy on data but seemingly completely devoid of strategy. After President Kennedy's assassination the Johnson Administration delineated a grand strategy to stop the expansion of communism and to create a bulwark against further expansion, but there was no strategy on the ground to achieve this overarching objective. Vietnam was not an obvious case at the time for the implementation of the new American policy of flexible response, which had been designed to counter the Soviets. But by 1964 the Chinese, rather than the Russians, were seen as the real problem vis-à-vis the expansion of communism. This assumption was made clear during the Korean conflict, and as NSC staffer Michael Forrestal argued the objective was to "delay China's swallowing up Southeast Asia until (a) she develops better table manners and (b) the food is somewhat more indigestible."[30] As already noted, the United States did consider using nuclear weapons in the

---

[26] Paul Edwards, *The Closed World: Systems Discourse* (Cambridge, MA: MIT Press, 1997), p. 155.
[27] George and Meredith Friedmans, *The Future of War* (New York: Griffin, 1977), pp. 52–59.
[28] John Lewis Gaddis, *Strategies of Containment* (Oxford: Oxford University Press, 2005), p. 255.
[29] Kaplan, *The Wizards of Armageddon*, p. 336.
[30] Gaddis, "Implementing Flexible Response," p. 231.

Vietnam conflict, in particular against China. But this option was eventually ruled out due to heavy lobbying by China experts that a nuclear war in South Asia was not worth the effort and that China would accept heavy losses rather than capitulate.[31]

While not inevitable, American involvement in Vietnam was long in coming. Johnson might have committed the United States to war in Vietnam, but American involvement in Indo-China predated Johnson by nearly twenty years. In 1944–1945 Ho Chi Minh asked the Americans for assistance against the Japanese, but FDR adopted a "hands-off policy." Following the conclusion of the War, the United States maintained this position, missing an opportunity to foment goodwill by letting the French attempt to reinstate colonial control over a polity that clearly wanted independence. The open conflict between the Vietminh and the French began in December 1946 when the French impounded a Chinese junk allegedly carrying arms to the Vietminh. In response the Vietminh constructed roadblocks in Hanoi that the French tried to bulldoze. When the French colonial authorities attempted to clear the road, they were attacked, which prompted the French to shell the city, and the Vietminh responded with terrorist attacks against targets across the city. On December 19 the Vietminh launched an assault on French bases across Indo-China. Over the next decade the Vietminh would wage a war of independence against France. This conflict between democratic, capitalist France and the communist Vietminh was a microcosm of the wider global struggle. In 1949 Mao Tse-tung was victorious over Chiang Kai-shek and China became communist. The French were fighting a losing war, Vo Nguyen Giap had been handed control of the communist forces by Ho, and Giap was successfully making use of insurgent tactics against French forces who were playing right into his hands. Despite the quality of the French military, commanders strung themselves across the length of the country in a series of outposts that weakened their force while preventing them from massing to oppose the enemy and securing any part of the country effectively.

---

[31] U.S. State Department, Office of Politico-Military Affairs, Memorandum for the Record, "Discussion with Mr. Rice on Far East Problems," April 26, 1966. Available at: www2.gwu.edu/~nsarchiv/nukevault/special/doc12.pdf (accessed July 1, 2014).

Having eluded the French and survived, Giap and Ho moved from stage one of an insurgency (survival) to stage two: attacks against government forces by irregular combatants. Rather than taking the French on with a conventional military, the Vietnamese communists decided to use a people's war to advance their objectives against France. According to Mao, the strategy of the guerrilla in stage two is to attack the enemy's flank and other vulnerable spots. Because the French were strung out in series of fortified bases, they made easy targets. Through continual harassment and a wearing down of the enemy forces, Giap was able to move into stage three, which was largely a conventional phase. In the autumn of 1950 Giap launched a full-on assault against French bases on the border with China, resulting in a total French defeat. Nonetheless, Giap had to fall back rather than pressing on with the conquest of the Red River Delta. Instead, he was forced to wait until 1954 and the siege of Dienbienphu to break the backs of the French in Indo-China.

Giap used a brilliant strategy of deception to attack French bases in Northwestern and Central Laos, followed by attacks in Upper Laos and the Red River Delta. The French fell into the trap and moved in to attack the Vietminh forces, at which time Giap launched the siege at Dienbienphu. As one commentator put it,

Thus it may be said that before a shot was fired at Dienbienphu the French were defeated. They had felt compelled to defend everywhere that the Vietminh attacked. They believed they could not afford to lose any more territory and feared the effect that any defeat in open battle by the 'inferior' Vietminh might have in Paris and on the world. So they allowed the Vietminh to isolate Dienbienphu, a fortress so firmly anchored in the "water" of a hostile peasantry that the French were never able to supply it by land.[32]

The French would eventually withdraw from Indo-China, and Vietnam would be divided between a communist north and a "free" south. It was a state of affairs not acceptable to the communists, who would soon be sending supplies and fighters into the south to upend the status quo.

Back in Washington, subsequent American administrations watched anxiously, but having only just extricated the country from the "mess in Korea" eight months prior, Washington policy-makers were not keen on getting involved in another Asian war. Army Chief of Staff General

---

[32] Robert Leckie, *The Wars of America* (New York: Harper & Row, 1981), p. 945.

Ridgway estimated that it would require eight divisions of infantry, which was about the maximum deployed in Korea, to intervene directly in Vietnam. President Eisenhower ruled out the option as well as ruling out the use of nuclear weapons to assist the French. American aid to the French in Indo-China would continue to pour in, but it would not be enough to stave off the inevitable. But the division of Vietnam set the stage for America's eventual involvement given the dominance of the domino theory in American strategic thought.

By the time Kennedy was sworn in as President of the United States in January 1961 the Free World was on the retreat from communist forces around the globe. The Soviets were leading in the space race, China had "gone red," Vietnam and Korea were divided and the Soviets had pounded Eastern Europe into submission. Washington was thus under some considerable pressure to put the United States on a new footing to upset the perceived communist advances. Kennedy himself was an amateur enthusiast of the small war. He saw that the communist strategy was to use people's war, guerrilla wars, to expand the communist sphere and he requested that the United States prepare better irregular forces – Kennedy wanted a new approach to American war.[33] Moving away from Massive Retaliation to Flexible Response the Kennedy Administration streamlined US conventional forces to make them more suited to "little wars" and also signed a nuclear test ban treaty in an effort to bring the nuclear arms race under control.

Under Kennedy, the curriculum at the Special Forces School at Fort Bragg would be expanded and within a year US Special Forces grew from 1,500 to 9,000.[34] As Kennedy put it, the wars of national liberation facing the United States required "a whole new kind of strategy, a wholly different kind of force, and therefore a wholly different kind of military training."[35] But the young president from Massachusetts failed to make a lasting impact on the American way of war. The pre-existing strategic culture of the American military stacked the deck against the young President. Instead of a new, small wars approach to the wars of national liberation that the communists favored, the United States would respond with "limited war" using large conventional

[33] *Ibid.*, p. 964.
[34] Russell Weigley, *The American Way of War* (Bloomington: University of Indiana Press, 1973), p. 457.
[35] *Public Papers of the President of the United States: John F. Kennedy, 1962* (Washington D.C.: Government Printing Office, 1963), p. 454.

forces. Civilian strategists would aim to implement the use of force in a graduated manner that relied on metrics, such as kill ratios, to evaluate their success while on the ground the military would wage a decidedly "Western" war against an opponent that refused to play by Western rules. The results would be paradoxical, a pyrrhic victory at best.

The American way of war in Vietnam

The bombing of Vietnam, according to Pape, "is a classic example of conventional coercion."[36] The US objective at the start of the conflict was to stop the material and manpower assistance flowing from communist North Vietnam to the support of the insurgency in "free" South Vietnam.[37] The ultimate goal was to force the North to the table to negotiate a final status agreement and end to hostilities. The bombing campaign, called Rolling Thunder, ran from March 2, 1965 to October 31, 1968.[38] Military and civilian leadership shared the goals of the bombing campaign, although they disagreed on the strategy. The civilians

---

[36] Robert A. Pape, *Bombing to Win: Airpower and Coercion in War* (Ithaca, NY: Cornell University Press, 1996), p. 174.

[37] This section makes use of numerous sources including: "The History of the Joint Chiefs of Staff: The Joint Chiefs and the Vietnam War, 1960–1969" DoD: Historical Division, July 1, 1970. Available at: www.dod.gov/pubs/foi/ International_security_affairs/vietnam_and_southeast_asiaDocuments/545–2. pdf (accessed July 1, 2014); Bui Tin, *From Enemy to Friend: A North Vietnamese Perspective on the War* (Annapolis, MD: Naval Institute Press, 2002); Clark Clifford and Richard Holbrook, *Counsel to the President: A Memoir* (New York: Random House, 1991); William J. Duiker, *Sacred War: Nationalism and Revolution in a Divided Vietnam* (New York: McGraw-Hill, 1995); W. D. Ehrhart, *Passing Time: Memoir of a Vietnam Veteran Against the War*, second edition (Amherst: University of Massachusetts Press, 1995); George C. Herring, *America's Longest War: The United States and Vietnam, 1950–1975* (New York: McGraw-Hill, 2001); David Hunt, *Vietnam's Southern Revolution: From Peasant Insurrection to Total War* (Amherst: University of Massachusetts Press, 2008); Mark Atwood Lawrence, *The Vietnam War: A Concise International History* (Oxford: Oxford University Press, 2008); Harry G. Summers, Jr., *On Strategy: A Critical Analysis of the Vietnam War* (Novato, CA: Presidio Press, 1982); William Westmoreland, *A Soldier Reports* (New York: Doubleday, 1976); Marilyn B. Young, John J. Fitzgerald and A. Tom Grunfeld, *The Vietnam War: A History in Documents* (Oxford: Oxford University Press, 2002); Samuel Zaffiri, *Westmoreland* (New York: William Morrow, 1994).

[38] "The Air Force in Vietnam, 1967," Office of Air Force History (December 1969), Top Secret, declassified 1986. Available at: www2.gwu.edu/~nsarchiv/NSAEBB/ NSAEBB248/alternatives_1967.pdf (accessed July 1, 2014).

advising Johnson advocated what could be labeled a "lenient" Schelling strategy, named after the writer-strategist Thomas Schelling, who advocated a model of coercive bombing focused on the populous and economic targets using a graduation of violence rather than a full-on campaign. Schelling was against destroying a target in one major operation: since "coercive leverage comes from the anticipation of future damage, military action must be careful to spare a large part of the opponent's civilian assets in order to threaten further destruction."[39] As Schelling put it, "to be coercive, violence has to be anticipated."[40]

This Schelling strategy was forcefully endorsed by Johnson's senior advisors such as Secretary of Defense Robert McNamara, NSC staffer John McNaughton, Chairman of the Joint Chiefs of Staff Maxwell Taylor, Director of Central Intelligence John McCone, Ambassador Henry Cabot Lodge, Deputy National Security Advisor Walt W. Rostow and Assistant Secretary of State William Bundy.[41] The Schelling approach merged well with the analytical and statistical mindset of McNamara's Pentagon. Pape argues that the American strategy was composed of four parts. First, the United States would threaten the total destruction of North Vietnam's emerging industry. As a memo from Walt Rostow to Dean Rusk indicated, "If, despite communist efforts, the U.S. attacks continued, Hanoi's leaders would have to ask themselves whether it was not better to suspend their support of Viet Cong military action rather than suffer the destruction of their major military facilities and the industrial security of their economy."[42] As such, the second aim was to maintain a stark division between north and south, rather than extensive attacks against North Vietnam. As McNamara argued, the US strategy depended on the "credible threat of future destruction" rather than the current bombing campaign.[43] Next the strategy would "gradually tighten the noose," increasing pressure on the North through graduated bombing of increasingly important targets. Finally, coercive bombing was to force the North to the table for a compromise, so it required extensive coordination

[39] Pape, *Bombing to Win*, p. 67.
[40] Thomas C. Schelling, *Arms and Influence* (Westport, CT: Greenview Press, 1977), pp. 2–3.
[41] Kaplan, *The Wizards of Armageddon*, pp. 332–335.
[42] "Memorandum for Secretary of State from W. W. Rostow," DDRS, Vol. 1988, No. 326, November 23, 1964, p. 2.
[43] "Memorandum for the President from Robert S. McNamara (TOP SECRET)," DDRS, Vol. 1987, No. 1344, July 30, 1965, p. 4.

between diplomacy and military action. This strategy was juxtaposed against two other options, one of which was premised on a strong, direct attack against North Vietnam. This option was preferred by the Air Force. Another option was to attack Hanoi's military vulnerabilities, a plan greatly favored by many in the Army. In the end the first strategy won out.

The irony of the war in Vietnam is that it was not supposed to be a ground war. Air power was chosen because it was seen to be less costly to the United States in terms of public opinion. Bombing would enable Washington to achieve its objective of stopping communism in a controlled fashion without the need to placate much public opinion. The US State Department had earlier argued against the presence of US troops.

We do not think the presence of US troops would serve to deter infiltrations short of overt armed intervention. There is not much reason for supposing the Communists would think our troops would be much more successful against guerilla operations in South Viet-Nam than French troops were in North Viet-Nam. Counter-guerilla operations require highly selective application of force; selection requires discrimination; and alien troops simply lack the bases for discriminating between friend and foe, except by the direction in which they shoot.[44]

The presence of US troops in Vietnam consequently did not start off as counterinsurgency operations, far from it. They were put on the ground at the behest of General William Westmoreland, head of the US assistance mission to Vietnam, who argued that the troops were necessary to guard the air base at Da Nang that was used to launch some of the strikes against North Vietnam. Never happy with the civilian's belief in the efficacy of limited war, Gaddis posits, the military argued for this "entering wedge" to secure a future Presidential mandate for a combat operation on the ground. The plan worked. Bundy authorized two brigades (approx. 3,500 men) to guard Da Nang. In April 1965 Johnson approved a combat role of US forces. By the end of 1967 there were 486,000 US troops in Vietnam.

One would expect nothing less from a military man such as William Childs Westmoreland, a southerner educated at West Point where he was captain of cadets. Westmoreland fought during World War II with the 9th Infantry Division all the way from North Africa, up through Italy and on to Normandy, the Battle of the Bulge and Remagen. He was

---

[44] Cited in Gaddis, "Implementing Flexible Response," p. 227.

made a one-star general during the war in Korea and then went on to command the 101st Airborne before a stint at West Point as superintendent. In 1964 Westmoreland was named the most senior US commander in Vietnam, officially charged with military assistance. As the insurgency escalated, the preference of the US military was an invasion of North Vietnam, but Westmoreland's civilian bosses for fear of open war with China did not sanction this plan, so the military was forced to fight a limited war in South Vietnam. This would prove next to impossible, not least because the North would provide a steady stream of supplies to Southern insurgents. More problematic was that Westmoreland failed to realize that his opponent refused to play by the same rules.

Giap would use the same tactics and strategy against the Americans that he used against the French. General Westmoreland, for all his familiarity with Mao's theory of the people's war and despite the presence of the American Small Wars Manual, would still commit several blunders that would cost the United States dearly. The United States would never lose a battle in Vietnam, but this would matter little as Giap's plan was not to defeat the American military out in the open, he simply wanted to bleed the country of the will to fight, a goal that he would succeed in obtaining. In 1968 the Free World forces including US, Australian, Korean, Thai, Filipino and New Zealand troops numbered 1.2 million yet they still could not overcome the North Vietnamese Army and Viet Cong fighters. Ho skillfully managed to turn the conflict from an internal war between the North and the South, to one predicated on "imperialist" Americans invading South Vietnam. This was accompanied by an outpouring of material support from the USSR with additional supplies from the PRC. Ho had a problem, however, in that the Viet Cong were not tremendously popular in the South where they had used assassination, terrorism and gunpoint recruitment much to the detriment of their own goodwill. Thus Ho was keen for Giap's men to get south to help keep the people on side, as much as he was to fight the Americans. As the Americans began to arrive, Giap was aiming to provide Ho with the victory he needed to subdue South Vietnam. The plan was to cut South Vietnam in half at the narrow point of the Central Highlands. Giap wanted a win similar to Dienbienphu to take the wind out of the Americans' sails before their involvement become greater.

General Westmoreland, to his credit, anticipated Giap's plans. Good intelligence provided American forces with the location and date,

somewhere between October and November 1965. Mobility would be
critical to the win, in Westmoreland's opinion, and he used the First
Calvary Division (Airmobile) to push back Giap's move. Giap would be
caught off guard. He had already faced a loss at the hands of the First
Marine Division on the Chu-lai coast, but he wrote this off to the fact
that his forces were up against a famous division in an environment that
favored the Marines rather than his jungle fighters. Giap attempted a
familiar ruse, attacking Plei Me and Pleiku to lure off the Americans to
facilitate the attack on their forces in the Ia Drang Valley. Westmoreland
was able to use his air mobility to hold off the two advanced assaults
before sending the air cavalry out to "search and destroy" the enemy.
Eventually Westmoreland forced Giap's forces to do battle in the shadow
of the Chu Pong Mountain where over the span of three days from
November 3 to November 6, 1965 the communist forces were decisively
defeated.

Westmoreland's military victory in the Ia Drang Valley would be
pyrrhic. He believed that the North Vietnamese were fighting stage
three of the insurgency, which they were in 1965. Following two successive defeats, Giap realized that the best option against the Americans was
to fall back to stage two, irregular warfare. Giap could not compete with
the Americans in terms of firepower, but he could in terms of resolve.
Moving back to stage two gave the initiative to Giap's forces: they could
decide when and where to attack US forces, rather than being blown into
dust by American artillery and bomber raids. The Americans for their
part made no attempt to stop the flow of supplies to the insurgents. North
Vietnam was subject to steady aerial bombardment but the limitations on
the bombing meant that Ho and Giap could work around the campaign.
Giap had total freedom to do what he wanted in North Vietnam,
Cambodia and Laos. As Leckie notes, "the enemy was never placed on
the strategic defensive, his staging areas and his heartland were safe from
total attack, and under these circumstances the only way to 'defeat' him,
that is to say, to deny him military victory, was to destroy his army: in a
word, to kill his soldiers."[45]

The need to kill the enemy pushed Westmoreland toward his now
controversial "search and destroy" strategy. The strategy rested on
massive military operations of brigade or division size. It ran counter

[45] Robert Leckie, *The Wars of America* (New York: Harper & Row, 1981), p. 980.

to the restrained, scientific approach to war the many civilian advisors wanted. At times they involved multiple divisions against enemy strongholds in South Vietnam. This network of bases was well into the hundreds, with approximately eighty major facilities all of which were well placed in swamps, mountains or jungle to maximize defensive ability. Many of them relied on a network of tunnels to keep the facilities supplied. The Iron Triangle 20 miles north of Saigon was one such network of bases. The Iron Triangle was an iron maze of tunnels through which men, supplies and weapons were moved for staging attacks against Saigon. The network was several decades old having been used first against the Japanese, then later the French and finally the Americans. It encompassed around 40 square miles of jungle-mountains that were bordered by dense jungle. Westmoreland's decision was to burn it down.

First, US aircraft poured chemical defoliants on the area, which was left to dry for a few months under the hot Southeast Asian sun. After warning insurgents to leave the area, Westmoreland had cargo aircraft douse the jungle with oil and gasoline, which was then set alight by combat aircraft using napalm and incendiary bombs. Unfortunately for Westmoreland the intense heat of the fire promoted an atmospheric reaction resulting in a huge tropical cloudburst that extinguished the fire. The general then sent a reinforced brigade composed of Americans, New Zealanders and Australians into the Iron Triangle. The brigade commander reported back the successful eradication of the enemy, but what was evident was that the insurgents had chosen not to fight the superior American force. Instead they moved off into the jungle to fight another day. The forces on the ground did not pick up this rather self-evident truth and the Americans continued with the search and destroy strategy. The goal was to find the enemy and fix him into location until American bombers could then bomb the fixed target. In 1966 B-52s made only sixty support sorties a month, but in 1967 they were in excess of 800 per month. As Max Boot reports, "the US dropped 8 million tons of bombs over Vietnam – twice the amount dropped by British and American bombers in all of World War II."[46] By 1966 the United States was spending $2 billion per month on conflict.

All of the US efforts were not entirely shaped by the American tradition of warfare. There was also a "small war" that was conducted

[46] Max Boot, The Savage Wars of Peace (New York: Basic Books, 2002), p. 301.

more in line with the principles of irregular warfare, but this strategy was only semi-successful and it was still subject to the Pentagon's penchant for quantification rather than understanding. Called the "pacification" program the aim was to create the "strong, free nation" that Johnson envisioned in South Vietnam. Under the rubric of "pacification" were several programs known first as Strategic Hamlets, and then as New Life Hamlets (Ap Tan Sinh), as well as Really New Life Hamlets, Rural Reconstruction, and Revolutionary Development, to name a few.[47] The goal of the Strategic Hamlets program was to push the Viet Cong from South Vietnamese villages, making them safe under government control.[48] This was not a new strategy. The French had attempted a similar program and the British had utilized a similar policy in Malaya with success, but in Vietnam the American efforts would fail.[49] The Strategic Hamlets program, for example, moved villagers from their traditional ancestral homes into the new communities. Because the South Vietnamese government liked the program, province chiefs worked overtime to construct more programs that were then chalked up as "successes" even though they were in reality Potemkin villages. Pacification was not a total failure: there were some areas, mainly those in the nearest proximity to Saigon, that did well and actually came under control. But the program never came close to winning the allegiance of the countryside that its proponents claimed. In fact, one of the negative side effects of pacification was the destruction of villages to remove hideaways of insurgents.

Westmoreland began to destroy villages to force insurgents out into the open in 1965 and he expected that the displaced peoples would go to government camps that had been especially prepared for them and where they could be more easily controlled and monitored. Instead by the end of 1967 approximately 3 million people – around 20 percent of South Vietnam's total population – had flooded into the cities of the South, which were ill-prepared for the influx. The result was shantytowns,

[47] Spencer Tucker, *The Encyclopedia of the Vietnam War: A Political, Social, and Military History* (Oxford: ABC-CLIO, 2011), p. 1070. See also Milton E. Osborne, *Strategic Hamlets in South Viet-Nam: A Survey and Comparison* (Ithaca, NY: Cornell University Press, 1965).

[48] David W. P. Elliot, *The Vietnamese War: Revolution and Social Change in the Mekong Delta, 1930–1975* (New York: M. E. Sharpe, 2003), p. 232.

[49] J. J. Zasloff, "Rural Resettlements in South Vietnam: The Agroville Program," *Pacific Affairs*, Vol. 35, No. 4 (Winter 1962–1963), 332.

disposed all about the urban centers. None of this helped the Americans to win "hearts and minds"; they desperately needed to shore up support for the government. In fact, the money and supplies that were poured into pacification programs often bred corruption not only in society, but also in the government and the military. The production of hamlets and the subsequent development programs instituted by the Civil Operations and Revolutionary Development (CORDS) program all became bits of information fed into computers in the Pentagon to determine the progress of the war. Regardless of the fact that such information did not necessarily provide context, systems analysis continued; often the quality of information was dubious. Gibson captured the failure of US efforts in this regard:

Collection departments received most agency budgets and collection departments represented their process in terms of how many "bits" of information they collected, or how many hours of radio messages were recorded. Since their work was so intangible and immeasurable, collection departments got the most. As one senior staff member of the National Security Council said, "95 percent of the US intelligence effort has been on collection, and only 5 percent on analysis and production [interpretation].[50]

By late 1967 General Giap was planning a major offensive that would be modeled on what one observer called "his own political-military-psychological masterpiece: the Battle of Dienbienphu."[51] Giap planned to distract US forces with a series of peripheral battles before launching his real assault, a series of coordinated attacks across South Vietnam. This plan was based on five assumptions. First, he calculated that Lyndon Johnson was not willing to send additional US troops. Second, the US President would not remove the caveats that he had placed on US forces in Vietnam regarding targeting of North Vietnam and subsequent escalation of the conflict. Third, if Giap could pull off a victory it would be disastrous for Johnson going into an election year. Fourth, Giap counted on the fact that the South Vietnamese Army would not put up a serious fight in Saigon and, finally, that a communist victory would incentivize the people of the South to revolt against the government. Consequently Giap started his peripheral attacks in November 1967 and the Americans hit back. Westmoreland and his commanders rather astutely determined that Giap's attacks were ruses, as was the case early in the war, and they

---

[50] Gibson, *The Perfect War*, p. 367.   [51] Leckie, *The Wars of America*, p. 1001.

suspected a concentrated attack on a more important target. The Americans decided that Khe Sanh, a Marine firebase located on a route from Laos toward Hue and Quang Trang, was the most likely target. The United States sent in waves of B-52 bombers, which dropped 100,000 tons of bombs on the jungle. Giap for his part continued to pound Khe Sanh with artillery and to move ever closer to the firebase. The Americans would eventually repel the Vietnamese, but Giap never had any intention of fighting to the end. His goal was to drive up domestic pressure on the Americans, a goal he successfully achieved.

Early in 1968 Giap would launch his follow-on attacks against the South. The plan was to attack on the Vietnamese lunar holiday of Tet – the most important and most sacred holiday of the Vietnamese year, which in 1968 fell on January 30.[52] Although Giap had planned a coordinated assault, because he wanted to protect the secrecy of the operation he did not notify his commanders of the precise plans until shortly before the operation began. As a result the attacks began over three days rather than in one swift instant. One part of the attacks was an insurgent raid on the US embassy. Although the raiders managed to breach the embassy's wall, they failed to capture it although initial US news reports indicated that the communists had indeed captured the compound. The psychological effect on the American people would be highly detrimental for US operations in Vietnam. In the end, the Tet Offensive, as Giap's operation would become known, was a total failure. The United States won big, killing 60,000 communists with three to four times that number wounded. The shadow government the communists had been nurturing was destroyed when they rose to aid the attacks. The Viet Cong were demoralized and significantly weakened. Civilians suffered greatly, with official figures indicating 7,721 civilians died, plus 18,516 casualties. Nearly 75,000 homes were destroyed and over half a million refugees fled the fighting. Property losses neared $200 million.

---

[52] Neil Sheehan, Hedrick Smith, E. W. Kenworthy and Fox Butterfield, *The Pentagon Papers* (New York: Bantam, 1971); Tran Van Tra, "Tet: The 1968 General Offensive and General Uprising," in Jayne S. Werner and Luu Doan Huynh (eds.), *The Vietnam War: Vietnamese and American Perspectives* (Armonk, NY: M. E. Sharpe, 1994); James H. Willbanks, *The Tet Offensive: A Concise History* (New York: Columbia University Press, 2008); James J. Wirtz, *The Tet Offensive: Intelligence Failure in War* (Ithaca, NY: Cornell University Press, 1991).

Despite the overwhelming US victory, the war was inevitably being lost to the communists. This process was developing long before the Tet Offensive. American forces continued with "search and destroy" operations that became a day in and day out trudge through miles of seemingly endless, humid South Vietnamese jungle in search of an elusive enemy that blended into the landscape. Westmoreland had "little sympathy" for the concepts of irregular war; he believed that the function of the infantry was to "seek out, pursue, and destroy enemy forces."[53] But Westmoreland's enemy was not stupid. Giap preferred to avoid full-on, symmetrical engagements that his forces would invariably lose to the Americans. As a result, soldiers traipsed over mountains and through swamps while being picked off by Viet Cong. They would pass deceptively peaceful villages full of women and children. It was from these same villages that sniper fire and motors would emerge to pick off Americans one by one. The Americans came to distrust the Vietnamese. The result was that when American soldiers felt threatened they had two options. They could lead a raid against a village, which might allow them to act more discriminately, but it also exposed the Americans to further attack. The other option was that they could pull back while calling in an air strike that would decimate the village but leave the Americans out of harm's way. The result was that the United States would increasingly make errors, killing hundred of civilians in an air strike in the pursuit of one sniper or a few insurgents. The American soldiers dehumanized the Vietnamese – they were all "gooks" and "slant eyes" and untrustworthy. The result was a downward spiral of US involvement that would result in brutality evidenced in the My Lai Massacre. It would seem at times that the American war in Vietnam was lawless, an image that films such as *Apocalypse Now* would enshrine in the public consciousness after the war. But the story is much more complex than popular culture makes it out to be.

A place for law in Vietnam?

Amid this mix of convoluted ideas that resulted from the American way of warfare in Vietnam – achieving body counts, and destroying villages, yet fighting in a semi-restrained way – was the requirement to apply the

[53] Gaddis, "Implementing Flexible Response," p. 233. See also Boot, *The Savage Wars of Peace*, pp. 286–317.

laws of war. Despite a reputation for being a heartless conflict, it is clear that there was a high level of concern by many members of the military leadership that the laws of war were fully applied to the conflict at the same time as soldiers were engaging in "pacification." As early as 1965 the Commanding General, Fleet Marine Force, Pacific, Lieutenant General Victor H. Krulak wrote: "I am anxious that all of our people are made fully aware of their obligations, under the Geneva Convention, as to the treatment of Prisoners. This point acquires particular importance now that the flow of replacements will bring you to a large group of new and uninitiated people each month." Two months later Krulak went on to write: "Ensure that every officer in the chain of command knows the rules, the reasons for the rules and the penalties for their violation, and then accept no compromise at all."[54] In this sense, despite whatever perceptions we have of the conflict, it is important to recognize that the Vietnam War did not occur in a legal vacuum.

Yet, it is clear that Vietnam posed serious challenges for the United States when it came to applying the laws of war, often with dire consequences. The prosecution of US soldiers for war crimes is one such area where difficulties arose. One military historian of the conflict counts 241 cases where Americans were alleged to have committed war crimes, of which 160 were found to be unsubstantiated on various grounds. Thirty-six war crimes incidents resulted in trials by court-martial on charges including premeditated murder, rape, assault with intent to commit murder or rape, involuntary manslaughter, negligent homicide and the mutilation of enemy dead. Of these thirty-six trials, sixteen (involving thirty men) resulted in not guilty verdicts or were dismissed after arraignment, while twenty cases (involving thirty-one men) resulted in conviction.[55] This picture, however, does not tell the whole story. The infamous case of My Lai, not included in the above counting, illustrates this point:

---

[54] Cited in Gary Solis, *Marine Lawyers and Military Law in Vietnam* (Quantico, VA: US Marine Corps Press, 1989), p. 34. Interestingly, Krulak's son, Charles C. Krulak, a retired Marine and commandant of the Marine Corps from 1995 to 1999, was one of the military voices speaking out against the mistreatment of prisoners and the use of torture in 2009. See Charles C. Krulak and Joseph P. Hoar, "Fear Was No Excuse to Condone Torture," *Miami Herald*, September 11, 2009.

[55] Frederic L. Borch, *Judge Advocates in Combat: Army Lawyers in Military Operations from Vietnam to Haiti* (Washington, D.C.: Office of the Judge Advocate General and Center for Military History United States Army, 2001), p. 22.

fourteen were charged with covering up information related to the massacre, but most of the charges were eventually dropped. Twenty-six men were charged with taking part in the massacre, but only Lieutenant William Calley was convicted of the crime.

Why did these failures occur? If, as we argue in this book, there is a set of competing imperatives behind the American way of warfare, one of which is the need for restraint, how can we explain law in Vietnam? There are several reasons that one may consider. First, it is clear that the US forces were suffering from serious problems related to demoralization and the breakdown of military discipline in Vietnam. Drafted into a difficult conflict that did not seem to have a clear military objective or a strategy against a deadly and creative foe, many young soldiers suffered from a sense of malaise and depression. During the conflict there were 11,058 arrests for non-war crime offenses – 1,146 involving hard narcotics such as heroin.[56] In addition, there were other serious problems such as racial tension between black and white troops, and "fragging" – the murder of officers by their own men became a serious issue. Enforcing basic military discipline (let alone the Geneva Conventions) in such an environment became extremely difficult.

Aggravating this problem was "Project 100,000," a scheme proposed by McNamara to accept men into the armed services who had previously been rejected, often because they had failed basic intelligence standards. As such, all of the military services were required to lower their standards in order to accept an additional 100,000 men. As W. Hays Parks notes, the average Marine or soldier involved in a serious incident or charge had fewer than ten years' formal education, was socially disadvantaged or had below-average intelligence. Where these "Project 100,000" recruits were met with weak or ineffective leadership, the results were disastrous.[57] One historian argues that weak leadership was "the most important single element, present in almost all incidents." The weak leadership led not only to weak discipline, but also inadequate planning of operations and loosely issued orders that resulted in the Rules of Engagement (ROE) not being consistently observed or implemented.[58]

[56] Gary Prugh, *Law at War, 1964–1973* (Washington D.C.: Department of the Army, 1975), p. 107.
[57] W. Hays Parks, "Crimes and Hostilities," *Marine Corps Gazette*, Vol. 60, No. 9 (September 1976), 38–39, p. 38.
[58] Guenter Lewey, *America in Vietnam* (New York: Oxford University Press, 1978), p. 330.

Poor and ineffective training did not help the problems of morale, discipline and weak leadership having a negative effect on the laws of war. This was one of the major findings of the "Report of the Department of the Army, Review of the Preliminary Investigation into the My Lai Incident" (otherwise known as the "Peers Report," named after General William R. Peers, who had been tasked with the investigation). The report made it clear that a major problem that may have led to My Lai was that the soldiers in the brigade involved in the incident were inadequately trained in the laws of war, specifically the obligation not to follow an order that was palpably illegal. Further, the report found that there was inadequate training in the obligations regarding the reporting of war crimes, the provisions of the Geneva Conventions, the handling and treatment of prisoners of war and the treatment and safeguarding of non-combatants.[59] Further, as Parks notes, the nature of the counterinsurgency operations in Vietnam required increased training on the protection of civilians, but such training was neither always effective nor consistent:

The effort was uneven and often personally driven. If a commander believed in the law of war, and in the importance of disciplined military force, law of war training was emphasized, as was the investigation and prosecution of incidents when they occurred ... Without positive command enforcement, and adequate realistic training, a law of war program is not likely to succeed. Where law of war training occurred in Vietnam, it occasionally left much to be desired.[60]

Put another way, in the systematized training program of the average American soldier, law was "tacked on" at the end rather than inculcated throughout the process.

Additionally, even where there was a desire to prosecute, the conditions on the ground in Vietnam did not make it particularly easy. Military lawyers, the Judge Advocate Generals (or JAGs), were deployed throughout South Vietnam, frequently with little more than a yellow legal pad and a Manual for Courts-Martial. Their mission was frequently unclear

---

[59] Department of the Army, "Report of the Department of the Army, Review of the Preliminary Investigation into the My Lai Incident" (Washington: Department of the Army, 1970; herein referred to as the "Peers Report"). See "Findings and Recommendations."

[60] W. Hays Parks, "The United States Military: Inculcating an Ethos," *Social Research*, Vol. 69, No. 4 (Winter 2002), 981–1015, p. 984.

and overseas communication was difficult, creating a situation where the
JAGs were frequently on their own.

The demands of irregular warfare meant that the "traditional" role of
the military lawyer was evolving. While duties such as helping ordinary
soldiers with wills, power of attorney, taxes, advice with domestic
relationships, claims for damaged property, etc. remained, the escalation of the war was changing the needs of the armed forces – even if they
were not entirely aware of it yet. First, given the large numbers of enemy
personnel being taken, there were concerns for the treatment of captured enemy personnel and how lawyers might help to ensure treatment
was in accordance with the Geneva Conventions. Secondly, given the
large number of war crimes being committed, it was clear that an official
policy and reporting war crimes was going to be needed. At first,
Directive 20–4, Inspection and Investigation of War Crimes, dealt only
with the escalation of war crimes being committed against US forces.
However, by mid-1965, American JAGs were advising all war crimes
investigations in Vietnam, including those committed by US forces.

Prosecuting crimes, whether ordinary criminal offenses committed by
US troops or war crimes, was not a straightforward process in Vietnam.
Instead, the remote location where many of the offenses occurred and a
constant turnover of military personnel meant that witnesses could
sometimes be hard to come by. While many witnesses were actually
sent back to the United States before they could testify, in cases involving Vietnamese villagers there were also frequently difficulties in locat-
ing witnesses who might have to travel for hours or days from their
villages. Further, the court-martial system of justice was very foreign to
many of these villagers, who did not speak the language of the court
(and finding translators could be difficult). Certainly, many would have
been intimidated by the prospect of facing the individual accused of
committing the crime, even in a formal, legal setting. As such, trying to
instil even the slightest bit of order through law in a very complex and
complicated conflict was a very difficult task.

There is no doubt that many of the problems originated in the fact that
the war simply did not meet the expectations of the Americans – it simply
did not look like war as they had known it in either World War II or
Korea. In 1951 the United States had ratified the Geneva Conventions
and incorporated them into its codes of military justice. However, neither
the Geneva Conventions (rooted in a view of warfare that mirrored
World War II rather than the "wars of national self-liberation" that

dominated the Cold War) nor US efforts to implement the laws of war had anticipated a conflict such as Vietnam where legal jurisdictions blurred with unconventional participants – who were frequently farmers by day but partisans by night. As Prugh notes:

The battlefield was nowhere and everywhere, with no identifiable front lines, and no safe rear areas. Fighting occurred over the length and breadth of South Vietnam, on the seas, into Laos and Cambodia, and in the air over North Vietnam. It involved combatants and civilians from a dozen different nations. Politically, militarily, and in terms of international law, the Vietnam conflict posed problems of deep complexity.[61]

As we argue throughout this and previous chapters, US assumptions of warfare were firmly grounded in a Western tradition where "proper" war fighting was done by soldiers in uniform who came out to the battlefield, carried their arms openly and distinguished themselves from the population. Anything else was simply not playing by the rules – indeed, the Viet Cong refused to issue a statement acknowledging that they would follow the Geneva Convention or where they agreed to be bound by international law. Although it was the position of the International Committee of the Red Cross (ICRC) that the Viet Cong were bound by the Geneva Conventions, the Viet Cong argued that they were not bound by these rules of war because they had not taken part in their negotiation.[62] As such, South Vietnamese soldiers were executed as a matter of routine, and captured US soldiers suffered terribly in North Vietnamese prisons where they were not seen as POWs, but "war criminals" who did not deserve international protections.

As such, a lack of understanding and cultural recognition of warfare, or even an agreement as to which rules applied, played a major role in many of the problems that the United States would have when it came to the laws of war in Vietnam. American soldiers on the ground, who had often been drafted into the conflict, were mistrustful of the villages they were sent to engage with; in a war with a shadowy enemy that refused to abide by the rules of war that marked civilized conduct, the basis of restraint was tenuous at best. The reputation of notions of

---

[61] Prugh, *Law at War*, p. 62.
[62] Geoffrey Best, *Law and War since 1945* (Oxford: Oxford University Press, 1994), p. 364.

law and restraint had suffered a serious blow in the minds of many US military commanders by the time the last American forces had left Vietnam.

Conclusion

In the wake of the Vietnam War there was a sense within the US military that never again should their country enter into such a conflict. After thirteen years of struggle and heartbreak, many simply wanted to forget Vietnam, or at least they wanted to view it as an aberration from the regular business of war. Indeed, while the CIA would find itself involved in similar counterinsurgency campaigns in Latin America and Afghanistan, the military quickly turned its attention back to how to fight a conventional and/or nuclear war in Europe against the Soviet Union.

Even if US military leadership wanted to forget Vietnam, the war still had a major impact on the way the US forces fought and it laid the groundwork for many of the changes to come in the 1980s, including the so-called Revolution in Military Affairs (RMA). If the United States had stumbled into Vietnam because of the application of computers, "rationality" and logic, by the end of Vietnam the application of computer technology to the battlefield was illustrative of the change in conventional warfare yet to come. The military that had previously been reluctant to embrace the new technology started to come around to the idea that technology could reduce the fog of war. The American faith in technology was nevertheless strengthened, for example, following the siege of Khe Sanh in 1968, where commanders calculated that without the sensors that had provided them with "sight" over the enemy, their casualty figures would have doubled.

This embrace of new technology, according to Michael T. Klare, was a direct result of the Army's failure to win against the irregular warfare of their opponent.[63] The "Battlefield of the Future" only glimpsed in Vietnam offered amazing possibilities to military leaders that had hitherto been reluctant to embrace new technology. General Westmoreland, Commander in Chief of US Forces in Vietnam, in a speech to the US

---

[63] Michael T. Klare, *War without End: American Planning for the Next Vietnam* (New York: Knopf, 1972).

Army Association waxed lyrical, and rather prophetically, about what was to come.

On the battlefield of the future, enemy forces will be located, tracked, and targeted almost instantaneously through the use of data links, computer assisted intelligence evaluation, and automated fire control. With first round kill probabilities approaching certainty, and with surveillance devices that can continually track the enemy, the need for large forces to fix the opponent becomes less important. I see battlefields under 24-hour real or near-real time surveillance of all types. I see battlefields on which we can destroy anything we can locate through instant communications and almost instantaneous application of highly lethal firepower ... In summary, I see an Army built up and around an integrated control system that exploits the advanced technology of communications, sensors, fire direction, and the required automatic data processing.[64]

But while the military would incorporate new technology into its war fighting the way it had for decades, it would fail to ask the seriously hard questions about the strategy deployed in Vietnam and why that strategy failed. Instead, the military would utilize technology to help it plan for what it saw as the next big conventional war; no more insurgencies in jungles was the lesson most in the military brass had learned from Vietnam. The preference within the American military was thus "go large or go home" and technology was there to fight wars bigger and faster than before, not to limit them in scope or application. Meanwhile, policy-makers would increasingly want to use limited force as a tool of policy as the passing of the Cold War led to a world of numerous risks that required limited military intervention. The American defeat in Vietnam did little to change the mindset within the military about the relationship between war and politics, nor did it change much about how to conceptualize victory.

Significantly, this technological revolution would be mirrored by what might as well be called a "legal revolution" in the US armed forces. Lawyers in the Department of Defense who had served in Vietnam had also been changed by their experience. They saw how law could have helped to prevent many of the problems that had occurred during the conflict, and how law might actually help US forces fight better and more efficiently rather than simply restrict their efforts. Together, the

[64] William Westmoreland, "The Battlefield of the Future," Address to the Association of the US Army, Washington D.C., October 14, 1969.

Revolution in Military Affairs or RMA and a legal revolution would merge in the 1980s to create a distinctly American legal-scientific way of warfare that would characterize how the nation fought (for better and worse) into the twenty-first century. How these changes, inspired by the American experience in Vietnam, occurred over the next decade is the subject of the next chapter.

4 | *Immaculate destruction: reorganization, revolution and re-enchantment of War*

Our strategy to go after this army is very, very simple. First we're going to cut it off, and then we're going to kill it.

Colin Powell, January 1991

The defeat in Vietnam, it can be fairly said, was an outcome that the US military essentially would choose to forget in the 1970s and 1980s. Abandoning the difficult lessons of irregular warfare and counterinsurgency in the jungles and deltas of Southeast Asia, American military leaders and service chiefs instead wanted to return to "proper," conventional warfare that, in their minds, would be fought in Cold War Europe against the USSR. Further, frustrated with what they saw as interference by civilian "Whiz Kids" during the war, military leaders sought to reform civil–military relations as they changed from a conscripted to a professional force.[1] However, there were other lessons of Vietnam that could not be ignored: the mistakes and errors caused by service infighting, a poor chain of command and weak military advice would continue to affect US military operations into the 1980s. Future US military operations were clearly in jeopardy unless urgent reforms to the Department of Defense were undertaken, despite objections from the military establishment. Although the reforms mandated by Congress were not always welcome, they transformed the US military into a much more efficient and effective military force. The 1991 Gulf War demonstrated the effectiveness of these reforms as the armed forces seamlessly blended superior military technology, law and their new, streamlined command structure into a lethal fighting force that utterly

---

[1] Gordon Goldstein, *Lessons in Disaster: McGeorge Bundy and the Path to War in Vietnam* (New York: Henry Holt, 2009); H. R. McMaster, *Dereliction of Duty* (New York: Harper Collins, 1998).

annihilated the Iraqi Army. Finally, it seemed, the US military had achieved a balance between annihilation and restraint in a perfect liberal war.

While the Gulf War demonstrated exactly what the US military could accomplish in a conventional conflict with its sophisticated weaponry, the conflicts of the remainder of the decade were very unlike the desert battlefields of Iraq. The 1993 "Battle of Mogadishu" and the chaotic and complex ethnic conflicts in the Former Yugoslavia and Africa reminded the US military just why it wished to avoid such messy, limited wars. But, starting with officials in the Clinton Administration, civilians began to see ways in which the technology employed by the US military could fight wars that were quick, low on casualties and could provide near instantaneous results. Two decades after the end of Vietnam, and having seemingly conquered its historical problem of balancing the competing imperatives of annihilation and restraint, the United States was "re-enchanted" with war.

This chapter traces the different military revolutions that occurred during the 1980s and how these contributed to an enhanced and effective military by the 1991 Gulf War. In particular, "revolutions" in civil–military relations, the most significant overhaul of the organizational structure of the US military since 1947 and a "legal revolution" combined with the most sophisticated military technology on the planet to create the world's most powerful army in the post-Cold War era. This chapter also traces how these "revolutions" led to a renewed belief in US military prowess and capabilities in *all* forms of conflict among many in the Administrations of William Jefferson Clinton and George W. Bush. Essentially, drawing upon a faith in the ability of US military technology to revolutionize the American way of war to deliver "clean" and convenient conflicts, the United States by the mid-1990s no longer viewed the use of force as an aberration from the norm.

A return to annihilation ...

The result of America's involvement in Vietnam's struggle for independence was far less than hoped for by the post-war generation of American civilian strategists. The military had been resistant to the idea of limited war conducted through advanced technology and air power, and many military officers believed that their view of war had been vindicated:

war was hell and there was no way around it; it could not be limited. If the United States was to engage in conflict, it had to be an absolute commitment, using every available means possible. Quite simply, the military could not allow itself to be hung out to dry again by politicians. There were two streams of discourse along these lines that dominated the interservices discussions of the US armed forces in the 1970s. The first was that politicians had not supported the military by rallying the public and the second was that the military had not been allowed to win the war due to the limited war paradigm pushed on them by civilians. As such, in the wake of Vietnam, the armed forces immediately set out to develop criteria for military action that ensured that the military would only be used in the most critical cases.

The first step was to change domestic hearts and minds by improving the relationship between society and the military. Creighton Abrams, Army Chief of Staff from 1972 to 1974, played an instrumental role in this regard. To ensure that politicians could not abandon the military in future in the same way the armed forces had been "abandoned" in Vietnam, General Abrams devised a system whereby the reserve forces of the military were tied into the active duty forces. He ensured that a number of Army divisions based in the United States were composed of both active duty personnel and reserve personnel. As such, to wage combat on a significant scale would require the President and Congress to send not just professional soldiers, but also the part-time soldiers of the reserves. The logic behind making reserve forces crucial to any deployment of regular forces was to put pressure on politicians to consider more fully any use of military force, since doing so would require not just the mobilization of professional soldiers, but also a contribution from the wider society.

The second development for the military was to improve relations with the civilian planners they had fallen out with during Vietnam. As such, effort was directed to restoring the civil–military relationship, but also redressing the imbalance between civilian planners and military planners. A chief fault with Vietnam, in the eyes of the military, was that the civilians had run amok with planning, casting aside the counsel of the military that repeatedly warned that the idea of limited war was a hopeless cause. This point of view is best captured by Colonel Harry Summers in his book *On Strategy: The Vietnam War in Context* where he argued, "our civilian leadership in the Pentagon, the White House and in the Congress evidently believe that military professionals had no worthwhile advice to give."[2] Rather than being dominated by academic political scientists and systems analysts in the defense bureaucracy, military leaders had to be reinstalled as the principal planners.

As former US Army Colonel, now professor at Boston University Andrew Bacevich argues that the armed forces did not just want to plan the wars; they also wanted a say in what wars to wage – a blurring of lines of civil–military control.

the officer corps sought not simply to reassert its primacy on matters relating to planning and conduct of operations; it also wanted to have a strong say in determining when and where US forces might be called upon to fight. Only influence there – prior to any actual decision to intervene – could prevent feckless civilians from committing the nation to wars or quasi-wars not to the military's own liking.[3]

After Vietnam, the military was extremely reluctant to counsel the use of force and was eager to define the parameters where the military could be used.[4] Andrew Bacevich put it, "the officer corps had a profound interest in curtailing any inclination on the part of civilian policy-makers to commit US forces to contingencies other than the defence of Europe, especially any contingency in which the likelihood of gaining a rapid and favourable decision appeared problematic."[5] To this end the military essentially codified what would eventually become known as the Weinberger Doctrine, named after President Ronald Reagan's Secretary of State Caspar Weinberger, who felt that the staff of the US National Security Council were spending "most of their time thinking up ever more wild adventures for our troops."[6] The doctrine, developed with the assistance of Colin Powell (at that time Secretary Weinberger's chief military

[2] Harry G. Summers Jr., *On Strategy: The Vietnam War in Context* (Carlisle, PA: US Army War College, 1981), p. 21. See also McMaster, *Dereliction of Duty*.

[3] Andrew Bacevich, *The New American Militarism* (Oxford: Oxford University Press, 2005), p. 47.

[4] See Peter D. Feaver and Christopher Gelpi, *Choosing your Battles: American Civil–Military Relations and the Use of Force* (Princeton, NJ: Princeton University Press, 2004).

[5] Bacevich, *The New American Militarism*, p. 47.

[6] Jeffery Record, *Making War, Thinking History: Munich, Vietnam, and Presidential Uses of Forces from Korea to Kosovo* (Annapolis, MD: Naval Institute Press, 2002), p. 29.

assistant), set an extremely high hurdle for the use of force.[7] The doctrine, as applied by Chairman of the Joint Chiefs General Colin Powell during his tenure at the pinnacle of the American military establishment, required an affirmative answer to eight questions to justify US military intervention.

1. Is a vital national security interest threatened?
2. Do we have a clear attainable objective?
3. Have the risks and costs been fully and frankly analyzed?
4. Have all other non-violent policy means been fully exhausted?
5. Is there a plausible exit strategy to avoid endless entanglement?
6. Have the consequences of our action been fully considered?
7. Is the action supported by the American people?
8. Do we have genuine broad international support?

Without eight affirmative answers, the United States should decline to use force, according to the chairman. These rules were the product of a long discussion in the military following Vietnam.

The Weinberger Doctrine also reflected and helped to institutionalize the kind of war the military had prepared for following Vietnam.[8] The goal in the late 1970s and 1980s was for the military to return to the zone between nuclear warfare and guerrilla warfare. Clearly, nuclear war was not a tenable option given the level of death and destruction that would ensue, and guerrilla warfare had resulted in Vietnam. As such military planners turned to Europe for their *raison d'état*. The Warsaw Pact in Europe under the leadership of the Soviet Union still represented a very real threat. Recalling that the use of force in Korea by the communists was short of nuclear war but was in every other sense a full-scale conventional war, planners prepared the Air Land Battle doctrine in 1982. The Air Land Battle doctrine was predicated on stopping and reversing a full-scale, conventional attack by the Warsaw Pact against Western Europe. In doing so, however, the military had essentially devised plans for a conflict that was so clearly defined and so highly improbable that it essentially eliminated the possibility that it might actually be utilized. As Martin van Creveld notes, given the alleged Soviet superiority in conventional forces, and the West German refusal to fortify their borders, most

---

[7] Kenneth J. Campbell, "Once Burned, Twice Cautious: Explaining the Weinberger–Powell Doctrine," *Armed Forces & Society*, Vol. 24, No. 3 (Spring 1998).

[8] Shultz arrives at a similar summary in his book: George P. Shultz, *Turmoil and Triumph: My Years as Secretary of State* (New York: Scribner's, 1993), pp. 649–651.

Western analysts had already concluded that a determined Soviet attack could only be stopped with the use of "tactical" nuclear weapons. As such, "during the last quarter century, much of the Western effort aimed at preparing a defense against the USSR has amounted to a gigantic exercise in make-believe."[9]

The armed forces had reverted to their largely pre-Vietnam tendency to think of war as an aberration and therefore as a break with politics, rather than a continuation of politics. The military was prepared for a war predicated on overwhelming force – a conventional conflict that the military believed it could win decisively in the American tradition. Fighting with one hand behind your back was no way to win a war, as General Westmoreland argued in his memoirs *A Soldier Reports*: "Bomb a little bit, stop it a while to give the enemy a chance to cry uncle, then bomb a bit more but never enough to really hurt. That was no way to win [Vietnam]."[10]

... Rethinking restraint ...

Although the US military leadership might have wanted to forget the lessons of Vietnam, not everyone at the Pentagon was so inclined. In particular, US military lawyers, especially JAGs deployed to Vietnam during the war, wanted to implement many of the lessons they had learned. They witnessed firsthand how improper attention to the laws of war and law of war training had led to political, military and moral disaster. From their view on the ground, and in reflecting on what had gone wrong in Vietnam, they began to recognize the many ways in which law could have given order to a chaotic conflict and ultimately helped US forces fight more effectively. What the United States needed to win wars was a new approach to law that emphasized smarter implementation – the law could facilitate war; it was not just a restraint.

This, however, was not a simple task. Like the notion of limited war, the laws of war had a bad reputation in the aftermath of Vietnam and were seen as a major factor in the United States "losing" the war. Lawyers within the Department of Defense after Vietnam were "confronted with

---

[9] Martin van Creveld, *The Transformation of War* (New York: The Free Press, 1991), p. 13.
[10] William C. Westmoreland, *A Soldier Reports* (New York: Doubleday, 1976), p. 410.

hostile clients" because "lawyers and the law of war were blamed for restrictions placed upon the use of military force during the Vietnam War."[11] In the minds of many American military leaders, limited war and legal restrictions were one and the same thing. As such, broaching the topic of reforming the way the United States implemented international law in the late 1970s was a project that seemed like a doomed endeavor.

Pentagon lawyers, however, were determined to challenge this view. Believing that the laws of war were neither cumbersome international obstructions nor a panacea that could cure all of the ills that occurred in Vietnam, they began the daunting task of rehabilitating the laws of war (and perhaps their own reputation) in the eyes of a military skeptical of anything that could limit war. A significant step toward this end was the establishment of a Department of Defense Law of War Program in 1974, a direct result of the military's attempt to respond to the recommendations of a government inquiry into the My Lai Massacre.[12] The Law of War Program was tasked with improving the implementation of the laws of war, including training. Immediately, lawyers undertook three separate tasks to implement these goals (including evolving their own position with the Department of Defense [DoD]) to ensure they fulfilled the new program's mandate.

First, lawyers embarked on studies of the legal aspects of military operations during Vietnam such as Operation Rolling Thunder and Operation Linebacker. As W. Hays Parks (a sniper and military lawyer who served in Vietnam and subsequently as a DoD civilian involved in these efforts) writes:

In each and every case, it was determined that the restrictions in question were the result of policy restrictions that were promulgated by either President Lyndon B. Johnson or Secretary of Defense Robert S. McNamara, or were restrictions that the combat commander-client had imposed on himself because he thought a particular course of action might violate the law of war, when in fact it did not.[13]

---

[11] W. Hays Parks, "The Gulf War: A Practitioner's View," *Dickinson Journal of International Law*, Vol. 10, No. 3 (1992), 393–423, p. 397.

[12] See DoD Directive 5100.77 (November 5, 1974). The DoD Law of War Directive has been updated throughout the years. The current directive (as of February 22, 2011) is 2311.01E.

[13] Parks, "The Gulf War," p. 397. The work of W. Hays Parks is significant here. He notes that many of the restrictions on attacks that had been put in place were there not because of the law, but because of political decisions or because of a mistaken

Principally, these papers on the interaction between international law and the conduct of military operations in Vietnam demonstrated that many of the restrictions imposed by the Johnson Administration were unwarranted by the laws of war. For example:

The focal point for much of the controversy over both targeting and bombing is that area of international law known as the law of war. Whereas the Johnson administration declined to authorize the attack of certain targets and imposed unprecedented restrictions on U.S. strike forces ostensibly to protect the civilian population of North Vietnam, the North Vietnamese were quick to allege that the United States was engaged in a campaign of indiscriminate bombing in violation of the law of war. Confusion over the state of the law persists. Draft contingency and operations plans I have seen routinely contain unwarranted restrictions apparently derived from the drafter's experience in Vietnam, misperceived to be based on the law of war. While lecturing at the U.S. military staff colleges, I have noted definite confusion among professional military officers regarding the source of many of the operational restrictions of the Vietnam War. While some of these restrictions may have been the result of law-of-war obligations accepted by the United States, most were not.

The United States is a nation of rule by law. Every member of the military is bound by oath to discharge his or her duties in accordance with the law, including the law of war. While some may question whether this measure of confidence in the law in the international sphere is warranted, it is essential to understand what the law provides and to distinguish the rights and responsibilities of the law of war from other restrictions.[14]

Essentially, Parks argues that it was not the laws of war that caused the United States to lose Vietnam, but ignorance of that law. Although the justification and redemption of the laws of war in these terms may sound harsh, what is significant in these arguments is the idea that the laws of war remain valid and legitimate standards, which the United States must apply. The law did not take away military advantage; the military was disadvantaged by the law's shoddy implementation. In essence, lawyers were making the point that the laws of war are not merely restrictions on state action, but also standards that preserve the rights of states in armed conflict.

belief that certain actions would violate the laws of war. See: W. Hays Parks, "Rolling Thunder and the Law of War," *Air University Review*, Vol. 33, No. 2 (1982) and "Linebacker and the Law of War," *Air University Law Review*, Vol. 34, No. 2 (1983).

[14] Parks, "Rolling Thunder and the Law of War."

These studies laid the groundwork for a second significant step for the military lawyers: the rebranding of "the laws of war" as "Law Affecting Military Operations" or "OPLAW" for short.[15] Having established that flawed understandings of the laws of war had led to poor decision making, military lawyers repackaged law as a tool that could actually help military operations run smoother. Intentionally or unintentionally reflecting the language of "Operational Research," Operational Law was defined as "that body of foreign, domestic and international law which impacts specifically upon the activities of the US Forces in war and operations other than war."[16] Although military lawyers argued that "Lest there be any doubt, OPLAW is a *new* concept,"[17] this de facto "rebranding" was designed to facilitate a transition from a position where the laws of war were understood as restrictions or outside impositions that burdened military commanders, to an appreciation of the law as a tool. In other words, the law could help the United States fight better.

Once the laws of war could be appreciated in this way, it became easier for military lawyers to argue that they should take an active part in not just the conduct of military operations, but also their planning and preparation. While senior military figures began to make the case that they should have a greater say in planning wars and in choosing which wars to fight, military lawyers argued that they too had a place in the war room. The advantage of a proactive JAG corps with direct access to military commanders was that they could ensure that legal problems that might negatively affect a particular mission could be identified and dealt with at an earlier stage and ensure that the United States properly implemented the laws of war.[18] As such, this rebranding of the laws of war was a way to ensure that they were taken seriously and implemented at all key levels of operational decision making. As Steven Keeva notes, it was an approach that brought "lawyers in the war

---

[15] On Operational Law see David E. Graham, "Operational Law (OPLAW) – A Concept Comes of Age," *The Army Lawyer* (July 1987); Parks, "The Gulf War" and Marc L. Warren, "Operational Law – A Concept Matures," *Military Law Review*, Vol. 152, 33–73.

[16] Graham, "Operational Law," p. 9.   [17] *Ibid.*, p. 8.

[18] Frederic L. Borch, *Judge Advocates in Combat: Army Lawyers in Military Operations from Vietnam to Haiti* (Washington D.C.: Office of the Judge Advocate General and Center of Military History, United States Army, 2001), p. 51.

room" rather than regarding law as an afterthought.[19] It was also a stance that required US military lawyers to be sensitive both to the needs of commanders and the need to achieve military objectives on the one hand, and the requirements of international law and the expectations of both the American and international public on the other.

A third measure US military lawyers carried out in the post-Vietnam era was an overhaul of the system of training soldiers in the laws of war. In the aftermath of the conflict, studies found that training in the laws of war during the Vietnam War was "abstract and academic, rather than concrete and practical"[20] and not necessarily in touch with the everyday realities of warfare. As Parks notes, law of war training prior to Vietnam placed more emphasis on the rights of American soldiers when captured than their responsibilities to any prisoners they might take. And while counterinsurgency operations required the protection of civilians not taking an active part in hostilities, this training was often uneven and inconsistent across different military units.[21] Therefore, rather than an afterthought, law was to be incorporated into the way that US soldiers were taught to do their jobs in the first place: soldiers would be taught to do their jobs and tasks in accordance with the laws of war from day one. In this way, the laws of war would be taught in a practical way rather than as a theoretical postscript.[22] The expectation of this concurrent approach

---

[19] Steven Keeva, "Lawyers in the War Room," *American Bar Association Journal* (December 1991).

[20] See Seymour M. Hersh, *Cover-Up: The Army's Secret Investigation of the Massacre at My Lai 4* (New York: Random House, 1972), p. 42. Hersh cites correspondence between General Bruce Palmer and General Harold K. Johnson, Army Chief of Staff in May 1968, who discussed problems related to law of war training.

[21] W. Hays Parks, "The United States Military and the Law of War: Inculcating an Ethos," *Social Research*, Vol. 69, No. 4 (Winter 2002), 981–1015.

[22] As Parks describes it in "The United States Military":

Thus a sailor "shovelling steam" aboard an auxiliary vessel would require less law of war training than an Army or Marine rifleman. At the outset, however, each person (whether enlisted, warrant officer, or officer candidate) receives a basic law of war presentation in accession training. The soldier or marine who proceeds to specialized infantry training would receive additional training, especially regarding the handling and safeguarding of enemy prisoners of war. Similar training is provided, as appropriate, in other military occupational specialty schools. Thus after initial exposure, the training is tailored to the individual's field. "Commensurate with his or her . . . responsibilities" also is rank conscious. As enlisted and officers advance through their respective ranks,

is that adherence to the laws of war is ingrained or inculcated within US military personnel so that observance of them will be automatic.

As such, US military lawyers, inspired by the (real and imagined) failures of Vietnam, developed pragmatic solutions to the problems that had emerged, and they developed solutions that were grounded in the everyday realities of soldiers and US military operational requirements. At the same time, the core assumption behind these developments is that the laws of war are professional standards to which the US military must adhere, but which would also ultimately help the United States fight better. The end result of these efforts by military lawyers in the post-Vietnam period led to a reimagining of how the US military could implement and adhere to the laws of war while also achieving its military objectives.

What can be said for this new approach? Importantly, during this time, DoD lawyers, whether active military or civilian veterans, were able to use their military experience to drive change and to repackage the laws of war to a skeptical defense establishment. In effect, they were able to debunk certain myths about the laws of war and leverage a "martial honor" that comes with active service to further their goals. This helped in garnering an audience for their ideas, and in formulating a strategy as to how they are implemented; martial honor gave military lawyers a voice of authority when speaking on what is often an unwelcome and uncomfortable subject. Yet, this "martial honor" is not limited to those within the Pentagon; as Mark Osiel notes, when US Senators with military experience (such as John McCain, John Warner and Lindsay Graham) speak on law-of-war issues (such as the treatment of prisoners of war), they do so in a way that emphasizes experience and honor:

All these men consistently emphasized the need for America to uphold standards of honourable conduct . . . The clear implication was that we should treat

---

additional training is provided at schools in their chain of advancement, such as (to use Army examples) the First Sergeant Course, at the Sergeant Major Academy, Officer Advanced Courses, the Warrant Officer Advanced Course, Command and General Staff College, and the Army War College. Each presentation is tailored to the individual's level of responsibility upon completion of the course. Other, specialized schools or special mission units also provide or receive tailored instruction. Law of war training is thus continuous throughout a soldier's career.

others honourably because that is how we may display our virtue. For virtue is a property of our character, not of our relations with others, even if evidenced in such relations. In arguing for national self-restraint, they thus sought not to minimize the threat that America faces – as did many critics of the Bush administration counterterrorism policies – but instead to suggest the need for courage in the face of it.[23]

Here Osiel is emphasizing the role of honor in enforcing the laws of war, specifically a form of martial honor that comes from active service with the US military. Osiel, however, is not uncritical of the concept or its use as the basis of the application of restraint in warfare. As he argues, during moments of crisis: "a sense of martial honor in the country's professional soldiers, joined to abstract notions of national self-respect not deeply shared in the country at large, is unlikely to provide sufficient counterweight to conflicting public pressures for 'getting tough.'"[24]

In other words, when there is a threat to the United States, or its values, the restraint that comes with martial honor is a problematic one. On issues such as torture, or treatment of detainees in the War on Terror, it is not at all clear that the martial honor upon which the DoD Law of War Program was at least partially based has been strong enough to carry the day with policy-makers and legislators.[25] Indeed, as incidents such as those at Haditha and Abu Ghraib or the revelation of a "kill team" (comprised of US soldiers who murdered civilians and took body parts such as teeth and fingers as trophies) in Afghanistan demonstrate, this approach, which relies on inculcating an ethos and martial honor, can fail dramatically on an individual level

---

[23] Mark Osiel, *The End of Reciprocity: Terror, Torture and the Law of War* (Cambridge: Cambridge University Press, 2009), pp. 351–352.

[24] Osiel, *End of Reciprocity*, p. 367.

[25] The debates between DoD and other government departments (such as Justice) and the Bush White House over issues regarding the laws of war in the War on Terror have been well documented. See Stephanie Carvin, *Prisoners of America's Wars: From The Early Republic to Guantanamo* (New York: Columbia University Press, 2010); David P. Forsythe, *The Politics of Prisoner Abuse: The United States and Enemy Prisoners after 9/11* (Cambridge: Cambridge University Press, 2012); Jane Mayer, *The Dark Side: The Inside Story of How the War on Terror Turned Into a War on American Ideals* (New York: Anchor Books, 2009).

when the fog and stress of war take hold and the scenarios covered in training no longer exist.[26]

But a second set of questions about this approach can be raised: Had this "legal revolution" turned the laws of war into a weapon rather than a restraint? Lawfare, as defined by Charles Dunlap (often credited with the modern definition of the term), is the strategy of using – or misusing – law as a substitute for traditional military means to achieve an operational objective. For some, lawfare is associated with liberal or left-leaning NGOs trying to use laws as a weapon against rule-of-law oriented societies in order to prevent them from resorting to force. In other words, lawfare may be understood as the use of law and legal tools (such as human rights tribunals) to create legal barriers that prevent states from using force.[27]

However, Dunlap's definition is different. For him "lawfare" is not "something adversaries seek to use against law-abiding societies; it is a resource that democratic militaries can – and should – employ

---

[26] This is not to imply that the fog of war/battle stress are any excuse for the war crimes that were committed on these three occasions. On Haditha see Charlie Savage and Elisabeth Bumiller, "An Iraqi Massacre, a Light Sentence and a Question of Military Justice," *New York Times* (January 27, 2012). Available at: www.nytimes.com/2012/01/28/us/an-iraqi-massacre-a-light-sentence-and-a-question-of-military-justice.html?_r=0 (accessed July 1, 2014); on Abu Ghraib see Carvin, *Prisoners of America's Wars*; Forsythe, *The Politics of Prisoner Abuse*; Mayer, *The Dark Side*. On the so-called "Kill Team" see Mark Boal, "The Kill Team: How U.S. Soldiers in Afghanistan Murdered Innocent Civilians," *Rolling Stone* (March 27, 2011). Available at: www.rollingstone. com/politics/news/the-kill-team-20110327 (accessed July 1, 2014).

[27] For example, human rights activists have used courts to try and stop militaries from conducting certain operations. In *Khan -v- SSFCA* (2012), the human rights organization Reprieve argued in the UK High Court that the sharing of intelligence with the United States that resulted in fatal drone attacks violates English and Welsh criminal law. (The Court rejected the plaintiff's arguments, although at time of writing, the case continues to work its way through the UK courts.) See www.judiciary.gov.uk/media/judgments/2012/khan-v-ssfca (accessed July 1, 2014) and Owen Bowcott, "High Court Rejects Challenge over UK Link to Drone Strikes in Pakistan," *Guardian* (December 21, 2012). Available at: www.guardian.co.uk/world/2012/dec/21/high-court-drone-strikes-pakistan (accessed July 1, 2014). Additionally, in September 2012 in the United States, the American Civil Liberties Union (ACLU) took the CIA to court for it to release more information on its alleged drone warfare program in order to enhance public accountability. See Tom Schoenberg, "CIA Role in U.S. Drone Strikes Scrutinized by Appeals Court," Bloomburg.com, September 20, 2012. Available at: www.bloomberg.com/news/2012-09-20/cia-role-in-u-s-drone-strikes-scrutinized-by-appeals-court-1-.html

affirmatively."[28] Law should not be seen as a hindrance, but as a tool that can enhance the way a nation fights. In fact, Dunlap argues that it is important for the militaries of military democracies to conceive of the role of law in more conventional military terms: "Understanding that the law can be wielded much like a weapon by either side in a belligerency is something to which a military member can relate. It facilitates accounting for law, and particularly the fact and perception of adherence to it, in the planning and conduct of operations."[29] Similar to the arguments made by DoD lawyers in the 1980s, Dunlap argues that law is not something that hurts America, or the ability of its armed forces to fight. Rather, it should be embraced by militaries as something that can help them fight better.

Interestingly, this argument and observation mirror a complaint of some in the "Critical Legal Studies" (LLS) school who argue that the current laws of war enable states rather than restrain them; they legitimize death and the use of violence rather than prevent it. As Roger Normand and Chris Jochnick argue:

In wars throughout history, belligerents have used law to legitimize conduct that might otherwise have received closer scrutiny. The legal lesson of the Gulf War is in degree rather than kind: a belligerent with overwhelming military superiority and a publicly professed commitment to respect the laws of war, especially in relation to the protection of civilians, nonetheless managed to kill an enormous number of civilians in attacks that had very little military significance. And for this the Coalition has been praised for conducting "the most legalistic war ever fought."[30]

Rejecting a liberal approach that is seen as trying to finesse war rather than prevent it, CLS scholars view the laws of war as codes written with combatants and not civilians in mind. As Judith Gardam argues, while the Geneva Convention does provide some protection for civilians in occupied territory, much of this is really focused on the maintenance of order rather than proper civilian protection. Further, women's rights and needs are barely given any consideration at all. Instead, any

---

[28] Charles J. Dunlap Jr., "Lawfare: A Decisive Element of 21st-Century Conflicts?", *Joint Forces Quarterly*, Vol. 54, No. 3 (2009), 34–39.

[29] *Ibid.*, p. 35.

[30] Roger Normand and Chris Jochnick, "The Legitimation of Violence: A Critical Analysis of the Gulf War," *Harvard Law Review*, Vol. 35, No. 2 (Spring 1994), 387–416, p. 409.

protections are geared toward the reproductive role of women, or issues that are, in reality, concerns for men:

Of some 34 provisions [in the Geneva Conventions] ostensibly providing safeguards for women, a closer inspection reveals that 19 of them are intended primarily to protect children. Moreover, the protections for women from sexual violence are couched in terms of their honour. In reality a woman's honour is a concept constructed by men for their own purposes: it has little do to with women's perception of sexual violence.[31]

CLS scholars are concerned about the perceived emphasis on the principle of "military necessity," over other principles, such as humanity. Military necessity recognizes that the goal of war is to win, and that this is a legitimate consideration when fighting in battle. It stipulates that attacks must be directed toward the defeat of the enemy and that they must be proportional to the military advantage anticipated. This is a concept central to the laws of war along with proportionality and discrimination – but clearly one that is also central to the US readoption of the laws of war in the 1980s.

It is interesting that the idea that the laws of war provide legal cover and justification for violence is something that US military and CLS scholars agree upon. Both see law as a weapon that complemented the return to conventional warfare in the 1980s. Yet, for the United States, law is a tool; for CLS scholars, this is a perversion and an outrage. For the purpose of this book, it is important to recognize that the laws of war are the established rules upon which arguing over the legitimacy of violent action in armed conflict – that is lawfare – is fought. Certainly, the rights granted and restrictions imposed by the laws of war would become a major area of contention in the War on Terror.

... and reorganization

But by the early 1980s, changes to improve relations between the military, American citizens and the government, as well as changes to the law, were simply not enough. Although many in the military laid blame with the civilian leadership (and DoD lawyers), it was clear to others within and outside of the Pentagon that there were structural issues responsible

---

[31] Judith Gardam, "Women and the Law of Armed Conflict: Why the Silence?", *International and Comparative Law Quarterly*, Vol. 46 (1997), 55–80, p. 57.

for serious problems in Vietnam that had more recently hampered the smaller missions being conducted abroad. As James R. Locher argues, the entire Pentagon structure desperately needed reform:

The military bureaucracy had tied itself in knots since World War II and lost outright the Vietnam conflict and three lesser engagements: the USS *Pueblo* seizure, the Desert One raid, and the peacekeeping operation in Beirut. The Korean War, *Mayaguez* rescue, and Grenada incursions were hardly resounding victories. Decision-making had become so convoluted, fiefdoms so powerful and inbred, lines of authority so confused, and chains of command so entangled that the military hierarchy had repeatedly failed the nation. Third-rate powers and terrorists had humiliated America. Tens of thousands of troops had died needlessly. Unprecedented levels of defense spending were not making the nation more secure.[32]

The United States' inherent distrust of its military in the early stages of the republic meant that little thought had been given to the structure of the armed forces, the services, the chain of command and civil–military relations. While it was clear that the military was subordinate to the civilian government, it was not clear how this should actually work in practice. The end result of this thinking was that problems in the chain of command and the ability to conduct joint operations between the services had become apparent as early as the Spanish–American War in 1898.[33]

The first major attempt at reform came in 1947 with the founding of the National Military Establishment (redesignated as "the Department of Defense" by Congress in 1949). The National Security Act designed a weak Secretary of Defense, legal standing to the Joint Chiefs of Staff (but no chairman) and, in effect, created a system that was dominated by the individual military services who worked to protect their fiefdoms

---

[32] James R. Locher III, *Victory on the Potomac: The Goldwater–Nichols Act Unifies the Pentagon* (College Station, TX: A&M University Press, 2007), p. 4.

[33] Locher, *Victory on the Potomac*, p. 16. However, as Martin van Creveld notes, the United States was in good company in this regard, arguing that "counterinsurgency" carried out by their Western allies failed in almost every case. The British failed in India, Palestine, Kenya, Cyprus and Aden; the French failed in Indochina and Algeria; the Belgians failed in the Congo; the Dutch lost Indonesia and the Portuguese failed in Angola and Mozambique. *The Transformation of War*, pp. 22–23. Truly, in light of the wars of national self-liberation, few Western nations had developed any significant counterinsurgency capability, other than perhaps a certain level of success of the British during the 1948–1960 "Malayan Emergency."

and downplay unified commands.[34] Subsequent efforts at reform in 1949, 1953 and 1958 aimed at further strengthening and centralizing civilian authority within the Pentagon, but left the services in "a divisive and contentious framework under the intentionally emaciated authority of a weakly centralized collectivity on the uniformed side of the defense establishment."[35]

The services preferred this arrangement so that they could more easily maintain control over their own affairs and their supporters in Congress, who also strongly resisted any attempt to promote a unity of command, "jointness" between services and a simplified chain of command. As such, between 1958 and 1983 there were no changes to the organization or structure of the military despite the fact that there were obvious flaws. The Joint Chiefs of Staff (JCS) continued to operate as something akin to the United Nations Security Council, where unanimous consent among the Services was required when it came to decision making or providing military advice to political leaders. Although there were those within the military who believed their advice had been ignored during Vietnam, Locher argues the real problem was the JCS' inability to "formulate quality advice" because of the required unanimity. Further, a lack of unified command in the field where every service considered the conflict to be its own war and sought to carve out a substantial mission for the individual service meant that advice was often conflicting and self-serving. Emotional controversies such as charges of undue civilian interference (as described earlier in this chapter), however, obscured many of these organizational lessons.[36]

Yet two factors seem to have been instrumental in bringing about change. First, as noted above, the smaller-scale skirmishes and conflicts that the United States would be involved in during the decade between 1975 and 1985 continued to demonstrate the very real and dangerous

---

[34] James R. Locher III, "Has It Worked? The Goldwater–Nichols Reorganisation Act," *Air Power Journal*, Vol. 1, No. 2 (Winter 2006), 156–179, p. 159.

[35] Vincent Davis, "Defense Reorganization and National Security," *Annals of the American Academy of Political and Social Science*, Vol. 517, New Directions in U.S. Defense Policy (1991), 157–173, p. 158.

[36] Locher, *Victory on the Potomac*, p. 29. That "the American military command structure was seriously flawed as it approached the conflict in Vietnam" resulting in a situation where "the U.S. fought four air wars in Southeast Asia" was also the conclusion of a study by the House Committee on Armed Services. See "Background Material on Structural Reform of the Department of Defense," 99th Congress 2d Session, March 1986, p. 2.

problems in the organization of the Department of Defense. The flawed rescue of the SS *Mayaguez* (which had been fired upon, boarded and seized by Cambodian pirates) resulted in eighteen dead and fifty wounded soldiers. Operation Eagle Claw, the doomed mission to rescue American hostages held in Iran, was complicated and suffered without either a clear command-and-control structure or a proper organization of joint aspects of the operation. As Charles Cogan notes:

Delta Force belonged to the Army. The transport aircraft, the EC-130 "Hercules," were from the Air Force. The helicopters, the RH-53D "Sea Stallions," belonged to the Navy. They were chosen because they had considerable range, but they had to be piloted for the most part by Marines, because Navy pilots were not used to fly them long distances over land.[37]

Further complicating matters was the fact that the CIA was responsible for the arrangements and intelligence inside Iran. Yet at the time of the Hostage Crisis, the Department of Defense did not have a proper joint command structure to coordinate the services and had to build an ad hoc one from scratch. A severe dust storm was ultimately responsible for the mission being called off, but during the evacuation two helicopters collided, killing eight personnel. The subsequent investigation by the Holloway Commission into the failure criticized the lack of centralization in planning, in particular, an insufficient number of helicopters as the specific cause of the failure. As Locher notes, however, it was clear that "disunity of effort was also glaring in administrative and support areas."[38]

Finally, two events in 1983 played a major role in developing the case for reform. The first of these was the US peacekeeping mission in Lebanon, viewed by the now very risk-averse Pentagon as another "limited" war being pushed by politicians in the Reagan Administration. During the eighteen months in which the United States was deployed in the country, 238 Marines were killed (220 in a terrorist attack against their barracks, along with a further eighteen sailors, three soldiers, a French paratrooper and a Lebanese civilian), 151 were injured "and the United States did not accomplish a single basic objective."[39] The mission clearly suffered from a convoluted chain of command, lack of unity of purpose between the

---

[37] Charles G. Cogan, "Desert One and Its Discontents," *The Journal of Military History*, Vol. 67, No. 1 (2003), 201–216, pp. 208–209.

[38] Locher, *Victory on the Potomac*, p. 30.   [39] *Ibid.*, p. 159.

services, and the sending of a not-mission-ready military force to Lebanon
without the requisite training assets and assistance for the counterterrorism
aspects of the operation there. The second such event was 1983's
Operation Urgent Fury, which, of all of the post-Vietnam missions before
1986, was clearly the most successful. However, once again a litany of
organizational issues arose – problems with jointness and unity and convoluted chains of command prevented the operation from running as
smoothly as it should. Believing that White House interference had caused
many of the failures of the Iranian Hostage Rescue, Reagan placed full
operational control of Urgent Fury in the hands of the Joint Chiefs of
Staff.[40] Yet, despite the lack of "political interference," which the military
had complained about since Vietnam, the operation demonstrated that, in
the words of Colin Powell: "Relations between the services were marred by
poor communications, fractured command and control, interservice paro-
chialism and micromanagement from Washington. The operation demonstrated how far cooperation among the services still had to go. The
invasion of Grenada succeeded, but it was a sloppy success."[41] As such,
General H. Norman Schwarzkopf, commanding the Army's 24th Infantry
Division (Mechanized) during the operation, concluded that friction
between the services resulted in the United States losing more lives than
it needed to. In his mind, the war revealed a number of shortcomings,
including "an abysmal lack of accurate intelligence, major deficiencies in
communications, flare-ups of interservice rivalry, interference by higher
headquarters in battlefield decisions ... alienation of the press, and
more."[42] Further, as Frederic Borch argues, the relative difficulties in
coordinating the invasion and subsequent legal issues (such as dealing
with prisoners of war, and issues related to the control of occupied
territory) were proof for US military lawyers (who still were not involved
in operational planning by the time of Grenada) that military lawyers had
a greater role to play in mission planning and in the war room.[43]

---

[40] *Ibid.*, p. 308. Locher argues that this was an incorrect assessment of the
problems that had affected Operation Eagle Claw.
[41] Colin L. Powell with Joseph E. Persico, *My American Journey* (New York:
Ballantine Books, 1996), p. 292, cited in Locher, *Victory on the Potomac*, p. 309.
[42] H. Norman Schwarzkopf with Peter Petre, *It Doesn't Take a Hero* (New York:
Bantam Books, 1992), pp. 246, 250, 254, 258, in Locher, *Victory on the
Potomac*, p. 310.
[43] On legal aspects of the US military mission in Grenada, see Borch, *Judge
Advocates in Combat*, especially Chapter 2, and Carvin, *Prisoners of America's
Wars*, pp. 118–121.

The second major factor that began to promote change was the will of military and political leaders. As a large bureaucracy, there was strong opposition within the DoD to any changes to its organizational structure, especially any that were seen as taking away powers from the Services and altering the JCS. However, there were those in the military who felt that things could not continue as they were. In February 1983, General David Jones, Chairman of the JCS, told a closed session of the House Armed Services Committee that "The system is broken. I have tried to reform it from inside, but I cannot. Congress is going to have to mandate necessary reforms." And shortly afterwards, the Army Chief of Staff, General Edward "Shy" Meyer, voiced support for fundamental reorganization.[44] These comments raised the concern of the House Armed Services Committee who subsequently embarked on a nearly five-year battle fraught with emotion, anger and frustration. Opposed by the Navy and the Marine Corps at first, but eventually all of the Services and the Reagan Administration, discussions were complicated and sensitive. Eventually a bipartisan consensus emerged in 1985, when Democratic Congressmen Les Aspin and William Flynt "Bill" Nichols, to push a pro-reform agenda, joined Republican Senator Barry Goldwater and Democratic Senator Sam Nunn. Further, the Reagan Administration seems to have gradually lessened its opposition as National Security Advisor Robert McFarlane convinced President Reagan to convene a commission to examine defense reorganization and Admiral William Crowe, a supporter of defense reorganization, became the Chairman of the JCS.[45] As such, the Goldwater–Nichols Department of Defense Reorganization Act was passed in October 1986.

The Act made several important changes aimed at fixing the many problems that had plagued US military operations for decades, particularly "the excessive influence of the four services, which had inhibited

[44] Locher, "Has It Worked?", pp. 162–163.

[45] *Ibid.*, p. 164. Executive Order 12526 established the Packard Commission to look at defense management and organization, which presented its results in a series of reports in 1986. The Reagan Administration indicated its cautious support in a message transmitted to the Committee on Armed Services on April 28, 1986. See Ronald Reagan, "Message From the President of the United States, Transmitting His Views on the Future Structure and Organization of Our Defense Establishment and the Legislative Steps That Should Be Taken to Implement Defense Reforms" (Washington D.C.: GPO, 1986). April 28, 1986. Message referred to the Committee on Armed Services and ordered to be printed. House Document 99–209.

the integration of their separate capabilities into effective joint fighting units."[46] As such, Congress identified nine purposes for the Act under this general theme: 1) strengthening civilian authority; 2) improving military advice; 3) placing clear responsibility on combatant commanders for accomplishment of assigned missions; 4) ensuring the authority of the combatant commanders is commensurate with responsibility; 5) increasing attention to strategy formulation and contingency planning; 6) providing for the more efficient use of resources; 7) improving joint officer management; 8) enhancing the effectiveness of military operations; 9) improving DoD management.

Of these nine purposes, the emphasis in the Act was ultimately aimed at the DoD's operational dimension, the provision of military advice, responsibility of authority of combatant commanders, contingency planning, joint operations management and the effectiveness of military operations.[47] First, there were substantial changes made to the role of the JCS and its chairman. Now, the Chairman of the JCS would be the principal military advisor to the President, the National Security Council, the Secretary of Defense and whomever else the President might designate. Significantly, the Chairman of the JCS was to do this as an individual, no longer representing the collective judgment (and frequently the lowest common denominator) of the JCS. As such, the JCS "became merely a committee of advisors to him, and he was free to accept, reject, or modify that advice."[48]

Additionally, there were steps taken to improve "joint" capabilities. The Chairman of the JCS would be in charge of the Joint Staff, and officers in the armed services were now required to work in a job designated as "joint" during certain periods of their careers if they were to later qualify for promotion to star ranks. To assist with the enlarged role of the Chairman of the JCS, the position of "vice-chairman" was created. Finally, the law put the Chairman in charge of the joint unified and specified command systems and in turn gave new substantial powers to the officers (known as the Commanders in Chief – or CINCs, aka combatant commanders[49]) heading each of the commands. This change greatly simplified the chain of command and reduced friction that had

---

[46] Locher, *Victory on the Potomac*, p. 437.   [47] *Ibid.*
[48] Davis, "Defense Reorganization," p. 159.
[49] CINCs were renamed "combatant commanders" by Secretary of Defense Donald Rumsfeld on October 24, 2002, reserving "CINC" for the President of the United States.

previously existed between the services.[50] Also, in accordance with the legal reforms that were taking place in the US military at this time, legal advisors to CINCs were given increased authority and responsibility, facilitating the input of lawyers in all stages of preparing and conducting military operations.[51]

The result of these efforts at reform amounted to the greatest shake-up of the organization of the United States' armed forces since 1947, if not the formation of the Continental Army. Yet it was not without controversy; one of the most criticized aspects of Goldwater–Nichols has been the elevation of the Chairman of the JCS, with some arguing that this position now effectively overshadows the Secretary of Defense. As Chris M. Bourne argues:

In practice, Goldwater–Nichols empowered the Chairman to act as the de facto equal of the Secretary of Defense and de facto member of the Armed Forces; it empowered military officers to formulate and influence policy far outside their proper sphere ... Intending to improve the effectiveness but not comprehending fully the complex interrelationships that effect civilian control, Congress failed to provide for the common defense with an establishment that reflects the basic values of the American government.[52]

James Locher, also heavily involved in the drafting and negotiations for the bill as a senior Congressional staffer, argues that this criticism is not valid as the Act clearly states that the Chairman is subordinate to the Secretary, leaving his authority in no doubt.[53] While conceding that "there is no doubt that the Joint Staff now overshadows [the Office of the Secretary of Defense, OSD], diminishing the civilian voice in the decision-making process," Locher attributes this to the fact that there has been a substantial improvement in the quality of Joint Staff work and a weaker performance by OSD. Therefore, "The solution to this problem is not to weaken military staff work but to improve civilian contributions." Additionally, as the Act clarifies the Secretary of Defense's authority, the military cannot resist the orders of this office as was done during the pre-Goldwater–Nichols era.[54] As such, "Disputes over the secretary's

---

[50] Davis, "Defense Reorganization," p. 160.
[51] William George Eckhardt, "Lawyering for Uncle Sam When He Draws His Sword," *Chicago Journal of International Law* (2003), 431–444.
[52] Christopher M. Bourne, "Unintended Consequences of the Goldwater–Nichols Act," *Joint Forces Quarterly* (Spring 1998), 99–108.
[53] Locher, *Victory on the Potomac*, pp. 437–450. [54] *Ibid.*, p. 439.

authority have ended; he is viewed as the ultimate power."[55] As evidence to back this assertion, Locher cites Richard B. Cheney, the first Secretary of Defense to fight a war under the Goldwater–Nichols Act, who claimed: "the Department of Defense is difficult enough to run without going back to a system that, in my mind, served to weaken the civilian authority of the secretary and the president ... Goldwater–Nichols helped pull it together in a coherent fashion so that it functions much better ... than it ever did before."[56]

The pro-reform movement in Congress went further after the passage of the Goldwater–Nichols Act. Bearing in mind the US experience of the 1980s in small skirmishes and limited war, and concerned that the Pentagon had not gone far enough in implementing the recommendations made by the Holloway Commission's report on Operation Eagle Claw, Congress passed the Nunn–Cohen Amendment to the Goldwater–Nichols Act on November 14, 1986. This Amendment created a unified combatant command for Special Operations Forces: the United States Special Operations Command (USSOCOM) based in Tampa Bay, Florida. As such, the Special Forces of the Army, Navy Seals and other Navy elements, and the Air Force's air commandos were reorganized and consolidated.

Like Goldwater–Nichols, this Amendment was passed in light of major opposition from the Department of Defense, who, as noted at the beginning of this chapter, wanted to stay out of "limited wars" and special operations after the problems of Vietnam, Eagle Claw, etc. Desiring to turn their attention to conventional wars in Europe, they had failed to implement any measures that would promote capabilities in these areas. Congress, sensing that such skirmishes would not be going away in the near future, and reflecting on the many failures over the previous decade, made certain that steps were taken to ensure that special operations capabilities were not neglected by the Department of Defense. Further, the Nunn–Cohen Amendment ensured that USSOCOM controlled doctrine, training and the budget (which could then not be siphoned off for non-special operations purposes) for all Special Operations Forces.[57]

---

[55] *Ibid.*
[56] Richard B. Cheney cited in "About Fighting and Winning Wars – An Interview with Dick Cheney," *U.S. Naval Institute Proceedings*, Vol. 122, No. 5 (May 1996), p. 33 in Locher, *Victory on the Potomac*, p. 439.
[57] Cogan, "Desert One," p. 216. It should be noted that, organizationally, the Marines are not considered part of Special Operations Forces.

The end result of the changes enacted by the military, military lawyers and Congress was a Department of Defense and military that, organizationally, had undergone major reforms by 1987. Quite simply, before a "Revolution in Military Affairs" could be complete, there had to be a "Revolution in Organization." Indeed, it's hard to imagine the Department of Defense engaged in the War on Terror without these reforms, but by the time these reforms were made the War on Terror was still over a decade away. In the meantime, the new approach to law and organization of the US armed forces seemed to immediately pay dividends by the successful Operation Just Cause in Panama in 1989. Here, a clear command structure and improved joint capabilities contributed to the success of the mission. Further, lawyers (now welcome "in the war room") successfully identified and provided legal advice on the operation while it was in the early planning stages. This included issues such as those surrounding armed civilians accompanying the Panama Defense Forces; circumstances under which civilian aircraft could be targeted; indirect fire in populated areas; the regulation of air-to-ground attacks in populated areas; and detainees.[58] Meanwhile, as the DoD was reorganized, technological developments continued apace and with a newly reconceptualized defense bureaucracy, the foundation was laid for the forthcoming technological revolution in military affairs.

Revolution and the re-enchantment of war

The final step to creating a new way of American warfare as it evolved in the 1990s was rooted in scientific developments that began to flourish in the 1970s. As we have seen, this change was a continuation of a much deeper tradition of applying science to make war more effective. Since the advent of nuclear weapons displaced conventional war, technological developments that continued apace in the mid- to late twentieth century were increasingly seen as ways to make war in the nuclear age "useable" once again. Technologies deployed extensively in the 1990s were actually products of an earlier era. Guided missiles, guidance systems and sophisticated sensors, for example, are associated with the 1991 Gulf War, but they were developed and first used during the

---

[58] Borch, *Judge Advocates in Combat*, pp. 96–97. For a discussion of legal issues during Operation Just Cause see Carvin, *Prisoners of America's Wars*, pp. 121–124.

Vietnam War as a part of Robert McNamara's buildup of conventional weapons during the Kennedy Administration. Satellites were used for reconnaissance in the early 1960s and for communications during the Vietnam War, while tactical computers came online in 1966. The Pentagon's efforts to link up computers, a forerunner of today's internet, started in the 1960s (and the first "email" was sent in 1972).[59] The first truly successful guided bombs were also dropped from American aircraft in 1972 during the Linebacker campaigns launched by the US Air Force at the end of the war. Although hardly "smart" bombs by today's standards, these "gravity-fall" weapons, dropped in the usual manner, had small fins and flaps affixed to them that made it possible to feed in small degrees of correction to what would otherwise be a free-fall ballistic trajectory.[60]

Following Vietnam the United States continued to make amazing progress domestically in the production of microtechnologies and conventional weapons. Much of the work done in this period, when a blurring of nuclear and conventional weapons systems began to appear, would further the foundation for today's modern technologies. Developments in miniaturization, a term first coined by Nobel Laureate Richard Feynman in 1959, precision guidance and propulsions systems that were utilized in the development of long-range cruise missiles in the 1970s would go a long way to furthering their integration across a range of weapons systems.[61] However, these developments did not go unnoticed by America's enemies.

The Soviet Union was concerned, noting that "advances in microelectronics, automated decision sensors, lasers and, especially, nonnuclear munitions so accurate and lethal that they could wreak levels of damage comparable to those attainable with tactical nuclear weapons" would render the manpower superiority and the nuclear assets of

[59] Lawrence Freedman, "The Revolution in Strategic Affairs," *The Adelphi Papers*, Vol. 38, No. 318 (1998), 21. Special issue: The Revolution in Strategic Affairs.

[60] Bernard and Fawn M. Brodie, *From Crossbow to H-Bomb: The Evolution of the Weapons and Tactics of Warfare* (Bloomington: Indiana University Press, 1973), p. 285.

[61] Richard Feynman, "There's Plenty of Room at the Bottom: An Invitation to Enter a New Physics," first presented at the American Physical Society at California Institute of Technology on December 29, 1959. Subsequently published in *Engineering and Science*, Caltech, February 1960.

the USSR irrelevant.[62] Indeed, as the USSR's economy stagnated and its army became stuck in an Afghan quagmire during the 1980s, the United States continued to plow considerable resources into developing sophisticated conventional weaponry with the express aim of applying advanced technology to compensate for whatever material advantages the Soviet Union possessed. The "Third Industrial Revolution" – the development of "nanotechnology" – was one that the United States would lead; the Soviets were right to worry.[63] By 1983 the United States had formally set up the Strategic Computing Program (SCP) related to the Strategic Defense Initiative (SDI) and its proposed artificial intelligence (AI) control system. The goal of SDI was to make more efficient use of space-based assets. For the most part, space was used for space-based telemetry to monitor the performance of flight vehicles and their components under operational conditions. Space was not yet the critical component it would become in the precision revolution, but technology was headed in that direction.[64] American military research capacity was tremendous with programs running across all branches of the armed forces and across the country from the Naval Center for Applied Research located in Washington D.C. to the Oak Ridge National Laboratory in Tennessee and the Lawrence Livermore National Laboratory in Livermore, California. Department of Defense computer spending totaled $14 billion by 1985 and by 1989 the Pentagon was operating over a third of a million computers. The projected expenses for digitalization at DoD were budgeted at $7.9 billion for 1995–2000.[65] Computing was predicted to make it possible to improve accuracy on the battlefield and to help create a more network-centric approach to war, which Norman Friedman defines as "picture-centric warfare, a kind of warfare based on using a more-or-less real-time picture of what is

---

[62] Thomas A. Keaney and Elliot A. Cohen, *Revolution in Warfare? Airpower in the Persian Gulf* (Annapolis, MD: Naval Institute Press, 1995).

[63] "Nanotechnology – Shaping the World Atom by Atom," The Committee on Technology, National Science and Technology Council, Washington D.C., 1999; B. C. Crandall and J. Lewis (eds.), *Nanotechnology, Research and Perspectives* (Cambridge, MA: MIT Press, 1992).

[64] Marvin Hobbs, *Fundamentals of Rockets, Missiles and Spacecraft* (New York: John F. Rider, 1962), p. 111.

[65] Chris Hables Gray, *Postmodern War: The New Politics of Conflict* (London: Routledge, 1997).

happening. How real time it must be depends on the pace and scope of operations."[66]

This advancement in technology and computing led to the rise of a belief in the United States that the country was going through, and leading, a military-technical revolution. This was then relabeled in the 1990s a "revolution in military affairs" before finally being called "military transformation" since about 2001 when the US Quadrennial Defense Review proclaimed that transformation was "at the heart" of the new American military posture.[67] Broad consensus exists within military studies that a revolution, or at least evolution, in military affairs of some type has been afoot since the mid-1980s.[68] There are a number of ways to define a revolution in military affairs, but for the sake of brevity a Revolution in Military Affairs or RMA can be defined as "the idea that dramatic changes in any number of variables of war, such as weapons technologies to cite but one, led to fundamentally radical and different approaches to the entire military structure and its *modus operandi*."[69] A

---

[66] Norman Friedman, *Network Centric Warfare: How Navies Learned to Fight Smarter through Three World Wars* (Annapolis, MD: Naval Institute Press, 2009), p. ix.

[67] Eliot Cohen, "Change and Transformation in Military Affairs," in Bernard Loo (ed.), *Military Transformation and Strategy: Revolutions in Military Affairs and Small States* (London: Routledge, 2009), p. 15; US Department of Defense Quadrennial Defense Review Report, September 30, 2001, p. 16. Available at: www.defense.gov/pubs/pdfs/qdr2001.pdf (accessed July 1, 2014).

[68] James Adams, *The Next World War: Computers are the Weapon and the Front Line is Everywhere* (New York: Simon & Schuster, 1998); John Arquilla and David Ronfelt (eds.), *In Athena's Camp: Preparing for Conflict in the Information Age* (Santa Monica, CA: RAND, 1997); Eliot Cohen, "A Revolution in Warfare," *Foreign Affairs*, Vol. 75, No. 2 (1996), 37–54; William S. Cohen, *Annual Report to the President and the Congress* (Washington D.C.: The Pentagon, 1999); Freedman, "The Revolution in Strategic Affairs," p. 318; Robin Laird and Holger Mey, *The Revolution in Military Affairs: Allied Perspectives* (Washington D.C.: National Defense University Institute for National Strategic Studies (1999); Michael O'Hanlon, *Technological Change and the Future of Warfare* (Washington D.C.: Brookings Institution Press, 2000); Barry Schneider and Lawrence Grinter (eds.), *Battlefield of the Future: 21st Century Warfare Issues*, Air War College Studies in National Security 3 (Montgomery, AL: Maxwell Air Force Base, 1995); Keith Thomas (ed.), *The Revolution in Military Affairs: Warfare in the Information Age* (Canberra: Australian Defense Studies Center, 1997); Alvin Toffler and Heidi Toffler, *War and Antiwar: Survival at the Dawn of the 21st Century* (Boston: Little, Brown & Co, 1993).

[69] Bernard Loo, "Introduction: Revolutions in Military Affairs: Theory and Applicability to Small Armed Forces," in Loo (ed.), *Military Transformation and Strategy* (Basingstoke: Routledge, 2009).

revolution in military affairs is not specific to our modern era. Indeed, a revolution occurs whenever new technologies are systematically applied to a range of military assets that then interact with new organizational structures and new operations concepts that fundamentally transform the way wars are fought.[70] This is evident in the development of the Western way of war and the early development of the American way of war discussed earlier. RMAs have occurred due to societal changes, changes in military doctrines and tactics and because of changes to the military industrial complex.[71] One of the critical ideas behind early thinking on the RMA is that a "system of systems" will collect, process and combine information to be applied to military force.[72] As Seymour Deitchman, then Vice President for Programs at the Institute of Defense Analysts, argued in 1985:

We are in the midst of a period of revolutionary change in the technology of the general purpose of military forces ... Over the next decade or two, those forces will be transformed radically in their doctrines, modes of operation, and capabilities ... The revolution in military affairs is driven by the same technological advances that are making startling changes in the civilian world. These advances include mainly the application of solid-state electronics to computation, sensing, guidance, communication, and control of all manner of devices and machines.[73]

The result, according to Lawrence Freedman, is that "military force will be directed in a decisive and lethal manner against an enemy still in the process of mobilizing resources and developing plans. The vision is of a swift and unequivocal victory in war achieved with scant risk to troops, let alone the home population and territory."[74] Such war will be dealt

---

[70] See Andrew Krepinevich, *The Army in Vietnam* (Baltimore, MD: Johns Hopkins University Press, 1986).

[71] MacGregor Knox, "Mass Politics and Nationalism as Military Revolution: The French Revolution and After," in MacGregor Knox and Williamson Murray (eds.), *The Dynamics of Military Revolution 1300–2050* (Cambridge: Cambridge University Press, 2001), pp. 57–73; Mark Grimsley, "Surviving Military Revolution: The US Civil War," in Knox and Murray, *The Dynamics of Military Revolution*; Clifford J. Rogers, "As if a New Son had Arisen: England's Fourteenth Century RMA," in Knox and Murray, *The Dynamics of Military Revolution*.

[72] William Owens, "The Emerging System of Systems," *US Naval Institute Proceedings*, Vol. 121, No. 5 (May 1995), 35–39.

[73] Seymour Deitchman, "Weapons, Platforms and the New Armed Services," *Issues in Science and Technology*, Vol. 1, No. 3 (Spring 1985).

[74] Freedman, "The Revolution in Strategic Affairs," p. 11.

with precision and the battle space will be less clearly defined as the attacker will be able to use parallel warfare to destroy critical targets simultaneously. In this model, ground forces simply become extensions of the machine, serving as sensors without needing to be "close with the enemy or seize territory."[75] Such thinking in the late 1980s and early 1990s was an extension of a much longer attempt to apply technology in the Western way of warfare to make it a more efficient practice, but all the while making it less and less of a humanistic endeavor.[76] The results were weapons systems that utilized precision guidance, remote guidance and control, target identification and acquisition, and significantly improved command-and-control operating systems. Electronics were applied not only to track enemy targets, but also to evade destruction. It seemed that the dream of achieving perfect information through full-spectrum dominance – the full control over all elements of a battlefield using land, air, maritime and space assets – was becoming a reality.

The promise of the RMA seemed to be fulfilled by the 1991 Gulf War. For the Pentagon, the circumstances could not have been better: in a clear violation of international law, Iraq's large conventional army had invaded another country. New guidance systems and the latest in missile technology allowed the Air Force to conduct a five-week bombing campaign against Iraq virtually unopposed. While not in the fields of Eastern Europe, the short ground war was in a large open battlefield by easily identifiable soldiers in easily identifiable targets. It was a war that exactly fitted the conventional capabilities of the Pentagon and, to a large extent, the laws of war period. While accidents tragically happen (and did happen[77]), the technological capabilities of the United States arguasly allowed it to follow the laws of war to the letter. The National Security Strategy of the United States outlined in 1990–1991 by the Bush Administration had actually called for small precision strike forces:

---

[75] *Ibid.*

[76] Christopher Coker, *Waging War without Warriors* (Boulder, CO: Lynne Rienner, 2002), p. 59.

[77] Perhaps the most noteworthy was the bombing of the Amiriya bunker on February 13, 1991 where approximately 400 civilians were killed. The bunker had been targeted by US Air Force commanders who noted that it had been used for military purposes in the Iran–Iraq War and who had not suspected that this had changed. Further, the Americans would maintain that the structure housed a command and control center from which military communications had been monitored for two to three weeks. Regardless, it was one of the most tragic targeting mistakes committed by the Allies during the conflict.

The growing technological sophistication of Third World conflicts will place serious demands on our forces. They must be able to respond quickly, and appropriately, as the application of even small amounts of force early in a crisis usually pays significant dividends. Some actions may require considerable staying power, but there are likely to be situations where American forces will have to succeed rapidly with a minimum of casualties. Force will have to accommodate the austere environment, immature basing structure, and significant ranges encountered in the Third World. The logistics "tail" of deployed forces will also have to be kept to a minimum, as an overly large American presence could be self-defeating.[78]

But it may be asked if the war's technical revolutionary nature oversold? For all the talk of precision and small force structure, the war against Iraq was surprisingly conventional: a big war waged by a big army (indeed a big coalition of armies). As Rochlin and Demchak argue, "ample time and high levels of redundancy were the keys to the coalition's success in the Gulf. Six months were needed to test, adjust, maintain and make fully operational many of the high-technology weapons systems."[79] As American General Omar Bradley once quipped, "Amateurs talk about strategy, professionals talk about logistics."[80] Rochlin and Demchak challenge the notion that the 1991 Gulf War was as revolutionary as people thought. "The apparent success led American military and political leaders to conclude that the new high-technology weapons were cost effective, and that US casualties can be minimized by substituting technology for people." The problem was that the entire system in the Gulf depended on a complex, highly integrated system that required months of set-up and logistical support, and in the end the enemy seemed not as determined to hamper operations as they could have been.[81] Furthermore, once the logistics and set-up were in place, a very conventional and extremely large invasion force undertook the actual 100-hour ground war. The United States had 532,000 troops, 2,000 tanks and over 1,800 fixed-wing aircraft in place. The UK contributed 42,000 troops with 350 tanks and 58 aircraft. Saudi

---

[78] George Bush, *The National Security Strategy of the United States 1990–1991* (Washington D.C.: Brassey's, 1990), p. 104.

[79] Gene Rochlin and Chris Demchak, "The Gulf War: Technological and Organizational Implications," *Survival*, Vol. 23, No. 3 (May/June 1991), 265.

[80] Cited in P. W. Singer, *Corporate Warriors* (Ithaca, NY: Cornell University Press, 2003).

[81] Rochlin and Demchak, "The Gulf War," p. 266. See also Duncan Anderson, "Chapter 4: The Build Up," in John Pimlott and Stephen Badsey (eds.), *The Gulf War Assessed* (London: Arms and Armour Press, 1992).

Arabia contributed 94,000 soldiers, 550 tanks and 180 aircraft, while
Egypt dispatched 40,000 troops with 400 tanks. Even Afghanistan sent
300 *mujahedeen* for the ground invasion. Approximately 844,650
ground troops with nearly 4,249 tanks were readied for Operation
Desert Sabre.[82] The ground force attacked Iraq only after *five weeks* of
aerial bombardment decimating Iraq's military forces, as well as hitting
strategic targets such as Iraq's air defense, command/control nodes and
transportation hubs. All in all, concluded R. A. Mason in his assessment,
"the air war in the Gulf tended to confirm forecasts and well founded
principles rather than produce surprises."[83]

From this perspective, the 1991 Gulf War was a highly conventional,
sequential air–land campaign far from the professed ideal of the RMA.
For all the talk of watching a cruise missile "turning left at the traffic
lights" by journalists,[84] the vast majority of the war was not particularly revolutionary. Military historian Stephen Biddle concurs, noting in
the conclusion to his book, *Military Power: Explaining Victory and
Defeat in Modern Battle*, that "the technological changes most often
cited as revolutionary, the increased lethality of precision guided weapons, the increased range of deep strike air and missile systems, and the
increased ability to gather and process information, are all extensions of
very longstanding trends." He ultimately concludes that the assumptions of the RMA theorists are faulty based on his vast empirical study
and that "traditional approaches to warfare are in fact essential on the
emerging battlefield, because the emerging battlefield is a further extension of the one for which traditional approaches were designed."[85]

Yet, this is not the lesson that most political officials or military
officers took away from the 1991 Gulf War. The war would be seen
not only as a military victory for the United States, but also a moral
one. Described as "a lawyers' war,"[86] even Human Rights Watch and

---

[82] William J. Taylor, Jr. and James Blackwell, "The Ground War in the Gulf,"
      Survival, Vol. 23, No. 3 (May/June 1991), 237.

[83] R. A. Mason, "The Air War in the Gulf," *Survival*, Vol. 23, No. 3 (May/June
      1991), 228. For more detail on the 1990–1991 Gulf Air War, see Richard
      P. Hallon, *Storm over Iraq: Air Power and the Gulf War* (Washington D.C.:
      Smithsonian Institution Press, 1992).

[84] Michael Ignatieff, *Virtual War: Kosovo and Beyond* (London: Chatto & Windus,
      2000), p. 92.

[85] Stephen Biddle, *Military Power: Explaining Victory and Defeat in Modern
      Battle* (Princeton, NJ: Princeton University Press, 2006), p. 197.

[86] Cited in Keeva, "Lawyers in the War Room," p. 52.

Greenpeace concluded that the conflict had largely been conducted in accordance with humanitarian law.[87] Representing a huge moral and military victory for the United States, the Gulf War seemed to signal a new era in American, if not Western, military superiority through advanced high-tech weaponry. The United States was finally able to annihilate its opponents in a legal way using technology – it was the perfect war.

The indispensable nation

The reforms of the 1980s began the transformation of the military from a Cold War to a post-Cold War army, even if the process of that reform was not always straightforward. Although technological prowess often dominates discussion of the reinvention of the US military during this period, it is clear that these technological developments should be situated within a wide range of reforms, affecting the organization of the military as a whole, as well as its approach to implementing law in battle. Nevertheless, it was the technological advancements that captured the imagination of the United States, offering what promised to be an unsurpassed advantage in conventional warfare.

The new post-Cold War world order was not straightforward either. While the US military was fixated on fighting conventional wars against other states, it became very clear that conflicts, often described as "new wars" or "ethnic violence," were becoming the dominant form of warfare.[88] The first indication of this for the United States came during its mission in Somalia: the empty battlefields and conventional militaries of planning exercises were replaced with child soldiers and warlords in a dangerous, crowded and uncertain urban environment. If the Gulf War in Iraq during 1990–1991 demonstrated how much the United States could accomplish, Somalia was a clear indication of just how far it still had to go, despite its technological superiority, and what the limits of its own war capabilities were. After the death of eighteen servicemen in the infamous Battle of Mogadishu (sometimes known as the "Blackhawk Down" incident) on October 3 and 4, 1993, the Clinton

---

[87] As stated by Chris Jochnick and Roger Normand, "A Critical Analysis of the Gulf War," *Harvard International Law Journal*, Vol. 35, No. 2 (Spring 1994), 409. It should be noted that both organizations remained critical of many aspects of the bombing campaign.

[88] Herfried Muenkler, *The New Wars* (Cambridge: Polity Press, 2005).

Administration, which had inherited the conflict from the George H. W. Bush Administration and was faced with a poor economy at home, ordered a withdrawal of all US troops and a review of US participation in peacekeeping operations. In May 1994 the Administration issued Presidential Decision Directive 25, a policy with the aim of limiting US participation in peacekeeping missions that did not directly serve US "vital national interests."[89] It would be this policy that would keep the United States from committing to full-scale intervention in the genocidal conflicts in the Former Yugoslavia and intervention in Rwanda over the next few years.

The US military treated Somalia as a reminder of its disdain for limited war or "low-intensity conflict" and, as the expression in the early 1990s had it, that "superpowers don't do windows."[90] Yet, despite reluctance on the part of many members of the Clinton Administration and the military, there were others who thought differently. These individuals were inspired and impressed by US military technological capability and prowess, particularly precision strikes. And rather than waiting for the next convenient conventional war to come along, they actually wanted to use US power to promote and protect a widened and expanded notion of what really constituted US interest. The solution to the chaos of the post-Cold War world was not to retreat, but to get involved, and superior US military technology and capability made this possible. One of the best examples of this way of thinking was the first female US Secretary of State, Madeleine Albright. As Slobodan Milosevic's forces began to attack Kosovar Albanians in 1999, she argued:

Upholding human rights is not merely a new form of international solidarity. It is indispensable for our security and well being, because governments which trample on the rights of their citizens sooner or later end up no longer respecting even the rights of others. Regimes which spread insecurity by oppressing their minorities also offer shelter to terrorists, deal in drugs, or secretly prepare weapons of mass destruction.[91]

[89] The full text of the Directive (also referred to as PDD-25) was declassified in 2009 and may be read at the Clinton Presidential Library website: www.clintonlibrary.gov/_previous/Documents/2010%20FOIA/Presidential%20Directives/PDD-25.pdf (accessed July 1, 2014).

[90] See, for example, John Hillen, "Superpowers don't do Windows," *Orbis*, Vol. 41, No. 2 (Spring 1997), 241–258.

[91] Quoted in Danilo Zolo, *Invoking Humanity: War, Law and Global Order* (London: Continuum, 2002), p. 40.

Clearly, any conflict in the Balkans, with its complex background and irregular nature, was not the kind of conflict that the US military was prepared to get involved with – it failed to pass the Weinberger safeguards. Yet it did not stop Secretary Albright from chiding then Chairman of the Joint Chiefs Colin Powell by asking, "What are you saving this superb military for, Colin, if we can't use it?" Albright felt that Powell's reluctance to use force in Kosovo was absurd. "The lessons of Vietnam could be learned too well," Albright wrote in her memoirs, noting, "with careful planning, limited force could be used effectively to achieve limited objectives."[92] The premise of this approach to politics, what would become known as the "Clinton Doctrine," was essentially that the post-Cold War world, no longer in stasis through the Great Power conflict of the Cold War, was increasingly interdependent and that the United States benefited most from this interdependency. Small regional threats, such as what emerged in the Balkans in the 1990s, could threaten to spin out of control, eventually damaging US interests in some way, shape or form. In this age of "risk," what German sociologist Ulrich Beck calls "the risk society," American foreign policy and force posture began to reorient at the policy level from a threat deterrent to a risk manager.[93] As such the Clinton White House would push to develop forces to manage multiple challenges from traditional threats to instability.

US civilian planners and policy-makers once again thought, as civilians in the 1960s had believed, that military force could be used in a limited "war" context, with a level of precision hitherto unknown, making it safer for civilians in the combat zone, not to mention for US troops. Using technology and small force packages the United States could avoid being hamstrung by a reluctant public afraid of being caught up in a quagmire overseas that unnecessarily risked American lives. This was the promise of warfare as glimpsed through the supposed "success" of the 1991 Gulf War. After all, the American experience in the Gulf War seemed to promise, in the words of veteran US foreign policy expert Leslie Gelb, "immaculate destruction."[94] Some even went

---

[92] Madeleine Albright, *Madame Secretary* (New York: Miramax Book, 2003), p. 182.

[93] Ulrich Beck, *The Risk Society* (Newcastle: Sage, 1992); M. J. Williams, *NATO, Security and Risk Management: From Kosovo to Kandahar* (London: Routledge, 2009).

[94] Peter Beinart, *The Icarus Syndrome: A History of American Hubris* (New York: Harper Collins, 2010), p. 259.

so far as to say that the digitalization of the battlefield meant the end of Clausewitz, since the "fog of war" would be permanently removed from the picture.[95] But not everyone was compliant with the demands of those who felt that the RMA, increasingly referred to as "transformation," meant that war was undergoing radical change.

Madeleine Albright's argument, while effective for mobilizing the use of force in Kosovo, was not good enough to manage the conflict as the commanding general Wesley Clark pointed out. The action in Kosovo violated what he considered the principles of war and this led to the muddle that the combat operations over Kosovo became. Clark wrote in his memoir of the war in Kosovo that:

As formulated in modern American studies, the Principles of War are defined to include having a clear *objective* and relying on *unity of command* to focus all efforts towards this aim. Plans and operations should be simple in conception, massing forces at the most critical points, relying on *economy of force* in the peripheral areas, and achieving *surprise* over the enemy. Forces must attend to their security. Decisive results are obtained through *offensive* action and *maneuver*.[96]

Clark's argument is textbook post-Vietnam US military thinking. But the Colin Powells and Wesley Clarks within the US Army suddenly found themselves losing ground. The Clinton years, with operations in the Balkans, were a prologue to a much more active and interventionist American foreign policy predicated on military force. This change in policy was once again the result of a growth in the influence of civilian military planners, coupled with significant developments in military technology. Albright and the Clinton Administration represented the first iteration of a way of thinking about America's role in the world labeled by Bacevich and Englehardt as the "Church of the Indispensable Nation." According to this argument, the "church" is: "A small but intensely devout Washington-based sect formed in the immediate wake of the Cold War. Members of this church shared an exalted appreciation for the efficacy of American power, especially hard power."[97]

[95] Cited in Benjamin Buley, *The New American Way of War: Military Culture and the Political Utility of Force* (London: Routledge, 2008), p. 85.

[96] Wesley Clark, *Waging Modern War* (New York: Public Affairs, 2002), p. 423. Emphasis original.

[97] Andrew Bacevich and Tom Englehardt, "Worshiping the Indispensable Nation." Available at: www.tomsdispatch.com/ost/174974 (accessed January 27, 2010).

The application of military force in the age of American unipolarity may have started under the Clinton Administration, but those on the opposite side of the political aisle welcomed it. Paul Wolfowitz, for example, who would become Under Secretary of Defense for George W. Bush in 2001, noted in 2000 the about-face of those who rejected the idea of a Pax Americana based on American military might during the Reagan years. "Strangely, just seven years later many of these same critics, without having visibly changed their minds, nevertheless seem very comfortable with a Pax Americana. They support – on occasion even clamor for – American military intervention in places like Haiti, Rwanda and East Timor, far before anything required by basic principles of the Regional Defense Strategy."[98]

The best confirmation of Wolfowitz's argument is probably Albright's proclamation in 1998 that the United States did not like to use force, but that it would when necessary: "But if we have to use force, it is because we are America; we are the indispensable nation. We stand tall and we see further than other countries into the future, and we see the danger here to all of us."[99] Those who thought that America should have an even more robust foreign policy than Clinton was pursuing at the time undoubtedly greeted Albright's words. These individuals would concentrate their efforts in an entity called "The Project for a New American Century" and they harangued the Clinton Administration for its failures: "We seem to have forgotten the essential elements of the Reagan Administration's success: a military that is strong and ready to meet both present and future challenges; a foreign policy that boldly and purposefully promotes American principles abroad; and national leadership that accepts the United States' global responsibilities."[100]

As Bacevich notes, "a more humane approach to warfare mattered a lot . . . [I]n the American hierarchy of values, humanitarian considerations

---

[98] Paul Wolfowitz, "Statesmanship in the New Century," in Robert Kagan and William Kristol (eds.), *Present Dangers: Crisis and Opportunity in American Foreign and Defense Policy* (San Francisco: Encounter Books, 2000), p. 310.

[99] Comments by Madeleine Albright, US Department of State. Available at: http://secretary.state.gov/www/statements/1998/980219a.html (accessed July 12, 2012).

[100] "Statement of Principles," Project for a New American Century. Available at: https://web.archive.org/web/20050205041635/http://www. newamericancentury.org/statementofprinciples.htm (accessed July 1, 2014).

did figure ... Americans in the 1990s did not harbor dreams of dominating through brute force as did the Fascists in the 1930s, but they did wish to perpetuate their nation's status as world's sole superpower."[101]

The scene was set for the perfect storm. A massive reorganization had transformed the American military establishment into a much more organized and well-oiled machine. Technological advancements were providing the United States with the capability to wield force ever more precisely, making it, in the eyes of many American policy-makers, an increasingly effective tool of policy. "Victory" in the Cold War, coupled with two decades of unipolarity, led to a bipartisan belief that the United States was a force for good in the world, the "indispensable nation." As Serena put it:

Technology and the RMA would come to be a panacea for successive administrations, congressional advocates, and army planners insofar as both inherently (and supposedly) increased capability and justified expensive weapons and sensor platforms that would enable the army to become the full-spectrum warriors envisioned in the Clinton Doctrine: equally capable of creating and restoring stability and conducting high-intensity conflict (HIC) against a near peer competitor anywhere on the planet.[102]

The core of this belief in the efficacy of force was "rooted in a national narrative on the successful role of force in preserving and promoting democracy during the Cold War, which is widely believed to have ended with an American 'victory.'"[103] Further, technological developments over two decades seem to promise the idea that the United States could engage in wars, but be shielded from any consequences of military engagement. Low-casualty conflict with minimal consequences to the civilian population, fought perfectly within the laws of war, sparked liberal dreams about the utility of force. But, the re-enchantment of war was making the United States a dangerous nation once more.[104]

---

[101] Bacevich, *The New American Militarism*, p. 170.
[102] Chad Serena, *A Revolution in Military Adaption* (Washington D.C.: Georgetown University Press, 2011), p. 34.
[103] M. J. Williams, *The Good War: NATO and the Liberal Conscience in Afghanistan* (London: Palgrave, 2011), p. 65.
[104] Robert Kagan, *Dangerous Nation* (New York: Knopf, 2006).

5 | Revolution denied: the "war" on terror

Kind-hearted people might of course think that there was some ingenious way to disarm or defeat an enemy without too much bloodshed, and might imagine this is the true goal of the art of war. Pleasant as it sounds, it is a fallacy that must be exposed: war is such a dangerous business that the mistakes which come from kindness are the very worst.

Carl von Clausewitz, *On War*

Following the success of Operation Desert Storm to oust Iraq from Kuwait, the US establishment felt that they had finally rid themselves of the dreaded body-bag syndrome that had haunted US policy-makers since the Vietnam War. Technology and the law had come together to wage a war so effective that the US military had managed to topple their adversary in a matter of days. The victory came with the loss of few American lives, the objective quickly met and the international coalition was successfully maintained. The campaign was critiqued from a number of angles, but the sum total of America's engagement was seen within the establishment as an unmitigated success. This experience would fuel those in the military establishment and the civilian policy world who felt that by harnessing newly emergent technology they could eliminate the "fog or war" identified by Clausewitz, giving the United States the ability to see the entire field of battle and to dominate it with high-end technology resulting in similar successes in future wars.

Civilians in the Pentagon and American foreign affairs establishment also became re-enchanted with war as risk management as a way to achieve policy goals. Initially, in the 1980s, there had been a good deal of hesitation in the Defense Department about what was known as the "military reform movement," but the positive evaluation of Operation Iraqi Freedom seemingly vindicated proponents of what would come to be termed the "Revolution in Military Affairs" (RMA) also known as "transformation." One key outcome of the US victory in the Gulf War was that the defense planning assumptions and trajectory of military

development since the Vietnam War was the correct course of action
and that policy should continue in the same direction. The future, it was
assumed, would look much like the past. As Chad Serena noted in his
study of American military adaption in Iraq,

the army pursued a relatively linear progression toward greater and expanded
combat capabilities by leveraging the so called revolution in military affairs to
transform the force into a refined instrument of combat. The army's relative
success in implementing the Clinton Doctrine in places like Haiti and Bosnia
and its overwhelming success in toppling the Taliban government in
Afghanistan only served to reinforce an institutional belief that the army
could adapt to any strategic requirement, counter any adversary, and conduct
operations in any operational environment. Unfortunately, this notion was
disproven rather dramatically in the plains and towns of Iraq.[1]

The problem facing the United States in 1992, however, was that aside
from a few "rogue states" such as Iraq or North Korea, there were very
few enemies that looked like the expected threat. For fifty years US
planning assumptions had been based on the perceived threat from
the Soviet Union. With the final collapse of the USSR in 1991, military
planners lost their foil. The strategic environment began to look very
different from previous planning assumptions and this presented new
challenges, as Paul Yingling argued:

to prepare for war, the general must visualize the conditions of future combat.
To raise forces properly, the general must visualize the quality and quantity
of the forces needed for the next war. To arm and equip forces properly, the
general must visualize the requirements for future engagements. To train
forces properly, the general must visualize ... future battlefields and replicate
those conditions in peacetime training.[2]

In 1992, the questions were: What opponent threatened to challenge
the United States? What sort of capabilities did the opponent possess?
What was the likely climate of conflict? There were no ready answers to
these questions. How could the US military exploit the RMA to prepare
for future missions if the future mission is unclear? How could military
lawyers draft protocol and regulations to manage US troops in operations

---

[1] Chad C. Serena, *A Revolution in Military Adaption: The US Army in the Iraq War*
    (Washington D.C.: Georgetown University Press, 2011), p. 5.
[2] Paul Yingling, "A Failure in Generalship," *Armed Forces Journal* (May 2007).
    Available at: http://www.armedforcesjournal.com/a-failure-in-generalship/
    (accessed July 1, 2014).

if the type of operation troops will be undertaking is not evident? Quite simply the sole superpower had no enemy to face down. The US military had no mission to prepare. Defense planning assumptions would remain the same and the American military and civilian leadership, by and large, would fail to recognize the changing strategic environment and the risks it could pose.

Technology rules!

As we recounted earlier, the United States has always been a nation of inventors and entrepreneurs, the two often coming together in a synergistic fashion to introduce critical new technologies. This national trend, coupled with a very strong Protestant work ethic based on efficiency and an initially small population, pushed Americans to develop technologies to compensate for lacking manpower. Not surprisingly this cultural trend has found its way into the production of technologies utilized in warfare. As the strategist Colin Gray argues, what can be more American than "technology rules!"[3] "Smart" bombs, while only a small percentage of the number of munitions used, hit their targets with never-before-seen precision. Stealth aircraft were able to penetrate Iraqi air defenses to bomb their targets with little risk to their crews. Information gathering in Operation Desert Storm had worked well as part of an integrated effort to know the battlefield and to develop a networked approach to war. US military planners expected thousands of casualties: instead the United States lost only 270 (including those who died in accidents). This number was 40 percent lower than the casualty figure would have been had the forces actually stayed at home based in the United States: more personnel would have died through traffic accidents, domestic incidents or crime back home in the United States than were lost in the war.[4] The law had been a guiding hand in helping the United States to wage war in a humane manner, compatible with its own internal norms and widely shared Western norms, helping to maintain robust support for the military operation domestically and

---

[3] Colin S. Gray, "Weapons for Strategic Effect," Occasional Paper 21, Center for Strategy and Technology, US Air War College (January 2001). Available at: www.au.af.mil/au/awc/awcgate/cst/csat21.pdf (accessed on July 21, 2012).

[4] Christopher Coker, *Humane Warfare* (London: Routledge, 2001), p. 12.

internationally. The war therefore offered several real breakthroughs in the conduct of war, but in the end, as argued in the last chapter, it was not revolutionary. It was a faster and more accurate form of war than that which had developed in the 1940s, but German, Russian and American generals from 1942 still would have easily recognized this form of warfare – even if they might have been astounded by new technical capabilities. The Gulf War, despite a host of new technologies, did not transform the tactics and strategy of the war.

One of the most exciting developments of this period was the growth of precision-guided munitions (PGMs) often called "smart" bombs. In reality, these weapons are not smart: they rely on targeting information to direct their flight path and target and they cannot deduce, for example, whether the building they have targeted is inhabited by sick and injured or enemy combatants. A smart bomb is only as smart as the intelligence that directs it to the target. If the intelligence is faulty, the targeting is faulty. Nonetheless, PGMs offer the United States the ability to pinpoint targets, reducing the number of bombs required for a mission, thereby reducing the number of bombers required for a mission, thereby reducing costs and risks to personnel. They also help to reduce civilian casualties, especially if the intelligence used to target the weapon is accurate and verified. The use of laser-guided bombs (LGBs) to strike targets was an important leap forward. This technology relied on targeting on the ground by military personnel and represented less than 10 percent of all munitions expended in the Gulf War; nevertheless they were extremely useful against hardened targets in densely populated urban areas. LGBs were not the only guided weapons used, however. The Tomahawk missile, used recently in the NATO strikes against Libya in 2011, made its debut in Desert Storm. The United States launched approximately 200–300 Tomahawk missiles (costing about $1 million each) at Iraqi targets. These weapons were launched remotely from the field of battle (as opposed to LGBs, which require that the bomber be in visual range of the target, increasing the risk to pilots). Launched from surface ships or submarines on position in the Persian Gulf, Tomahawks relied on satellite guidance to direct their movements, allowing the United States to adequately destroy targets from several hundred miles away. Finally, the use of more traditional dumb weapons retrofitted with a Global Positioning System (GPS), an internal inertia measurement device and tail fins made for a cheap, "smart" bomb. These systems became known as Joint Direct Attack Munitions (JDAMs) and cost around $16,000 each – a big cost saving over the Tomahawk. JDAMs were not as accurate as LGBs, but they also did not need a clear line of sight like the LGB did, which made them ideal weapons for the inclement conditions of the desert prone to sandstorms.

These munitions and the crews that directed them were also linked up in a manner never before seen in combat. General Westmoreland might have dreamed about the battlefield of the future back in Vietnam, where the US military would be joined up in a network utilizing information and advance technology to dominate the battlefield, but General Norman Schwarzkopf lived it. The use of unmanned aerial vehicles (UAVs) gave the United States the ability to collect information with little risk to US forces. UAVs were not a new invention; they were used in Vietnam where drones such as the Ryan Model 147 Lightning Bug enjoyed great success. But at the time they were limited in range and were more of a stand-alone reconnaissance unit rather than part of a larger efficiently connected network.[5] A few decades later much changed. Contemporary UAVs, when coupled with the more synergistic networked systems of the late twentieth century, made it possible for the United States to conduct extensive missions for surveillance and target-strike assessment. In Operation Desert Storm UAVs served, similar to in Vietnam, only to observe, but a decade later the UAV would be adapted also to launch strikes against targets, closing the "sensor-to-shooter cycle," making them a deadly and rather risk-mitigating piece of weaponry. All of this was underpinned by a massive communications system that linked together a diverse assortment of US and coalition assets. The system relied on space, air and ground assets to collect and disseminate information to the military leadership and their soldiers on the ground. The coalition would eventually make use of over 2,000 personnel in fifty-nine communication centers to manage the process. During the course of the war there were approximately 7,000 radio frequencies in use and nearly 20 million phone calls were logged.[6] The complexity of the endeavor was astounding. But for all the success in Desert Storm, and

[5] Nova, "Spys that Fly," PBS, November 2002. Available at: www.pbs.org/wgbh/nova/spiesfly/uavs.html (accessed on July 22, 2012).
[6] Lukasz Kamieski, "Gulf War (1990–1991)," in Christopher Sterling (ed.), *Military Communications* (Santa Barbara, CA: ABC-CLIO, 2007), pp. 201–204.

the technological developments of the 1990s, the United States would come up short in the next two major wars it would undertake.

In 2003, as the United States stood on the precipice of war in Iraq, Paul Starr reflected on the transformation of war and the impact that technological developments had upon the willingness of the American people to resort to force. He observed that war had transformed from an activity led by "gentlemen" with limited firepower, aimed at men in uniform, into "total war," directed at civilians and soldiers alike, requiring the all-out mobilization of the entirety of a nation's resources. At the dawn of the twenty-first century, however, war had transformed into a remote activity, seen as having little to no impact on American society: "Our technological edge is so great that we anticipate few casualties among our own troops, and with precision-guided bombs we can minimize 'collateral damage' to civilian populations. There is no mass mobilization at home, no draft, no rationing. Although wars usually come with tax increases, the Bush administration promises an ever greater bounty of tax cuts."[7] Starr refers to this state of affairs as the promise of "easy war." Technology had rendered warfare "easy" in terms of the sacrifices it demanded of a society – easy on conscience, easy on pocketbooks. "There is no sense that we will have to bear any burden whatsoever in fighting it."[8]

Shock and awe

Following the 2000 election of George W. Bush to the US Presidency the US military embarked on a further radical reformation of the armed forces under the leadership of Bush's new Secretary of Defense, Donald Rumsfeld. Rumsfeld was no stranger to Washington, nor was he unknown in military circles. Previously Rumsfeld had been a four-term member of the House of Representatives, he was Chief of Staff in the White House, a counselor to the President, US Ambassador to NATO and Secretary of Defense from 1975 to 1977. During the campaign, then-Governor Bush had made it clear that he did not think the US military should be used for the sorts of missions that President Clinton had dispatched it on. Condoleezza Rice, Bush's foreign policy tutor, and later National Security Advisor, summed up the mentality of

[7] Paul Starr, "The Easy War," *The American Prospect* (March 2003).
[8] Starr, "The Easy War."

the future Bush Administration during the campaign when she wrote that "the 82nd airborne did not exist to escort kids to school."[9] The US military was a lethal weapon to wage war – it was not a tool of humanitarian assistance. Furthermore, Bush felt that the military was in need of reform. "Our forces," said Bush in a campaign speech,

in the next century must be agile, lethal, readily deployable, and require a minimum of logistical support. We must be able to project our power over long distances, in days or weeks rather than months. Our military must be able to identify targets by a variety of means, from a Marine patrol to a satellite. Then be able to destroy those targets almost instantly, with an array of weapons ... On land, our heavy forces must be lighter. Our light forces must be more lethal.[10]

As Thomas K. Adams put it, Bush's speech was "the most emphatic pro-transformation statement yet from a national leader."[11] Behind Bush were an array of senior figures, with Secretary Rumsfeld at the pinnacle, who were intent on transforming the military. Rumsfeld, the man charged with effecting this change, was an obvious choice for the job given his background and the fact that he was an ardent believer in the RMA.

Rumsfeld and Deputy Secretary of Defense Paul Wolfowitz were intent on making real change, and the men charged Andrew Marshall, the dean of RMA scholarship in the United States, to conduct the 2001 Quadrennial Defense Review (QDR) to identify the way forward. Change was afoot and Rumsfeld was clear about where the problem lay. He argued that there was an opponent out to destroy the military, an opponent that "attempts to impose its demands across time zones, continents, oceans and beyond." "The opponent was opposed to new ideas, he went on; that opponent, stated Rumsfeld, was the Pentagon bureaucracy."[12] Unsurprisingly, this argument was not very popular at

---

[9] *Ibid.*

[10] George W. Bush, "A Period of Consequences," The Citadel, South Carolina (September 23, 1999). Available at: www3.citadel.edu/pao/addresses/pres_bush. html (accessed July 1, 2014).

[11] Thomas K. Adams, *The Army after Next: The First Postindustrial Army* (Palo Alto, CA: Stanford University Press, 2008), p. 95.

[12] "DOD Acquisition and Logistics Excellence Week Kickoff – Bureaucracy to Battlefield," Remarks as Delivered by Secretary of Defense Donald H. Rumsfeld, The Pentagon, Monday, September 10, 2001. Available at: http://www.defense. gov/speeches/speech.aspx?speechid=430 (accessed June 29, 2014).

the Pentagon, despite the fact that Rumsfeld was correct in asserting that bureaucracies do not like change and they change slowly.

Furthermore, while the military enjoys cutting-edge equipment and advanced technology, these were normally conceived of, and applied, within a rather conventional approach to military affairs instead of in a truly revolutionary manner. While there were an increasing number of RMA supporters within the Pentagon, it is important to note that the entire institution was not wholeheartedly enamored of the idea. Instead, much of the bureaucracy viewed the idea of wholesale transformation as a threat to personal fiefdoms, each with its own pet equipment programs and priorities. The military brass was content with a big military, ready to wage big wars in the defense of the nation – Rumsfeld's change made many of the top military brass nervous. As such the field of battle over the future of the US military within the Pentagon was readied.

However, the showdown between recalcitrant military leaders and senior Pentagon civilian leadership was not to be. Hours after Rumsfeld's speech the Al Qaeda terrorist network launched the most daring and deadly terrorist strikes against US civilian targets and the Pentagon in the American homeland. The nation would soon be officially at war and the debate on military transformation – which would have been good for the nation – was sidelined. Instead, the Bush Administration moved forward with a radical new "war on terror." The subsequent doctrine that flowed from the Bush White House was not all that different from the Clinton years, in that the Bush Administration felt that the American military had to deal with both traditional and non-traditional threats to maintain security. But whereas the Clinton Doctrine viewed action as flexible and optional, the Bush Administration now felt compelled to protect American interests from terrorism.

America at war: Afghanistan

The US-led operations against Taliban-controlled Afghanistan in October 2001 were once again held up as a template for the "new" American way of war. The goal was to use comparatively small numbers of US troops, with some handpicked international Special Forces soldiers, paired up with indigenous forces on the ground. This composite military force would be assisted by the American technological advantages in communications, munitions and delivery capacity to create regime change in Afghanistan. The goal was to avoid the overexposure of US forces in a risk-averse environment, to maintain freedom of movement internationally by not committing a large US force to Afghanistan and to avoid enraging the Afghan population with a large foreign force on their soil.

With the 9/11 attacks falling in mid-September, US military planners had a limited timeline to plan operations before the weather conditions in South Asia became exceedingly adverse. They also wanted to strike quick to keep the Taliban forces off balance, ensuring that the Taliban did not have too much time to retrench and prepare a defense against the US invasion. With winter likely to start in November, the timeline for planning and implementing the operation was extremely tight. Such circumstances created what seemed to be a fortuitous scenario for the "Rumsfeld Revolution" – the idea that the military could do more with less; that technology would make up for numbers, agility for sheer mass. It would be difficult for the bureaucracy to oppose Rumsfeld now that the nation was at war. The United States would fight smarter, not harder, to exact revenge for 9/11. Afghanistan presented an excellent opportunity to illustrate the true effectiveness of the RMA, building on the successes in the Persian Gulf in 1991 and Kosovo in 1999. General Tommy Franks, commander of US Central Command in Tampa, Florida, was responsible for the campaign in Afghanistan and he supported Rumsfeld's approach.

In the planning discussions for Afghanistan it became clear to some members of the planning staff that "a sharp stiletto" of military force would be used and that nation-building was "not a dominant conversation."[13] Echoing his National Security Advisor's statements on the proper use of the American military, President Bush stated with regard to Afghanistan, "I don't want to nation-build with troops."[14] Across the Administration the President's senior political appointments supported keeping the United States out of a long nation-building campaign in Afghanistan. Washington was on a counterterrorism mission, not a state-building enterprise. The Secretary of Defense was inclined toward a light, quick operation, and the apolitical culture of the American military supported this predilection.[15] There was little thought as to what would

---

[13] Author's interview with US Military Officer on Pentagon Panning Staff, Washington D.C., April 17, 2008.
[14] Bob Woodward, *Bush at War* (New York: Pocket Books, 2003), p. 241.
[15] *Ibid.*

follow the military campaign – a reality that would become evident by 2006 as the security situation spiraled out of control.[16]

US-led military operations against Afghanistan began on October 7, 2001 and were conducted by an extremely limited number of US and select international forces (it was a "coalition of the willing," as it would become known, rather than a fixed alliance such as NATO). These forces included regular air and naval assets, supplemented by Special Forces units. The vast majority of ground forces were comprised of Afghan fighters. Allies on the ground included the UK's Special Air Service as well as contributions from Germany, France, Australia and Denmark. NATO invoked Article 5 on September 12, 2001 offering assistance to the United States in any retaliatory military action, but the Bush team declined the offer. There would be no repeat of the 1999 operations in Kosovo where the European allies contributed only 10 percent of the effort and still had 100 percent of a say in planning and conduct of the operation. Senior Bush Administration officials agreed that if Kosovo had taught them anything it was that NATO should "never do such an operation again." The Bush team rejected US General Wesley Clark's argument that although alliance politics made the military operation more complex, it ultimately strengthened the case against Milosevic. Secretary Rumsfeld was adamant that NATO would not be involved.[17]

US-led Special Forces teams infiltrated Afghanistan to set about gathering intelligence and recruiting allies on the ground. A substantial number of warlords opposed to Taliban rule had been waging war against the Taliban since the start of the group's ascent in 1996. By 2001 these groups were generally limited to northern Afghanistan, the Taliban having successfully occupied the rest of the country. Despite the heterogeneous composition of the different factions they represented, the forces were collectively known as the "Northern Alliance." The Pentagon planned that these forces would form the major land-war component necessary to oust the Taliban, while avoiding casualties to US forces.[18] As one British military officer who dealt with Washington during this period put it, "the war was essentially being fought by special

---

[16] Seth Jones, "The Rise of Afghanistan's Insurgency," *International Security*, Vol. 32, No. 4 (Spring 2008), 7–40.
[17] *Ibid.*   [18] *Ibid.*

forces with suitcases full of money."[19] In the north of the country the US forces teamed up with Generals Abdul Rashid Dostum and Atta Mohamed. The generals' Afghan forces, accompanied by limited numbers of US Special Operations Forces, carrying upwards of 40 pounds of equipment each, rode Afghan mountain ponies through the treacherous mountain passes toward Mazar-e-Sharif via Dar-ye Suf and the Balkh River valleys. Although US bombing began on October 7, the first actual ground combat operations against Taliban placements did not occur until October 21, when Dostum's forces attacked Bishqab. This pattern – bomb first, invade second – followed the format of the First Gulf War in 1990–1991 as well as the 1999 Kosovo engagement. A series of successive engagements followed at Cobaki on October 22, then Chapchal on the 23rd and Oimetan on the 25th. Momentum slowed as Northern Alliance fighters encountered entrenched Taliban fighters in old Soviet positions in and around Bai Beche. However, combined air–ground operations eventually overran these defensive emplacements. Simultaneously with General Atta's maneuver to Ac'capruk, located on the Balkh River, the attack against Mazar-e-Sharif was launched. The final assault on Mazar was briefly delayed by the Bush Administration so that Pakistan President Pervez Musharraf could evacuate Pakistan intelligence officials from the Inter-services Intelligence (ISI) working *with* the Taliban *against* US and Northern Alliance forces.

The fall of Mazar signaled the undoing of the Taliban in northern Afghanistan. The group had never been popular with the people in the north of the country, and the locals' impression of the Taliban did not improve with the harsh treatment of the population during Taliban rule. There was also little sympathy based on kinship, given that the Taliban were predominantly Pashtun, an ethnic group from southern Afghanistan traditionally bent on ruling over the other Afghan ethnicities. In southern Afghanistan, however, the Taliban were more at home and it was to their native lands that the battle for Afghanistan now turned. The southern city of Kandahar, at the crossroads of South Asia, was the home of the Taliban and their spiritual leader, the one-eyed cleric Mullah Omar. Omar despised Kabul, preferring the quieter and spiritually purer Kandahar in the south to the chaos of Kabul in the northeast.

---

[19] Author's interview with British military officer, London, April 24, 2008.

In southern Afghanistan US military forces worked primarily with two different groups: one led by Gul Agha Shirzai; the other by a man named Hamid Karzai. Karzai's forces marched on Kandahar from the north, initiating battles at Tarin Kowt (November 18) and Sayed Sim Kaly (December 2 and 4). South of the city there were concurrent battles from December 2 to 6 along Highway Four. The night of December 6 senior Taliban leadership, including Mullah Omar, fled the city, effectively ending the Taliban's official rule in Afghanistan. US forces pursued groups of Taliban fighters into the White Mountains near Tora Bora and a series of battles ensued over a sixteen-day stretch. Combat operations stopped on December 16, despite the fact that Osama bin Laden evaded capture and was now believed to be hiding out with Taliban elements in the mountains.

From late December 2001 through March 2002 there was relative quiet across Afghanistan. However, in March 2002 Taliban and Al Qaeda forces were discovered hiding in the Shar-e-Kot Valley and the mountains to the east of Gardez, which prompted the Pentagon to launch Operation Anaconda. Anaconda was a combined offensive utilizing infantry from the US 10th Mountain Division and the 101st Airborne, Special Operations Forces from several allied countries, as well as indigenous Afghan forces. In just six months, and with a limited number of US and allied Western ground forces, the coalition ousted the Taliban from Afghanistan. The war was widely heralded as a success for the American way of war.[20] As Eliot Cohen put it: "The Afghan achievement is remarkable – within two months to have radically altered the balance of power there, to have effectively destroyed the Taliban state and smashed part of the al Qaeda – is testimony to what the American military and intelligence communities can do when turned on to a problem."[21] Cohen was not alone in his praise; the historian Max Boot also argued that the war in Afghanistan was evidence of a new way of American war:

The transformation of the American military was showcased in Afghanistan in 2001. Instead of blundering into terrain that had swallowed up past

[20] See Max Boot, "The New American Way of War," *Foreign Affairs*, Jul./Aug. 2003; Michael O'Hanlon, "A Flawed Masterpiece," *Foreign Affairs*, Vol. 81, No. 3 (March/April 2002), 47.

[21] Eliot Cohen, "World War IV: Let's Call This Conflict What It Is," *Wall Street Journal* (November 20, 2001). Available at: www.opinionjournal.com/editorial/feature.html?id=95001493 (accessed January 30, 2010).

invading armies, the United States chose to fight with a handful of special operations forces and massive amounts of precision-guided munitions. This skillful application of American power allowed the Northern Alliance, which had been stalemated for years, to topple the Taliban in just two months. Although generally successful the Afghan war also showed the limitations of not using enough ground forces. Osama bin Laden and other top terrorists managed to escape during the battle of Tora Bora, and even after a new government was established in Kabul, warlords were left in control of much of the countryside.[22]

The Brookings Institution's Michael O'Hanlon labeled the US-led efforts in Afghanistan a sterling example of "military creativity and finesse."[23] These three analysts, typical of a much wider literature, all viewed the US-led military operation from October 2001 to March 2002 within the very American split dichotomy of war and peace. The analysis conforms to the dominant strategic culture of the United States discussed earlier in this book, and the subculture of the American military, whereby war is seen as a suspension of politics (in the Jominian sense) and when the battles are won the politics return.

There were others, however, that did not see the American campaign in Afghanistan as revolutionary. One of the earlier, more outspoken critics of the war in Afghanistan was Stephen Biddle, then a military analyst at the Council on Foreign Relations in New York and now professor at the George Washington University. Biddle argues that the Afghan War of 2001–2002 was a "surprisingly orthodox air–ground theatre campaign where heavy fire support decided a contest between two land forces."[24] From Biddle's perspective, the problem with understanding military operations in Afghanistan is that those who adhere to the concept of transformation tend to oversell the revolutionary nature of the development when it comes to the war. The US forces benefited from the country's technological edge, but Washington also made extensive use of indigenous forces that were well suited for conflict on the ground against the Taliban. Without the ample supply of indigenous

---

[22] Boot, "The New American Way of War," pp. 42–43.

[23] O'Hanlon, "Flawed Masterpiece," *Foreign Affairs* (May/June 2002), 47. Available at: www.foreignaffairs.com/articles/58022/michael-e-ohanlon/a-flawed-masterpiece (accessed July 1, 2014).

[24] Stephen Biddle, "Afghanistan and the Future of Warfare," *Foreign Affairs* (March/April 2003), 6. Available at: www.foreignaffairs.com/articles/58811/stephen-biddle/afghanistan-and-the-future-of-warfare (accessed July 1, 2014).

ground forces that campaign would not have worked. Seizing on the "success" of Afghanistan a number of observers in Washington began to suggest that Enduring Freedom could be a template for other conflicts. Biddle argued against this notion, countering that one should not assume that the RMA enabled Washington to pursue a neo-imperial foreign policy based on "cheap but effective military intervention on a potentially global scale."[25] Further, he was cognizant that victory in battle (whether or not it was "revolutionary") was different from strategic victory. The technological emphasis on warfare within the US approach is overly tactical, rather than strategic, which has contributed to the overall failure to reach strategic objectives on more than one occasion over the last fifty years.

Another scathing critic of US military culture in the wake of the Afghanistan invasion was US Army Major H. R. McMaster. McMaster argued that the logic behind the RMA and military transformation could really only be effective if the enemy has no say in how war is waged. The "organizations within the US military, such as the US Army's battle labs and J9, the concepts development branch at Joint Forces Command, focused on how US forces might prefer to fight and then assumed that preference was relevant to the problem of future war."[26] The focus of their plans occurred in a strategic-cultural bubble. They assumed victory in a conventional battle would equate to victory in war since the historical experience the US military chooses to recognize is one based on conventional war between states utilizing the laws of war and technology to pursue their objectives. Utilizing this framework, defeat means settlement of the conflict, not a shift to irregular methods.

Not everyone overlooked the problem of conflating victory in battle with strategic victory. As early as the mid-1990s a number of reports suggested that transformation might be of limited use in conflicts of lesser scale than major war.[27] The Pentagon's assumptions regarding

[25] Biddle, "Afghanistan and the Future of War."

[26] H. R. McMaster, "On War: Lessons to be Learned," *Survival* (Feb./Mar. 2008), 21.

[27] Steven Metz and James Kievit, "The Revolution in Military Affairs and Conflict Short of War," US Army War College, Strategic Studies Institute, July 25, 1994. Available at: www.strategicstudiesinstitute.army.mil/pdffiles/pub241.pdf (accessed January 30, 2010); and Jeffrey R. Cooper, "Another View of the Revolution in Military Affairs," US Army War College, Strategic Studies Institute, July 15, 1994. Available at: www.strategicstudiesinstitute.army.mil/pdffiles/PUB240.pdf (accessed January 30, 2010); Steven Metz, "America's

future conflict were woefully incorrect and this "self-delusion about the character of future conflict weakened US efforts in Afghanistan and Iraq as war plans and decisions based on flawed visions of war confronted reality."[28] RAND analyst Chad Serena supports this conclusion arguing that:

Military planning tends to follow a projection of future trends, especially if these trends are considered responsible for past success. Likewise, military planning also has a tendency to circumvent past mistakes either through avoiding situations that might provoke similar errors or by studiously ignoring the causes of these errors. Late Cold War and early post-Cold War planning decisions were no exception to this rule.[29]

In short, although the military possessed technology that enabled them to do a lot, in the end, as Thomas Mahnken of the US Naval War College argues, the services chose how to apply the technology rather than technology shaping the services.[30] Thus the assumptions the military made about conflict could not be overcome by technology since the technology they chose and how they applied it flowed from their view of conflict.

Therefore, while it is true that the United States did manage to remove the Taliban from power, they had not actually won the war. If war is the use of force to achieve a political end, the goal was not simply the removal of the Taliban. The actual goal needed to be the establishment of an indigenous political process to institute a legitimate government to rule Afghanistan. Instead the United States had decapitated the Taliban leadership, without any thought about the work needed following major combat operations that makes up the immediate post-combat phase – otherwise known as Phase IV peacekeeping and stabilization operations.

In fact, it would soon become evident that not only did the US military fail to achieve true strategic victory, but that the force the US Army built during the 1990s proved woefully inadequate to conduct any operation other than major combat. Furthermore, there was little effort to build a military that could work effectively on Phase IV operations with other

Defense Transformation: A Conceptual and Political History," *Defense Studies*, Vol. 6, No. 1 (2006).
[28] McMaster, "On War," p. 19.
[29] Serena, *A Revolution in Military Adaption*, p. 33.
[30] Thomas G. Mahnken, *Technology and the American Way of Warfare* (New York: Columbia University Press, 2008).

branches of the Federal government.[31] In the first phase of the Afghan War, the United States failed to alter the balance of power in Afghanistan in any lasting manner. The enemy was not eradicated, nor was it delegitimized except in those areas where it was already unpopular. Washington also failed to dismantle the regional framework supporting the Taliban government. The United States had essentially no plan for the country after the ousting of the Taliban, as a November 27, 2001 planning memo from the US Department of Defense on the pending Iraq invasion notes.[32] The war was far from won and already Secretary Rumsfeld and General Franks were working on diverting resources from Afghanistan to Iraq. Civilians in the Bush Administration should have ensured that there was a post-conflict plan in place, but they did not. Although the military was not solely responsible for the invasion of Afghanistan, the decidedly astrategic and apolitical culture of US forces identified earlier in this book meant that Washington's quick win in Afghanistan would result in inevitable failure.

It was pretty much inevitable that the United States and its allies would oust the Taliban and Al Qaeda fighters in a conventional war. Why the Taliban and Al Qaeda even bothered to fight the coalition forces in a semi-conventional manner is bewildering, given that they stood essentially no chance against better-trained, better-equipped and better-led soldiers. Had the Taliban been well versed in tactics and strategy they might well have simply pulled back even sooner into safe havens from which they could launch an unconventional campaign against US targets. This is eventually what the Taliban did following their ousting from power in 2002. From 2002 to 2003 the Taliban, and to a lesser extent international fighters from Al Qaeda, began to regroup in Pakistani safe havens. As NATO assumed control of the International Security Assistance Force (ISAF) in Afghanistan, the Taliban began to make inroads along the Afghanistan–Pakistan border and in southern Afghanistan. As NATO attempted to expand the remit of the Afghan government beyond Kabul and northern Afghanistan it began to run up

---

[31] M. J. Williams, "Empire Lite Revisited: NATO, the Comprehensive Approach and State-Building in Afghanistan," *International Peacekeeping*, Vol. 18, No. 1 (2011), 64–78.

[32] U.S. Department of Defense, Notes from Donald Rumsfeld, [Iraq War Planning], November 27, 2001; Annotated. Source: Freedom of Information Act: Available at: www2.gwu.edu/~nsarchiv/NSAEBB/NSAEBB326/doc08.pdf (accessed July 1, 2014).

against not insignificant numbers of Taliban forces. Interestingly the Taliban launched a large-scale, conventional assault against European and Canadian forces in southern Afghanistan in 2006. Many speculate that the Taliban felt that the Europeans, Canadians, Australians and Kiwis would turn tail and run. But despite the NATO mission being undermanned and lacking key enablers and desired fighting power, the Alliance forces routinely defeated the Taliban attacks.

To root out the Taliban, in July 2006 NATO launched Operation Medusa in the "Pashmul Pocket" around the village of Pashmul west of Kandahar city. Complementing this was a joint US–Afghan operation, "Mountain Fury," that focused on the east-central Afghanistan territories of Paktika, Khowst, Ghanzi, Paltia and Logar Provinces. The international forces defeated the Taliban, but failed to eradicate the group. This was partially because of the assistance and shelter Taliban forces received from sympathetic parties in Afghanistan as well as a host of external support (both official and unofficial) from Pakistan. NATO continued to suffer with a lack of resources – including shortages of troops as well as key enablers such as rotary lift capacity – and confused lines of command. Throughout 2006, at the height of the insurgency across Afghanistan, the United States and NATO were failing to earn strategic victories on the back of hard-fought tactical wins. The strategy to defeat the insurgency was purportedly "clear, hold and build" but the light footprint of NATO and US forces meant that while NATO managed to clear areas, it could not hold most of them. The security was limited to a select few areas. The NATO ISAF commander, UK General David Richards, is on the record declaring that if the Taliban had utilized more maneuver warfare in the summer of 2006 they might have actually landed a couple of victories against NATO given the critical shortages in the Allied Forces, Combined Joint Statement of Requirements (CJSOR). Following the summer fighting season of 2006, the Talibs (and whatever Al Qaeda remained to assist them) switched to increasingly unconventional tactics, seeking to foil NATO's conventional superiority. This shift in tactics worked, and after seven years of war, progress in Afghanistan remained largely stalled by 2008. All sixteen American national intelligence agencies concurred in an October 2008 report that Afghanistan was in a "downward spiral." The US inter-agency intelligence report doubted that the Afghan government could overcome the presence of the Taliban, and intelligence analysts criticized the United States and Europe for a lack of leadership in conducting the war. Tragically, a similar downward spiral was simultaneously taking place in Iraq.

America at war: Iraq

After US forces quickly toppled the Taliban regime in Afghanistan, the US government and military were bolstered, despite warnings, in their determination to apply this model to the next conflict – and the civilian leadership in the Bush Administration were adamant in the wake of 9/11 that Iraq was a problem the United States needed to solve. Citing Saddam's sponsorship of terrorism in the Middle East, as well as his past behavior (including the invasion of Kuwait, chemical weapons programs and ethnic cleansing of his own people), they forcefully argued that Saddam needed to be eliminated. In his 2002 State of the Union address, the President made this clear where he described an "axis of evil" that included Iraq, Iran and North Korea. The President went on to say:

States like these and their terrorist allies constitute an axis of evil, arming to threaten the peace of the world. We'll deliberate; yet time is not on our side. I will not wait on events while dangers gather. I will not stand by as peril draws closer and closer. The United States of America will not permit the world's most dangerous regimes to threaten us with the world's most destructive weapons.[33]

As Congressional Representative Ike Skelton, the then ranking Democratic member on the House Armed Services Committee, put it, "That was a declaration of war."[34] Planning for the war in Iraq had begun soon after the invasion of Afghanistan, and the victory in Afghanistan was seen as a template for what would follow in Iraq. Unfortunately, the same flaws as in the Afghanistan plan – the use of technology to win a tactical victory at the expense of any strategic thought and planning – would be repeated once more. As a memo from Matthew Rycroft, advisor to British Prime Minister Tony Blair, to David Manning said, "There was little discussion in Washington of the aftermath after military action."[35]

[33] George W. Bush, The State of the Union, 2002. Available at: http://edition.cnn.com/2002/ALLPOLITICS/01/29/bush.speech.txt/ (accessed July 1, 2014).
[34] Thomas Ricks, *Fiasco: The American Military Adventure in Iraq* (New York: Penguin Books, 2007).
[35] United Kingdom, Matthew Rycroft, Private Secretary to the Prime Minister, Cabinet Minutes of Discussion, S 195/02, July 23, 2002. Source: Printed in *The*

The run-up to and political history of the Iraq War are well documented elsewhere[36] and our focus here is on the belief within the ranks of civilian advisors and military leaders in the efficacy of US military force. In particular, the belief of US officials in the American way of war – the use of high technology to enable a relatively small military force to topple the enemy and win the war – dominated the discussion.

The commander of US Central Command (CENTCOM), General Tommy Franks, who had just led the war in Afghanistan against the Taliban, ultimately ended up crafting a new Iraq war plan quite different from the one developed by previous CENTCOM Command, General Anthony Zinni. The plan developed under Zinni's leadership, named Operation Desert Crossing, was developed following the 1998 strikes against Iraq in Operation Desert Fox.[37] Desert Crossing called for three heavy armored divisions. The new plan developed under Franks would rely on only one heavy division to launch the attack supported by attack helicopters from the 101st Airborne as well as an assortment of support from part of the 82nd Airborne, some US Marines and some British forces.

Importantly, the planning under Frank's supervision discounted a number of concerns raised in the much more detailed Desert Crossing plan. For example, emails exchanged related to the operational plan indicate a concern over some planning assumptions such as political support for US forces in Iraq, the legitimacy and support of neighboring

Sunday Times, May 1, 2005, Downing Street Documents: Available at: www2. gwu.edu/~nsarchiv/NSAEBB/NSAEBB328/II-Doc14.pdf (accessed July 1, 2014).

36 See Michael R. Gordon and Bernard E. Trainor, *Cobra II: The Inside Story of the Invasion and Occupation of Iraq* (New York: Random House, Inc., 2007); Thomas E. Ricks, *Fiasco* and *The Gamble: General Petraeus and the American Military Adventure in Iraq* (New York: Penguin Press, 2009); Ron Suskind, *One Percent Doctrine: Deep Inside America's Pursuit of Its Enemies Since 9/11* (New York: Simon & Schuster, 2006); and Bob Woodward's three books on the George Bush Presidency: *Bush at War* (New York: Simon & Schuster, 2002), *Plan of Attack* (New York: Simon & Schuster, 2004) and *State of Denial: Bush at War III* (New York: Simon & Schuster, 2007).

37 Operation Desert Crossing, Pre-War Game Intelligence Conference, April 29–30, 1999. Available at: www2.gwu.edu/~nsarchiv/NSAEBB/NSAEBB207/Desert% 20Crossing%20Pre-Wargame%20Intellgence%20Conference_1999-04-29.pdf.
Desert Crossing, After Action Report (U), June 28–29, 1999. Available at: www.gwu.edu/~nsarchiv/NSAEBB/NSAEBB207/Desert%20Crossing%20After %20Action%20Report_1999-06-28.pdf.
Desert Crossing After Action Report Briefing, July 22, 1999. Available at: http://www2.gwu.edu/~nsarchiv/NSAEBB/NSAEBB207/ (all accessed July 1, 2014).

countries and the need for firmer strategic assumptions. As one email put it: "Doesn't Kosovo give us a historical truth that everything may take longer and more effort (political will) to accomplish than originally planned for? ... Desert Crossing seems to be lacking in details about Multi National Force support for US efforts and requirements."[38] Certainly, the plan was not perfect, but the overall Desert Crossing plan utilized a large number of forces and was far more detailed and gamed than the plan that was brewing in the Pentagon in 2002–2003. Secretary Rumsfeld asked US Central Command to revise the Iraq war plans numerous times.[39] As Joyce Battle and Malcolm Byrne of the National Security Archive at the George Washington University note, "Rumsfeld wanted the Iraq invasion to be an exemplar of modern technological warfare, so the troop levels recommended by planners for a successful invasion were downgraded over time during the planning phase in accordance with the secretary's philosophy."[40]

The first war-gaming for the Iraq invasion following 9/11 was undertaken under the name "Prominent Hammer." Each of the games took three to four days to conduct and they looked at the immediate campaign as well as the second and third order effects of the war. The conclusion of the war games was that a second conflict would greatly stretch the military. As the *New York Times* reported in May 2002: "The highly classified war game uncovered worrisome shortages in military equipment, including that used for surveillance and electronic-jamming, as well as refueling tankers and transport aircraft that would be required to conduct a war on the scale of attacking Iraq or North Korea."[41] The study led one participant, a senior Air Force official, to say, "Everyone is much better informed of the overall health of the system and everyone

---

38 Desert Crossing, Miscellaneous Emails, May–August 1999, p. 7. Available at: www2.gwu.edu/~nsarchiv/NSAEBB/NSAEBB207/Desert%20Crossing% 20Misc%20emails_May-Aug%201999.pdf (accessed July 1, 2014).
39 U.S. Central Command Slide Compilation, ca. August 15, 2002; Top Secret / Polo Step, Tab K [1003V Full Force – Force Disposition], Source: Freedom of Information Act. Available at: www2.gwu.edu/~nsarchiv/NSAEBB/ NSAEBB214/ (accessed July 1, 2014).
40 Joyce Battle and Malcolm Byrne, "The Iraq War Ten Years After: Briefing Book No. 418," National Security Archives, The George Washington University, March 19, 2013. Available at: www2.gwu.edu/~nsarchiv/NSAEBB/ NSAEBB418/.
41 Thom Shanker and Eric Schmitt, "Military Would be Stressed by New War, Study Finds," *New York Times* (May 24, 2002). Available at: www.nytimes. com/2002/05/24/international/24GAME.html?pagewanted=all.

has a better sense of the risks," adding that the gaming pinpointed "what areas need to be shored up. It reaffirmed areas where we need help."[42]

Civilian leaders were insistent this operation could be done with less. As Thomas Ricks recounts in *Fiasco*, Secretary Rumsfeld countered the military planning with a plan from General Downing that called for just 10,000 troops. As Ricks wrote, "he [Rumsfeld] was going to make the military fight for every incremental increase in the size of the force."[43] Within the Pentagon a real struggle was under way on two key issues: to what extent would civilians as opposed to the military do the military planning? and, secondly, what number of troops were necessary for the invasion? On this second question, the numbers advocated by civilians were not in sync with what the military felt was required. As Ricks argues, civilians "were into precision targeting, use of proxy forces, and minimizing ground forces."[44]

James Fallows captured the difficulty of the situation in an article titled "The Fifty-First State?" published in the *Atlantic Monthly*, questioning the "cake walk" assumptions of the pro-war camp. Confessing that he too had felt that the war was a necessity as he set out to research the piece, he was now less certain over this course of action. As Fallows put it:

the day after a war ended, Iraq would become America's problem, for practical and political reasons. Because we would have destroyed the political order and done physical damage in the process, the claims on American resources and attention would be comparable to those of any U.S. state. Conquered Iraqis would turn to the U.S. government for emergency relief, civil order, economic reconstruction, and protection of their borders.[45]

Fallows was just one of many who thought the nation needed to ponder the Administration's message of a high-tech war that overwhelmed the enemy and resulted in a quick victory at little expense. In a conference at the conservative American Enterprise Institute, defense analyst Michael O'Hanlon countered the arguments by fellow panelists, including Ahmed Chalibi, that the war would be easy and require few troops:

We have to go in and win this war quickly, and then be prepared to help stabilize Iraq over an indefinite period, five to ten years, at a minimum, I believe, using a large fraction of American forces. This is a major undertaking. It's

[42] *Ibid.*   [43] Ricks, *Fiasco*, p. 38.   [44] *Ibid.*, p. 41.
[45] James Fallows, "The Fifty-First State," *Atlantic Monthly* (November 2002). Available at: www.theatlantic.com/magazine/archive/2002/11/the-fifty-first-state/2612/.

going to require a number of steps that among other things make the importance of Saudi bases and international participation central.[46]

O'Hanlon believed that the post-war occupation force would need to
start at 150,000 troops and would most likely stay above 100,000 for a
decade.[47] The dissent in planning for the Iraq invasion in the public
sphere was also reflected at the official level. While some senior and
mid-level military officials were happy to sign off on the demands of
Rumsfeld and other members of the Bush Administration such as US
Deputy Secretary of Defense Paul Wolfowitz, Vice President Dick
Cheney and Under Secretary of Defense for Policy Douglas Feith (to
name some of the most prominent proponents of the "shock and awe"
approach that would be implemented), a number of military officers
were at great unease about the planning that was (or was not) occurring.
While the military and civilian leaders traditionally are not critical of
Administration plans in public, the nature of the debate and the need for
transparency in planning operations meant that some of this private
unease and disagreement spilled over into the public sphere.

For example, General Eric Shinseki, Chief of Staff for the Army,
appeared on Capitol Hill for a hearing on force structure and budgets
on February 25, 2003. Although the topic of the hearing was not in and
of itself all that exciting, Shinseki expected that there would be discussion of what size military force would be required for the impending
invasion of Iraq since it was his job to make sure the US Army was well
resourced. Shinseki requested that Army historians look at the data on
post-conflict troop numbers in Germany and Japan after World War II
so as to provide him with an estimate of a probable troop number. The
researchers estimated that the United States would need to place
approximately 250,000 soldiers on the ground. Shinseki also drew
on his experience in the Balkans where he served in Bosnia. In Bosnia
the ratio had been one soldier for every fifty Bosnians. Applying that
ratio to Iraq meant around 300,000 troops would be required for post-
invasion stabilization operations. Shinseki was therefore prepared,
when Senator Carl Levin, the ranking Democrat on the Senate Armed
Services Committee, asked, "General Shinseki, could you give us some

---

[46] Conference Transcript, "The Day After: Planning for Post-Saddam Iraq," American
Enterprise Institute (October 3, 2002). Available at: http://chenry.webhost.utexas.
edu/oil/fall02/resources02/msg00150.html (accessed on July 18, 2012).
[47] *Ibid.*

idea of the magnitude of the Army's force requirement for an occupation of Iraq following a successful completion of the war?" Shinseki was prepared. First, the general responded, "In specific numbers, I would have to rely on the combatant commander's exact requirements." When pushed for a less specific figure, the general then answered, "I would say that what's been mobilized at this point, something on the order of several hundred thousand soldiers, are probably, you know, a figure that would be required."

Shinseki's civilian leaders in the Pentagon were not happy with the general's statement. Wolfowitz was telling senior Army staff that there would only be around 30,000 troops required for post-war Iraq. The Under Secretary quickly contradicted Shinseki at a hearing on Capitol Hill two days later, saying: "There has been a good deal of comment; some of it quite outlandish, about what our postwar requirements might be in Iraq. Some of the higher end predictions that we have been hearing recently, such as the notion that it will take several hundred thousand U.S. troops to provide stability in post-Saddam Iraq, are wildly off the mark." Wolfowitz justified this, because: "it was hard to conceive that it would take more forces to provide stability in post-Saddam Iraq than it would take to conduct the war itself and to secure the surrender of Saddam's security forces and his army – hard to imagine."[48]

General Shinseki was not the only senior military official to question the civilian thinking in the Bush White House on Iraq. About two weeks before General Shinseki testified on Capitol Hill, over in Foggy Bottom a memo landed on the desk of US Under Secretary of State Paula Dobriansky on Iraq contingency planning.[49] The three interagency experts that drafted the memo were concerned about "serious planning gaps for post-conflict public security." US Central Command (CENTCOM) was focused solely on "primary military objectives" with a reluctance to take on "policing roles" that the interagency experts thought necessary to secure post-invasion Iraq.[50] But the idea that technology could replace

---

[48] Testimony from PBS Frontline, "Rumsfeld's War," October 26, 2004. Available at: www.pbs.org/wgbh/pages/frontline/shows/pentagon/etc/script.html (accessed June 29, 2014).

[49] State Department Information Memorandum for Paula J. Dobriansky, Under Secretary of State for Democracy and Global Affairs, *Iraq Contingency Planning*, February 7, 2003. Available at: www2.gwu.edu/~nsarchiv/NSAEBB/ NSAEBB163/ (accessed July 1, 2014).

[50] *Ibid.*

troops on the ground was a seductive one for many civilian planners in the administration, and it had already taken hold. Retired US Army Colonel and now Professor of Strategic Studies at Boston University, Andrew Bacevich, put it this way:

Here may be the clearest manifestation of OSD's [Office of Secretary of Defense] contempt for the accumulated wisdom of the military profession and of the assumption among forward thinkers that technology – above all information technology – has rendered obsolete the conventions traditionally governing the preparation and conduct of war. To imagine that PowerPoint slides can substitute for such means is really the height of recklessness.[51]

Some time later, immediately after the invasion, retired US General Jay Garner arrived in Iraq to start the reconstruction mission. Upon arrival Garner, who had years of experience in conflict and post-conflict zones, met with Lawrence Di Rita, one of Rumsfeld's closest aides. Di Rita quipped to one of Garner's staff in response to a planning query from the General, "Don't bother. Within 120 days we'll win this war and get all US troops out of the country, except 30,000." Apparently the Secretary of Defense "viewed Haiti, Kosovo, Bosnia, and even Afghanistan as failures, and this wasn't going to be their failure."[52] As the situation decayed, top political officials as well as many of the leading military commanders failed to see that Iraq was descending into chaos. When an envoy from Washington was sent to meet with Paul Bremmer, head of the Coalition Provisional Authority (CPA), the body set up to administer Iraq post-Saddam and prior to new elections, Bremmer discounted the envoy's suggestion that Iraq was at the precipice of an insurgency. Wolfowitz (who was rather slowly and belatedly realizing the situation in Iraq was not going according to his post-war "plan") sent Anderson, the retired Marine colonel who served as an assistant to Rumsfeld, to pitch the idea. When he suggested some programs that worked well in the latter half of the Vietnam War, Bremmer, according the *New York Times* reporter Tom Ricks, exploded. "Vietnam? Vietnam! I don't want to talk about Vietnam. This is not Vietnam. This is Iraq!" Anderson, reflecting on the incident, told Ricks, "I don't think he, or Sanchez (the commander of Coalition Forces in Iraq), ever fully grasped the danger of it."[53]

[51] Ricks, *Fiasco*, pp. 75–76.   [52] *Ibid.*, p. 106.   [53] *Ibid.*, pp. 187–188.

120 days ...

US forces invaded Iraq on March 21 (March 20 in the United States) 2003. The invasion force was a fraction of what many military planners, external analysts and historians felt was necessary. The invasion force came in at just under three American divisions, plus one large Marine division and a British division. Approximately 247 tanks and roughly the same number of Bradley fighting vehicles were included in the assault. Including UK forces, the total invasion force was about 145,000. This was half of what was allocated under the previous Iraq invasion plan, Desert Crossing, drafted while Anthony Zinni was CENTCOM commander. US forces included one heavy Army division, the 3rd Infantry Division, as well as one light division, the 101st Airborne and two infantry brigades, the 82nd Airborne and 173rd Airborne. The US Army's total manpower contribution was 65,000. Another 60,000 US Marines were involved and the 1st Armored Division of Great Britain added another 20,000 personnel. The Special Ops troops drove west to stop the scud missiles sites from targeting Israel before going north to join up with Kurdish fighters who would assist in the battle to oust Saddam.

The 3rd Infantry Division (3ID) struck first, composed predominately of heavy tanks and other armored vehicles rather than conventional infantry. The 3ID set out from Kuwait, through the desert to An Nasiriyah, seizing a critical airfield and a number of bridges crossing the Euphrates River. The US Marines then occupied these assets, freeing 3ID to race up the Euphrates north past An Najaf and on to Karbala. The ultimate goal of 3ID was Baghdad, some 350 miles from the start of the attack on the Kuwait–Iraq border. The logistics to facilitate such a long supply line were impressive and the delivery of them by the US military was excellent, reflecting the skill of modern US forces. Meanwhile, additional Marines were busy in the south securing the oil fields before moving north to cross the Euphrates around Nasiriyah and going on to launch a number of attacks at targets between the Tigris and Euphrates Rivers. Eventually the 1st Marine Division would close on Baghdad from the east and 3ID would strike from the west. British forces left Kuwait bound for Iraq's second largest city, Basrah, the gateway from Iraq's inland to the Persian Gulf.

In line with the shock and awe doctrine, CENTCOM's plan was based on simultaneous air, land and sea strikes to overwhelm the Iraqi forces. The main aerial assault actually came once US forces were already deep inside Iraq on their way to Baghdad. This was a clear departure from the 1991 Gulf War where weeks of pounding preceded the ground invasion. Also different from previous US war efforts, such as those in World War II, the military did not seek to take land and secure it through occupation. Instead the forces rapidly descended on what were deemed key targets, passing through large swathes of land, leaving much of it under no control whatsoever. This decision would mean that in the post-combat phase of the operation (Phase IV) there would be little to no US or UK presence across most of the country. Such forces were not needed, because as Vice President Cheney and Under Secretary of Defense Wolfowitz argued, US forces would be "greeted as liberators."[54]

The simultaneous attacks of air, sea and land forces represented a major step forward in the American way of warfare from the 1991 Gulf War. Developments had made precision-guided missiles even more precise. Additionally, in 1991 there was very little synergy between the ground and air efforts. They occurred in a sequential manner (air strikes, followed by ground invasion) and the Air Force was unable to provide close support due to weather conditions. Furthermore, in 1991 there were no PGMs available to strike from a high altitude, unlike in 2003 where the use of technology had advanced to such a degree that a wide range of PGMs allowed the Air Force to assist the Army and Marines in a much more synergistic and effective manner. Finally, Saddam's air defense forces were significantly worse in 2003 than in 1990–1991 following ten years of sanctions and no-fly zones in the north and south of the country.

By April 9, only nineteen days after the campaign began, it was clear that Saddam Hussein's Ba'ath power structure had entirely collapsed. Large amounts of Iraqi military hardware, including 100 tanks in Baghdad, simply sat unused. US forces moved about the capital preparing for the Phase IV operations under the control of the Coalition Provisional Authority. President Bush officially declared combat operations at an end on May 1, 2003 when he landed, in full flight gear, on the USS *Abraham Lincoln* off the coast of California and announced

---

[54] Kurt Eichenwald, "Perpetually Wrong, Paul Wolfowitz Is Still Convinced He Knows What Would Have Happened in Iraq If We Hadn't Invaded," *Vanity Fair* (March 19, 2013). Available at: www.vanityfair.com/online/eichenwald/2013/03/paul-wolfowitz-still-convinced-he-knows-what-would-have-happened-in-iraq (accessed July 1, 2014).

"mission accomplished." But, while the mission of ousting Saddam from power had been achieved, the war was far from over. As Gordon and Trainor scathingly put it,

Bush, Cheney, Rumsfeld, and Tommy Franks spent most of their time and energy on the least demanding task – defeating Saddam's weakened conventional forces – and the least amount on the most demanding – rehabilitation of and security for the new Iraq. The result was a surprising contradiction. The United States did not have nearly enough troops to secure the hundreds of suspected WMD sites that had supposedly been identified in Iraq or to secure the nation's long, porous borders. Had the Iraqis possessed WMD and terrorist groups been prevalent in Iraq as the Bush administration so loudly asserted, U.S. forces might well have failed to prevent the WMD from being spirited out of the country and falling into the hands of the dark forces the administration had declared war against.[55]

The US Administration felt that it had won the "war," but the reality was that the mission was far from over. US forces decidedly defeated Saddam Hussein's conventional military forces, but the military would fail to provide for stability in the period following major combat operations, paving the way for a widespread insurgency. The ranking American military leadership, including General Franks, and the top American civilians from the President on down failed to connect the use of military force to wider political objectives and how the post-combat phase would reinforce this supposedly stunning American military victory. Although the United States conducted several studies on the future of Iraq, these studies were largely divorced from the military campaign. Furthermore, many of these studies, such as the "Future of Iraq: Oil and Energy," made rather optimistic assumptions that failed to reflect reality.[56] The seeds of failure were sown in Washington well before the first American troops set foot on Iraqi soil; the price would be paid by thousands of dead American soldiers and possibly hundreds of thousands of Iraqi civilians over the course of the coming decade. The war that was supposed to self-finance and be over in a matter of weeks, with few US troops in Iraq, would stretch on for nearly a decade

[55] Michael R. Gordon and General Bernard E. Trainor, *Cobra II: The Inside Story of the Invasion and Occupation of Iraq* (New York: Pantheon Books, 2006), pp. 503–504.

[56] "The Future of Iraq: Oil and Energy Working Group Summary Report," April 20, 2003, United States Department of State. Available at: www2.gwu.edu/~nsarchiv/NSAEBB/NSAEBB198/FOI%20Oil.pdf (accessed July 1, 2014).

and cost the United States direct and indirect expenses of approximately $1.5 trillion. As Bacevich argues, "The Bush administration's misplaced confidence in the efficacy of American arms represents a strategic misjudgment that has cost the country dearly."[57] The 2003 invasion of Iraq was quite simply the worst strategic decision ever made in the history of the United States.

In their evaluation of the combat phase of the Iraq War, when the conflict was still in a relatively early phase, military historians Williamson Murray and Robert H. Scales sounded off what should have been obvious to Pentagon civilians in 2002–2003, but was patently not the road taken.

The conflict in Iraq engaged an enemy who had virtually no military capabilities left after an air war of attrition lasting over twelve years. Consequently, the conventional phase of the conflict was extremely lopsided and brief. The aftermath, however, is proving more troublesome and unmanageable, and in this phase of the conflict cruise missiles are of little value. The ability of bombers and strike aircraft to hit a number of targets with precision does indeed represent a significant step forward in technological capability; and once air supremacy is achieved, these capabilities allow the project of almost unlimited firepower against specific targets of value to the enemy. Nevertheless, unless advances in air power are coupled with intelligent thinking – by planners on the ground – about the nature of one's opponent and of wars and their aftermath, past, present and future, these improved technologies will ensure only that political and military defeats will come later, and at greater cost.[58]

The Pentagon had never planned for anything but the best-case scenario and this became obvious soon after Baghdad fell. "There was a mindset by the first part of May," according to an officer on the Joint Staff at the time. "Major combat operations are over, let's think about drawing down the force."[59] But commanders on the ground had far too few resources to stop the unrest that was destabilizing the military victory. There were no troops to stop the looting of ministries, museums and shops because they were preoccupied in the south protecting supply lines and keeping watch over prisoners of war. An internal Pentagon

---

[57] Andrew Bacevich, *The Limits of American Power: The End of American Exceptionalism* (New York: Henry Holt and Company, 2008), p. 126.
[58] Williamson Murray and Robert H. Scales, Jr., *The Iraq War: A Military History* (Cambridge, MA: The Belknap Press, 2003), p. 183.
[59] *Ibid.*

review, conducted by two former US Defense Secretaries James Schlesinger and Harold Brown, concluded that in Iraq "there was not only a failure to plan for a major insurgency, but also to quickly and adequately adapt to the insurgency that followed after major combat operations."[60] What makes this all the more confusing is that Secretary Rumsfeld was more than aware of the potential complications that might follow-on from the US invasion. A classified memo dated October 15, 2002 detailed very perceptively twenty-nine challenges including: failure to find WMD, drawn-out conflict lasting eight to ten years, the outbreak of ethnic conflict and a diminution of US influence in the world.[61]

The failure in Iraq thus had two parts, with blame to be apportioned to both civilians in the US government as well as the military. The first failure was mainly that of Bush Administration civilians who refused to heed, and indeed deliberately undermined, the advice offered to them by some members of the military establishment. There were ample officers within the DoD and external analysts and historians who argued the planning assumptions for the Iraq invasion would not be a problem in the first phase of the war, but that trouble would arrive in the post-combat phase.

Yet, once it became apparent that the situation in Iraq was rapidly spiraling out of control, the civilian leadership in the Department of Defense, the Bush Administration and the military failed to adapt. This was the second major failure. Civilian leaders did not supply the number of forces that military commanders needed to adequately provide security against looting and instability, followed by insurgency. Military leaders fell back to their default operational mindset, predicated on the type of wars the US military wanted to fight, rather than the war they confronted. As Thomas Ricks notes: "the Bush administration's tendency was to suppress the dissent and paper over differences, substituting loyalty for analysis, so the war continued to stand on a strategic foundation of sand. Nor had the president been well served

---

[60] "The Reach of War: Excerpts of DOD Report on War in Iraq," *New York Times* (August 25, 2004). Available at: www.nytimes.com/2004/08/25/world/reach-war-findings-abu-ghraib-prison-sadism-deviant-behavior-failure-leadership. html?pagewanted=all&src=pm (accessed on July 20, 2012).

[61] Donald Rumsfeld, "Iraq: An Illustrative List of Potential Problems," Secret Memo, October 15, 2002. Available at: www2.gwu.edu/~nsarchiv/NSAEBB/ NSAEBB418/docs/7%20-%20Iraq%20-%20An%20illustrative%20list%20of %20potential%20problems%20-%2010-15-2002.pdf (accessed July 1, 2014).

by his generals, who with a few exceptions didn't seem to pose the necessary questions."[62] Therefore, as the insurgency took hold, the strategy remained the same. As Coker argues, the American soldiers inspired fear, but also appeared fearful in their layers of body armor and sitting mounted in tanks and armored vehicles – distant and foreign to the Iraqi people they were supposed to protect.[63] And as Ricks notes:

"The civilian leadership did not foresee the need for extensive Phase IV operations, and thus did little planning beyond near-term relief," said one Pentagon official who was involved in war-gaming the invasion plan and who later analyzed its failures. "This was fine with the military, which had traditionally focused on Phase III operations, did not want to do Phase IV operations, and figured that someone else would step in."[64]

The American experience in Iraq was a failure of the American military as well as the civilians, who, as in Vietnam and the Philippines before, failed to appreciate the true nature of the war they were fighting and failed to realize that technology could not guarantee victory in warfare. Although technology had once again handed the United States a quick military victory over Iraqi forces, similar to the first Gulf War in 1991, the first war was based on a much sounder overall strategy. The size of the force used in 1990–1991 was commensurate to the task, the political objectives were clearly and precisely defined and the campaign was waged to achieve these objects. In 2003 the military edge the United States possessed over Iraq was far greater. "Because of the army's transformation and force modernization program, the force that entered Iraq in 2003 was a faster and more lethal version of the force that defeated Iraqi forces in 1991. Battlefield victory was all but a fait accompli of the order to invade."[65] The problem with the military was that even though the civilians failed to plan for the post-war environment in Iraq (and also previously in Afghanistan), the military deluded itself for nearly two decades into thinking it was prepared to wage major operations other than war (MOOTW). This was simply not the case.

The forces retained after the reduction in force (during the Clinton Administration) were almost exclusively conventional and structured either for combat, combat support (CS), or combat service support (CSS). One of the few exceptions to this rule was the retention of SF, which at that time had been

---

[62] Ricks, *The Gamble*, p. 14.   [63] Coker, *Human Warfare*.
[64] Ricks, *Fiasco*, p. 151.   [65] Serena, *A Revolution in Military Adaptation*, p. 4.

stripped of many of its unconventional missions and was instead being used almost solely in conventional support of corps and separate operations.[66]

The war in Iraq was doomed to fail even before the United States invaded in March 2003. The Bush Administration viewed technology as the solution that provided for a cheap and effective use of military force. Both military and civilian planners were beholden to a Jominian, tactical mindset that equated victory in battle with strategic success, and the American military had fooled itself into believing that despite little focus on MOOTW the US armed forces could fight major wars and minor ones with the same level of skill and success. The result was predictable: technology could not compensate for a lack of strategic understanding or planning. The stage was set for the tragedy to follow.

Law and the lessons of Iraq

From the start of the war in March until May 1, 2003 only 139 American troops were killed and 542 injured.[67] However, while the United States initially seemed to be in control, it faced a number of security challenges – lawlessness and banditry, internecine conflict between religious sects, indigenous and international Islamist extremists and, of course, supporters of the old regime – in the months that followed. Given that none of the emerging armed groups possessed a capability to challenge US forces in a conventional manner, they rationally utilized irregular warfare to leverage their weakness as strength and US military strength as weakness. Consequently, as US forces were confronted with a way of warfare against which they were poorly trained, not properly equipped and for which they were mentally unprepared, they were unable to counter a growing insurgency that spread after the invasion. This in turn led to overreaction by US troops on the ground, followed by frustration and eventually human rights abuses and even war crimes. By 2006, news stories about US failure to curtail the violence in Iraq were often accompanied by stories of terrible abuses at places such as Haditha and Abu Ghraib. How did this happen?

[66] *Ibid.*, p. 34.
[67] Ujala Sehgal, "Eight Years Ago Bush Declared Mission Accomplished in Iraq," *The Atlantic Wire* (May 1, 2011). Available at: www.theatlanticwire.com/national/2011/05/mission-accomplished-speech/37226/ (accessed on July 21, 2012).

There is no question that along with a willingness to stretch the credibility of intelligence about Iraq to suit their political goals, there was also a willingness to downplay the relevance of the Geneva Conventions to a "war on terror." Civilian lawyers such as David Addington (General Counsel to Vice President Dick Cheney), Jay S. Bybee (Assistant Attorney General for the Office of Legal Counsel), Robert J. Delahunty (Special Counsel), the then-White House General Counsel Alberto Gonzales, William J. Haynes II (General Counsel to the Secretary of Defense) and John Yoo (the then-Deputy Assistant Attorney General) participated in a general discussion and wrote a series of memos on the laws of war in late 2001 and early 2002. In these documents, an argument emerged that the Geneva Conventions (including the special fundamental guarantees found in Common Article 3 that essentially amount to a prohibition of inhumane treatment) did not apply to the War on Terror because the drafters of the Conventions had not anticipated that there could be an insurgency movement that was not a nation-state, nor a global war on terror, and that it was not clear that Congress would support the application of the Conventions to such a conflict. As Gonzales wrote in a memo in January 2002, "In my judgment, this new paradigm renders obsolete Geneva's strict limitations on questioning of enemy prisoners and renders quaint some of its provisions."[68] Further, this series of memos argued that the President had the authority to declare combatants beyond the protections of international law.[69]

---

[68] The series of memos has been collected and published in Karen J. Greenberg and Joshua L. Dratel, *The Torture Papers: The Road to Abu Ghraib* (Cambridge: Cambridge University Press, 2005).

[69] Such a view is consistent with a neo-conservative, or what Peter J. Spiro calls a "New Sovereigntist" view of international law. Peter J. Spiro, "The New Sovereigntists: American Exceptionalism and Its False Prophets," *Foreign Affairs*, Vol. 79, No. 6 (November/December 2000), 9–15. Briefly, such a view can be said to subscribe to believing in the supremacy of constitutions (particularly the US Constitution) over international law. International law is seen as vague, unaccountable, undemocratic and unenforceable. As a result of this, countries may opt out of any international legal regime as a matter of power, legal right and constitutional duty. The ultimate emphasis is on the sovereignty of the state and preventing any international law that may take away from US sovereignty. Sovereignty is seen as a moral virtue that guards the way of life a nation chooses for itself. Ergo, anything that violates or betrays this sovereignty (including international law) is unconstitutional and should be resisted. From this standpoint, the President has the authority to reject the application of the Geneva Conventions because the United States was engaged in a war of self-defense,

The process by which these changes were made may seem bureaucratic, but the impact they had was profound. As discussed in this book, US military lawyers had spent years, if not decades, reforming the way the laws of war were implemented within the American armed forces. Having witnessed the chaos that can emerge from undisciplined troops, poor implementation of legal rules and the failure to see the potential and advantage that international law can bring to the fight, military lawyers and their allies had struggled to bring about the reforms that made the First Gulf War a relative legal success. These gains, however, had been taken away at the stroke of a pen, marked by the release of a February 2002 memo that announced the new rules for treatment of detainees in the War on Terror.[70] For all that military lawyers had struggled to be in the war room and contended that "operational law" was a valuable tool that could help the United States fight better, their argument had fallen on deaf ears in the Bush Administration with the attacks of 9/11.

But beyond shattering much of the work that military lawyers had done, this revision of the American approach to the laws of war immediately began to create problems that have plagued the United States ever since. As the War on Terror began to span across the globe, the new, harsher treatment regimen, intended to gain actionable intelligence from Al Qaeda and the Taliban leadership captured on the battlefields of Afghanistan, had the unfortunate effect of spreading confusion with regard to which detainee treatment rules were in effect, where they applied and to whom. Detainee treatment guidelines (later found to violate DoD policy) meant solely for Guantanamo prisoners eventually found their way to Bagram prison in Afghanistan as well as Iraq where

---

protecting its way of life. See, for example, John Bolton, "The Global Prosecutors: Hunting War Criminals in the Name of Utopia," *Foreign Affairs*, Vol. 78, No. 1 (1999); Jack Goldsmith and Eric E. Posner, *The Limits of International Law* (Oxford: Oxford University Press, 2005); Jeremy Rabkin, *Law without Nations: Why Constitutional Governance Requires Sovereign States* (Princeton, NJ: Princeton University Press, 2005).

[70] See the memo released February 7, 2002, "Humane Treatment of Al Qaeda and Taliban Detainees." Available at: www2.gwu.edu/~nsarchiv/NSAEBB/ NSAEBB127/02.02.07.pdf (accessed July 1, 2014). Although the argument downplaying the significance of international law itself was not new and had been gradually emerging since the 1990s. See Stephanie Carvin, "Linking Purpose and Tactics: America and the Reconsideration of the Laws of War during the 1990s," *International Studies Perspectives*, Vol. 9, No. 2 (2008).

they played a major role in the maltreatment of prisoners at Abu Ghraib.[71]

This chain of events, and the abuses that followed, were a result of the Bush Administration replacing a constant and steady argument that the United States follows and adheres to the Geneva Convention (even if this adherence could sometimes be quite literal) with their new legal regime, designed by White House lawyers without consultation with the Pentagon. The downplaying of the laws of war in light of a new war on terror conveyed a confusing message as to the status of international law in the conflicts that were now spreading across the globe.

The precise circumstances that led to the downplaying of the laws of war in the War on Terror have been discussed elsewhere.[72] But what is particularly important to highlight for the purpose of this book is that there is a clear connection between a failure to appropriately plan for the consequences of the Afghan and Iraq Wars, a misplaced belief in the ability of technology to compensate for manpower and deliver "clean wars" and serious breaches of the laws of war committed by the US personnel.

The story of Abu Ghraib prison highlights this connection. The prison, already notorious in Saddam's time, was utilized by the United

---

[71] This was a finding of the August 2004 "Final Report of the Independent Panel to Review DoD Detention Operations" (aka the Schlesinger Report). It is not clear to what extent this was a deliberate policy or accident. See David Rose, *Guantanamo: The War on Human Rights* (London: Faber and Faber, 2004). A fuller description of the circumstances that lead to the downplaying of the laws of war in the War on Terror and the consequences of these actions has been provided elsewhere. See Stephanie Carvin, *Prisoners of America's Wars: From The Early Republic to Guantanamo* (New York: Columbia University Press, 2010); David P. Forsythe, *The Politics of Prisoner Abuse: The United States and Enemy Prisoners after 9/11* (Cambridge: Cambridge University Press, 2012); Jane Mayer, *The Dark Side: The Inside Story of How the War on Terror Turned into a War on American Ideals* (New York: Anchor Books, 2009). For a critical take suggesting that the legacy of Abu Ghraib is directly linked to the policies advocated by the Bush Administration and its betrayal of the long-standing commitment to the laws of war, see Seymour M. Hersh, *Chain of Command: The Road from 9/11 to Abu* Ghraib (New York: Harper Collins Publishers, 2005); Philippe Sands, *Lawless World: America and the Making and Breaking of Global Rules* (London: Allen Lane, 2005) and *Torture Team: Uncovering War Crimes in the Land of the Free* (London: Penguin, 2009).

[72] The circumstances that lead to the downplaying of the laws of war and the consequences of such actions have been discussed extensively (see previous note). See Carvin, *Prisoners of America's Wars*; Forsythe, *The Politics of Prisoner Abuse*; Mayer, *The Dark Side*.

States to hold common criminals, terrorists and "security detainees," often as a mixed population. In early 2004, pictures were leaked to the press of US military prison guards physically and psychologically abusing terrified prisoners. At first glance, it seemed as if this group had decided to sadistically abuse the prisoners for their own amusement. However, as the scandal progressed, it soon became clear that Abu Ghraib was the result of several failed aspects of US policies toward Iraq.

First, because of the low numbers of troops initially committed to Afghanistan and Iraq, as well as a desire to control costs associated with these conflicts, the United States has relied heavily on private military companies (PMCs) and contractors. Yet, despite their omnipresence in military operations, in many cases there is no guarantee that private actors have proper (or any) training in the laws of war. Further, as private actors they are largely unaccountable under any framework of international or domestic law when and if they do violate it.[73] For example, until a renegotiated Status of Forces Agreement (SOFA) in December 2008, Iraqi authorities had no control over companies such as Blackwater despite the fact that they were involved in hundreds of shooting incidents. Nor are PMCs subject to the Uniform Code of Military Justice. Such actors could, and did, get away with law of war violations with no punishment other than being sent back home and having their contracts cancelled. At Abu Ghraib, private contractors in the prison reportedly encouraged guards to engage in activities that violated the laws of war.[74] When questioned about their actions, PMCs have repeatedly refused to provide answers, arguing that their companies are immune due to a lack of jurisdiction.

Second, due to poor planning, a shortage of troops arose, leading to reserves being called up for duty and sent to the theater of operations without having completed their training, including training in the laws of war. This was the finding of several reports that looked at the Abu

---

[73] On problems regulating PMCs, Sarah Percy, *Regulating the Private Security Industry*, Adelphi Paper 384 (London: International Institute of Strategic Studies, 2006); P. W. Singer, *Corporate Warriors: The Rise of the Privatized Military Industry* (Ithaca, NY: Cornell University Press, 2003).

[74] The March 2004 "Article 15–16 Investigation of the 800th Military Police Brigade" (aka the Taguba Report) was one of several that looked into the abuse at Abu Ghraib, and argued that the Virginia-based CACI was partially responsible for what took place.

Ghraib scandal.[75] There was a shortage of qualified prison guards and the soldiers that were sent to the prison did not complete their training before they were sent to Iraq. Further, what training soldiers did have was inadequate for the complicated situation they were met with. One of the reports notes that the 800th MP Brigade (the brigade from which most of those charged with war crimes at Abu Ghraib came) was originally designed to conduct standard prisoner of war operations in Kuwait and that the doctrine used on military personnel was out of date. Rather than a rowdy, crowded prison in the middle of a war zone, training had proceeded on the grounds that the troops would be working in a conventional war scenario where prisons were far removed from the battlefield and prisoners were largely compliant and self-disciplining.[76] The result of this inadequate training meant that many of the soldiers sent to Abu Ghraib had a serious lack of knowledge of the Geneva Conventions, and other law of war obligations. Further, a shortage of qualified prison guards meant that prisons, already over-crowded by a mix of criminals, insurgents and "security detainees," meant that the facility was constantly understaffed, placing additional stress on the situation.

Third, the shortage of troops and bad planning that resulted in Coalition forces losing control of major cities as the country plunged into civil war created exceptionally poor conditions upon which to maintain security, let alone a prison in the middle of a war zone. US barracks, infrastructure and assets (including prisons) were constantly being shelled and under attack. Weeks and months of exposure to constant shelling created a high-stress environment for soldiers in the prison that greatly complicated the job of the guards. Almost every US military report looking into the controversy notes that the prison was often under attack by insurgents and inhabited by prisoners that were very hostile to their captors. Additionally, many of the reports note that there was poor-quality food for prisoners and military personnel alike, and a lack of resources (such as secure radios for communication, an internet connection and, in some cases, clothes).[77]

---

[75] Specifically, this was a finding in the July 2004 "Department of the Army, The Inspector General – Detainee Operations Inspection" (aka Mikolashek Report), Schlesinger and Taguba Reports.

[76] This was a conclusion of the Taguba Report.

[77] This was a finding of the Taguba Report, which included a "Psychological Assessment," included in an annex that looked at conditions in the prison.

Noting these factors is not to downplay the responsibility of individual soldiers for their actions in abusing prisoners and engaging in activities that, since their exposure in the media, have hung as a shadow over American efforts in Iraq. Instead, it is to note that there is a direct, traceable connection between belief in the efficacy of a new high-tech American way of warfare that seemed able to unlock almost limitless military capabilities and war crimes such as Abu Ghraib.

Essentially, the situation comes down to this: it is relatively easy to arm a Marine, tell him how to use his high-tech weapons and train him to take a city. However, once that city has been taken, does that soldier have the skills to run it? And what happens when tensions in the city begin to mount, or armed gangs take advantage of the situation? Does his training account for that? How should the laws of war be enforced then? These are not theoretical questions – many young Marines found themselves in this position in 2003. In other words, although soldiers are trained in how to use their weapons, and how to use them legally, can their training account for conditions that are less than ideal? A Marine captain may be trained in leadership and how to conduct operations, but what happens when his job description radically changes in the light of an unpredictable conflict? What happens when they have to think outside the box?

The answers are not always pretty. A survey conducted by the Army Surgeon General's office in 2006 on the mental health and ethical outlook of soldiers and Marines in Iraq found that a third of its 1,767 respondents believed that torture should be allowed if it helped gather important information about insurgents, and more agreed that torture should be used if it helped save the lives of fellow soldiers. Two-thirds of Marines and half the troops surveyed indicated that they would not report a team member for mistreating a civilian or destroying property. Perhaps most disturbingly, 10 percent said that they had personally mistreated a civilian.[78]

The US fixation with conventional, high-tech warfare means that much of the planning and training for law of war issues has been built upon the assumption that this is the kind of warfare soldiers will be engaging in. The end result is clear in both Afghanistan and Iraq: in the

---

[78] See Thomas E. Ricks and Ann Scott Tyson, "Troops at Odds with Ethics Standards," *Washington Post* (May 5, 2007) and Ricks, *The Gamble*, pp. 7–8. See also, Carvin, *Prisoners of America's Wars*, p. 214.

conventional, invasion phase of both conflicts, the implementation of the law of war is good, if not excellent.[79] Although it was certainly the case more in Iraq than Afghanistan, in both conflicts the expectations demanded by the US-conventional paradigm of warfare were met to a large degree. However, once these conflicts transitioned from a conventional to irregular conflict, serious problems arose. While more problems with law of war issues might be inherent in an irregular/guerrilla warfare scenario, it is clear that there was a lack of training for soldiers when the conventional warfare framework they were trained in disappeared.

Once again, this points to the importance of the cultural recognition of warfare in the US historical experience and in the legal-scientific way of war. As in the case with the Native Americans, Filipinos and Vietnamese, where a cultural recognition of warfare was not met (i.e. the means used to engage in conflict were not recognized as "war" proper), there were serious problems for the implementation of the laws of war. And this goes beyond just the US military: high-level civilian lawyers in the Bush Administration (and their supporters) passionately argued that those who did not fight by the laws of war did not deserve their protections, they were merely terrorists, brigands and criminals, undeserving of the "niceties" of international law. Essentially, the same argument made in the nineteenth century was being made in the twenty-first. Over 250 years later, America has still not resolved the problems of applying the laws of war outside the framework of activities they understand as war.

Tossing a COIN

By 2006 it was clear that the Coalition's efforts in Iraq were crumbling. These difficulties dramatically increased on February 22 with the bombing of the Golden Dome Mosque in Sammara, a very important shrine for Shias in Iraq and the global Shia diaspora. The bombing was widely seen as the beginning of the civil war phase of the Iraq conflict and, within the next few weeks, hundreds and eventually thousands would

---

[79] For a summary of issues regarding the 2003 invasion, see Michael N. Schmitt, "Conduct of Hostilities during Operation Iraqi Freedom: An International Humanitarian Law Assessment," *6 Yearbook of International Humanitarian Law* (2003), pp. 73–110.

die as sectarian violence took hold. The Americans were overwhelmed by events and, as this chapter has discussed, too undermanned to do anything about them. By mid-2006, insurgents were detonating approximately 1,000 roadside bombs every week, and the period between mid-2006 and mid-2007 proved to be the bloodiest of the war for the Americans yet, with 1,105 troops killed and an unknown yet certainly high number of Iraqi civilian deaths (estimated to be many times this number of US casualties.) Shias turned on Sunnis and attempted to force the latter to flee Baghdad, and Sunnis turned to violent extremist groups to protect them.[80]

Yet, it was not until fall 2006 that the United States even began to re-evaluate its strategy in Iraq, despite substantial evidence that current one was not working. The mindset that the United States would win through the use of lightly armed, high-tech troops in military bases was firmly rooted. This approach was fully reflected in the US engagement with the Iraqis. As one commentator noted, "there is little dispute that U.S. forces in Iraq over this period were more offensively minded than their Coalition counterparts. For a start, U.S. Rules of Engagement (ROE) were more lenient than other nations, thus encouraging earlier escalation."[81] In other words, when it came to solving problems, "kinetic" solutions were the default option, rather than engaging affected individuals to find an explanation and resolution to the problem. Soldiers were encouraged to *destroy* the enemy, not *defeat* him through other means.[82] Unfortunately, it was not until a number of former military officers, academics and conservative think-tanks began an effort to persuade the President that thinking and planning for the war needed to change that a new approach to the conflict was gradually devised at the end of 2006.

The 2007 "Surge" was controversial and represented a major change in strategy for the United States as it tried to salvage the now deadly situation in Iraq. It was rooted in a turn to counterinsurgency, or COIN, warfare – something we can by now recognize as anathema to conventional US thinking on warfare at this time. It is true that by the end of the conflict in Vietnam the United States had developed a wide range of knowledge and understanding of guerrilla warfare and

[80] Ricks, *The Gamble*, p. 45.
[81] Nigel Aylwin-Foster, "Changing the Army for Counterinsurgency Operations," *Military Review* (November–December 2005), 2–15, p. 4.
[82] *Ibid.*, p. 14.

counterinsurgency. Yet, as this book has argued, the scars of the conflict resulted in this knowledge being lost – downgraded to the category of "Operations Other than War."

The new COIN strategy of the United States was developed at Fort Leavenworth in February 2006 in a meeting convened by General David Petraeus of 135 experts on irregular warfare to develop a new manual on COIN operations, suited for the Iraq War. This manual, *FM 3–24* (the first in twenty years for the Army, and twenty-five years for the Marine Corps), aimed to outline an approach to insurgency as:

a mix of offensive, defensive, and stability operations conducted along multiple lines of operations. It requires Soldiers and Marines to employ a mix of familiar combat tasks and skills more often associated with nonmilitary agencies ... Soldiers and Marines are expected to be nation builders as well as warriors. They must be prepared to help reestablish institutions and local security forces and assist in rebuilding infrastructure and basic services. They must be able to facilitate establishing local governance and the rule of law. The list of such tasks is long; performing them involves extensive coordination and cooperation with many intergovernmental, host-nation, and international agencies.[83]

Essentially, it was an approach to combating the insurgency where military units must interact and live with the target population, live among them and convince the population that they are there to protect them and ensure their security. Such an approach required US troops to leave their bases, engage and mix in the population and exercise a much greater deal of sympathy for civilians in the conflict. Put simply, in targeted areas US troops should not break down doors, but knock on them; they would have to lower their shields, even in the midst of a chaotic situation, and engage with religious and civilian leaders and earn their trust.

Despite the grim associations with guerrilla warfare, the COIN manual made it clear that respect for human rights and cultural understanding are central to the success of a COIN campaign. As argued in *FM 3–24*:

7–25. A key part of any insurgent's strategy is to attack the will of the domestic and international opposition. One of the insurgents' most effective

---

[83] Headquarters, Department of the Army, "Foreword," *FM 3–24/MCWP 3–33.5: Counterinsurgency*, December 2006.

ways to undermine and erode political will is to portray their opposition as untrustworthy or illegitimate. These attacks work especially well when insurgents can portray their opposition as unethical by the opposition's own standards. To combat these efforts, Soldiers and Marines treat noncombatants and detainees humanely, according to American values and internationally recognized human rights standards. In COIN, preserving noncombatant lives and dignity is central to mission accomplishment. This imperative creates a complex ethical environment.[84]

The Manual was clear that this was not an easy task, and it would require new emphasis on cultural understanding – something at which the US forces, with their emphasis on science, technology and engineering, were not particularly adept. Brigadier Nigel Aylwin-Foster, British Army (who worked with US forces in 2004), argued at the end of 2005 that while soldiers were "almost unfailingly courteous and considerate, at times their cultural insensitivity, almost certainly inadvertent, arguably amounted to institutional racism."[85] The US military would now have to teach its soldiers to engage with a people and a culture that was foreign to many, indeed, most.

Although Aylwin-Foster acknowledged that the United States would have to maintain its conventional capability, even as it had to adapt to COIN warfare, Bacevich argued in 2008 that this approach was, in fact, the future face of warfare:

Although advanced technology will retain an important place in [conflicts such as Afghanistan and Iraq], it will not be decisive. Wherever possible, the warrior will rely on "non-kinetic" methods, functioning as diplomat, mediator, and relief worker ...

The soldier on the ground will serve as both cop and social worker. This prospect also implies shedding the sort of utopian expectations that produced so much confident talk of "transformation," "shock-and-awe," and "network-centric warfare" – all of which had tended to segregate war and politics into separate compartments.[86]

This approach was combined with political efforts to reach out to the Sunnis, who by this time were growing frustrated with the violent extremists in their midst. Although groups such as Al Qaeda in Iraq were extremely able at targeting coalition and Iraqi government personnel as

---

[84] Department of the Army, *FM 3–24*.
[85] Aylwin-Foster, "Changing the Army," p. 3.
[86] Bacevich, *The Limits of Power*, pp. 134–135.

well as Shia militias, they were also just as keen to target Sunni moderates and leaders they disagreed with. As tribal elders came to the realization that the Sunni extremist groups they had relied on for security were unreliable and untrustworthy, the Surge was able to take advantage of this "Sunni Awakening." As trust in the coalition-led efforts grew, Sunnis were eventually convinced to take part in a political process that was aimed at bringing some kind of stability to the country.

Conclusion

Despite significant progress by 2011, by no means can it be concluded that the United States won the war. Reflecting on events of the previous two years, Ricks observed: "it is unclear in 2009 if [Petraeus] did much more than lengthen the war. In revising the U.S. approach to the Iraq war, Petraeus found tactical success, that is, improved security, but not the clear political breakthrough that would have meant unambiguous strategic success."[87] Indeed, after US troops departed at the end of 2011, neither the security nor the political situation in Iraq seems to have stabilized. Within months of the US withdrawal, a survey conducted by Minority Rights Group International revealed that minority groups in Iraq still felt at risk, did not trust that the institutions of government could or would protect them, and were still more confident and secure by arming their own ethnic militias.[88] Complicating matters, Iraqi President Nouri al-Maliki has been accused of an increasingly authoritarian approach to governance, again alienating the Sunnis from an already fragile political process. Further, the success of the Islamic State of Iraq and Levant (ISIL – the new name of the group formerly known as Al Qaeda in Iraq) in capturing territory in June 2014, following an eighteen-month period of escalating terrorist violence in Iraq, demonstrates the ongoing weakness, if not outright failure, of the country following the departure of US troops. While the Surge may have had some successes, the United States was unable to translate these into a strategic victory in the form of a true political

[87] Ricks, *The Gamble*, p. 9.
[88] Emma Eastwood, "Months after US Withdrawal, Iraq's Minorities Fear for Safety, Distrust Security Forces and Call for Justice, New Report," *Thomas Reuters: Alernet*, July 19, 2012. Available at: www.trust.org/item/?map=months-after-us-withdrawal-iraqs-minorities-fear-for-safety-distrust-security-forces-and-call-for-justice-new-report (accessed July 1, 2014).

settlement for the country that could at least better enable it to defend itself against extremist groups within its borders.

Although the Americans had hoped to leave some residual forces behind, an inability to secure a basing agreement with the Iraqi government meant that US forces were required legally to leave the country. Now, the main questions surrounding the conflict are what the lessons of the War will be for the US government, the American people and US military.

In the aftermath of Vietnam, a series of US military lawyers sought to bring about change in the way the United States implemented and considered the laws of war. However, the lessons that other military officers took from the conflict were that guerrilla conflicts were something that the United States should try to avoid at all costs in the future, an understandable sentiment, but such a policy proved to be impossible.

So what will be the lessons for a new cadre of upcoming US military leaders, who have gained their experience in the villages of Afghanistan and streets of Iraq? Has COIN moved from "Operations Other than War" to "war"? Will emphasis continue to be placed on "full-spectrum dominance" or counterinsurgency and cultural awareness? Can the United States adjust from a "kinetic"-based force with its core focused on the "annihilation" of its enemies, to one that can find a path to winning its goals while restraining the use of force?

The history recounted in this book suggests that change will be extremely difficult. The US military has been shaped by its history and experience to fight large-scale intra-cultural land wars. An appreciation for wars outside of the Western cultural context is lacking, except in passing reference to such conflicts in military journals. There has been no widespread culture within the US military for understanding non-Western ways of warfare, perhaps because, as historian Victor Davis Hanson hubristically put it, "the West is best."[89] This sort of mindset does not cultivate an understanding of different ways of warfare. The preference for large, set combat warfare within the Western model and predicated on a Western rationality and a Western normative and legal framework also means that unconventional warfare, itself not foreign

---

[89] Victor Hanson Davis, *Why the West Has Won: Culture and Carnage from Salamis to Vietnam* (New York: Faber and Faber, 2002).

to war in the Western world, is also highly discounted. Time and time again the American military (and other Western militaries) have needed to adapt to unconventional or irregular warfare. But the lessons of previous wars have not been internalized. Only time will tell if this event and the lessons learned will make a difference in future military behavior.

6 | Back to the future?

Reportedly fed up with complicated and protracted operations overseas, top Pentagon officials acknowledged this week they were desperate to be given just one straightforward, no-nonsense military engagement they could really knock out of the park.

"Given all these messy, ambiguous conflicts we've been fighting against enemies you can't even put your finger on, what we could really use right now is a plain old war against a clear-cut bad guy employing conventional tactics and weaponry," said Gen. Martin Dempsey, chairman of the Joint Chiefs of Staff. "No roadside bombs or plainclothes militants hiding out among innocent civilians – just a fair fight where two sides shoot at each other and someone wins. That's it."

Citing the country's long history of winning wars against sovereign nations with actual standing armies, the Pentagon's top brass repeatedly assured reporters they would "completely wipe the floor" with such an opponent if given the chance, and promised they would make America "very, very proud."

The Onion, March 28, 2012

The story of the United States at war is a tale of a country greatly influenced by its liberal political culture, geographic position and history. The United States uniquely adapted a specific Western way of war, starting in the early days of the republic, to wage war in a manner compatible with its liberal norms. Isolated geographically, and with a history of military engagements conceptualized as "all or nothing struggles," the American people, American politicians and the American military developed a view of war as an aberration – a necessary struggle to be won quickly, but to also be won in a more or less humane way. A liberal nation, enthralled with science and technology, it has sought to apply its technological prowess to achieve this goal. This has worked in some cases, principally where the opponent fights by the same normative standards, but it has failed spectacularly in others, mainly those that are inter-cultural in nature. Today's challenges, and those of the medium term, are no different.

Droning on and on . . .

This book began with the targeted killing of Anwar al-Awlaki in Yemen in September 2011. The story of al-Awlaki's death embodies the principal challenge facing the United States today: How should Washington combat a continued perceived threat from international terrorists in an era when the public is tired of war and insurgency? Policy-makers believe the insecurity of terrorism remains a primary obstacle that must be dealt with, but their options are limited. Once more the United States has turned to technology as a solution to maintaining security. Drones fit the American way of warfare and its legal-scientific approach to conflict – they are precision-guided weapons that may be used to surgically strike at threats while promising to avoid excessive civilian casualties. Further, rather than requiring the deployment of military troops and the necessary infrastructure that accompanies them, and which can cause problems and resentment in host countries, drones require few, if any, boots on the ground. The risk to American soldiers is minimal. They are seemingly the perfect legal-scientific weapons.

This is not to say they are without their detractors. Many believe the use of drones in this way is immoral and, in reality, little more than assassination.[1] They argue contrary to claims of proportionality and

---

[1] For both sides of the moral and legal debate on drones and targeted killing, see Kenneth Anderson "Predators over Pakistan," *The Weekly Standard* (March 8, 2010), 26–34; Steven R. David, "Fatal Choices: Israel's Policy of Targeted Killing," *Mideast Security and Policy Studies*, No. 51 (2002), "Israel's Policy of Targeted Killing," *Ethics and International Affairs*, Vol. 17, No. 1 (2003), 111–126 and "If Not Combatants, Certainly Not Civilians," *Ethics and International Affairs*, Vol. 17, No. 1 (2003), 138–140; Alan Dershowitz, "Targeted Killing Vindicated," *Huffington Post* (May 2, 2011). Available at: www.huffingtonpost.com/alan-dershowitz/targeted-killing-vindicat_b_856538. html; Michael L. Gross, "Fighting by Other Means in the Mideast: A Critical Analysis of Israel's Assassination Policy," *Political Studies*, Vol. 51 (2003), 350–368 and "Assassination and Targeted Killing: Law Enforcement, Execution or Self-Defence?", *Journal of Applied Philosophy*, Vol. 23, No. 3 (2006), 323–335; Nils Melzer, *Targeted Killing in International Law* (Oxford: Oxford University Press, 2008); Mary Ellen O'Connell, "Unlawful Killing with Combat

distinction made by the Obama Administration that the vast majority of casualties remain civilians.[2] And they express concerns that there are simply no legal grounds for these activities in international law. Further, the al-Awlaki killing has been singled out and criticized by some on the grounds that the United States has targeted one of its own citizens without any due process.[3]

Beyond whether or not the program is morally and legally right or wrong, there are quite simply many unknowns about it, including the central question as to whether or not drone strikes are an effective counterterrorism tactic. Although there have been some studies of the effectiveness of drone strikes published in academic journals, we are still far away from a clear answer to this question.[4] First, as a covert government program, much information about it and its effects are still unknown. Second, even if we could measure the immediate effects of

Drones: A Case Study of Pakistan, 2004–2009," Notre Dame Legal Studies Paper No. 09–43, 2010. Available at: http://papers.ssrn.com/sol3/papers.cfm? abstract_id=1501144, Michael N. Schmitt "Drone Attacks under the Jus ad Bellum and Jus in Bello: Clearing the 'Fog of Law,'" *Yearbook of International Humanitarian Law*, Vol. 13 (2011), 311–326; Yael Stein, "By Any Name Illegal and Immoral," *Ethics and International Affairs*, Vol. 17, No. 1 (2003), 127–137.

[2] See for example the investigation by the Bureau of Investigative Journalists, "Covert War on Terror." Available at: www.thebureauinvestigates.com/category/projects/drones/.

[3] The American Civil Liberties Union has filed a lawsuit on behalf of al-Awlaki's father. Their concerns/arguments are presented on their website. Available at: www.aclu.org/blog/tag/anwar-al-awlaki (accessed July 1, 2014).

[4] There have been a number of studies published in the last ten years. For example, Daniel Byman, "Do Targeted Killings Work?", *Foreign Affairs*, Vol. 85, No. 2 (2006), 95–111 and "Do Targeted Killings Work?", *Foreign Policy* (July 2009). Available at: www.foreignpolicy.com/articles/2009/07/14/do_targeted_killings_work (accessed July 1, 2014); Mohammed M. Hafez and Joseph M. Hatfield, "Do Targeted Assassinations Work? A Multivariate Analysis of Israeli Counter-Terrorism Effectiveness during Al-Aqsa Uprising," *Studies in Conflict & Terrorism*, Vol. 29, No. 4 (2006), 359–382; Patrick B. Johnston *International Security*, Vol. 36, No. 4 (2012), 47–79; Jenna Jordan, "'When Heads Roll' Assessing the Effectiveness of Leadership Decapitation," *Security Studies*, Vol. 18 (2006), 719–755; Lisa Langdon, Alexander J. Sarapu and Matthew Wells, "Targeting the Leadership of Terrorist and Insurgent Movements: Historical Lessons for Contemporary Policy Makers," *Journal of Public and International Affairs*, Vol. 15 (Spring 2004), 59–78; Aaron A. Mannes (2008), "Testing the Snake Head Strategy: Does Killing or Capturing its Leaders Reduce a Terrorist Group's Activity?", *Journal of International Policy Solutions*, Vol. 9 (Spring 2008), 40–49. For a summary and critique of the Drone/Targeted Killing debate up to 2012, see Stephanie Carvin, "The Trouble with Targeted Killing," *Security Studies*, Vol. 21, No. 3 (2012), 529–555.

drones, it is not necessarily the immediate effects that should concern us. It is the second and third order effects of the strikes that may take years, or even decades, to materialize – what will be the effect of drones on civilian populations in ten years' time? It seems that few considered the long-term implications of arming the *mujahedeen* in Afghanistan, and pouring millions of dollars of weaponry into the country. However, it is indisputable that this policy had a major effect on subsequent events. Will the United States be dealing with a similar situation when it comes to drone strikes down the road?

In one sense drones are conventional weapons like any other: they are fired at a target with the aim of eliminating them. On the other hand, their use in the form of targeted killing poses potentially radical implications for the future of war fighting. The current US policy, driven by a legal-scientific warfare paradigm, essentially amounts to a gamble that the future implications of this policy will not be severe and that the technology will continue to help the United States achieve its immediate and long-term objectives.

Yet, reflecting on this book, we can contextualize, if not understand, the turn once again to technology as a solution to the problems posed by war and, specifically, the problems presented by the ongoing War on Terror (even if no politician wants to use this Bush era phrase).

Lessons learned?

As we have argued, the American way of warfare is one imbued with the liberal values of its Revolution and its Enlightenment origins. This has, however, produced two conflicting imperatives: first, to protect itself and its liberal values at all costs (an imperative we have referred to as *annihilation*); second, to do so in a way that is acceptable to liberal/ Enlightenment values, including respect for human rights and the rule of law (an imperative we have referred to as *restraint*). To reconcile these two conflicting imperatives, the United States has increasingly turned to science to create weapons and methods of fighting with the aim of achieving overwhelming victory in a liberal, humanitarian way. This way of war is unique to the United States, but it draws on a wider Western tradition. Other Western states have also used technology to wage war in both humane and inhumane fashions, but today the United States exemplifies this type of warfare given that the rest of the West has largely demilitarized.

As is clear from the history recounted in this book, despite possessing the most advanced and powerful military technology on the planet, problems continue to emerge when policy-makers in Washington use military force as a tool of policy. Significantly, the emphasis on technology as a solution by civilian policy-makers and some senior military leaders created the impression of "cost-less" wars: wars with zero or minimal casualties and wars that can be quickly fought by small numbers of high-tech soldiers. This logic was behind the 1999 Kosovo bombing campaign, the 2001 Afghanistan invasion and the 2003 Iraq War. In all three cases this logic has been shown to be wanting at best. War can never be "costless" in terms of blood and treasure.

The focus on technology as a solution to the challenges of warfare has meant that the United States has difficulty with the "non-kinetic" aspects of warfare and inter-cultural understanding. As such, despite high levels of technology and overwhelming military force, the United States continues to have problems when it encounters enemies that do not meet its cultural expectations of warfare. This reflects a historical trend going as far back as the wars against the Native Americans, the insurgency in the Philippines, Vietnam through to the recent battles in Iraq and Afghanistan. The United States expects to fight a symmetrical military conflict and when it decisively defeats opponents on the field of battle, Americans expect the enemy to surrender. This, however, is not always the case as recent and more historical cases illustrate. The United States has a long history of fighting irregular wars, but Washington never institutionalizes the lessons taught in these conflicts.

Is contemporary history different? Has the United States finally learned from its recent past? The turn to drones and Special Forces operations by the Obama Administration (as well as a professed strategy of "leading from behind") suggests that it is anxious to avoid major wars. At the same time, as argued above, the turn to drones fits perfectly within a pattern of a turning to technology to enhance war fighting and security, even when the consequences of these actions are not clear, and is consistent with the legal-scientific way of warfare described in this book.

It is hard to imagine the United States giving up its technological prowess and focus. As a nation that produces the largest number of patents, has a strong research and development culture and which values its inventors, science and technology remain at the very heart of American values. However, just like US military lawyers who returned from Vietnam convinced that the DoD could do better in terms of implementing and utilizing the laws of war, there may be a generation of officers within the US military who have learned from their experiences in Iraq and Afghanistan and who wish to bring about reform as to how the US military operates. It will be interesting to see if the new generation of officers that have come through the wars of the last decade decide to emphasize the need to improve cultural and historical understandings of other peoples, nations and countries and to emphasize "non-kinetic" skills necessary for successful COIN operations. Or, just like many of the previous generation who fought in Vietnam, will they draw the lesson of "never again," and encourage the military to continue to aim at preparing for the next conventional war?

We do not yet have an answer to this question. While it is likely that the technological focus of the armed forces will remain, it is possible that "non-kinetic" skills may be emphasized alongside it. In fact, in a sign that things may be changing, the US Army released in July 2012 a new "manual" on preventing civilian casualties in warfare. *Army Tactics, Techniques, and Procedures 3–37.31 on "Civilian Casualty Mitigation"* is a first for the US armed forces,[5] and the culmination of a year-long project by Colonel (Ret.) Dwight Raymond of the Army's Peacekeeping and Stability Operations Institute. The Manual has been reported as having received strong support from within the Pentagon.[6] Drawing on the lessons of Iraq and Afghanistan, it seeks to prevent the causes of some otherwise preventable civilian casualties in warfare. Technically the document is not a "Field Manual" (such as *FM 3–24 on Counterinsurgency*), and as such not "doctrine," although it may evolve into doctrine at some point. While this new document is indicative that the US military may be moving in this direction, however, one must also be skeptical as to how much this will really change the overall culture of the military. This attempt at knowledge transfer related to Operations Other than War is an important first step, but it seems that larger social drivers will push war in a different direction – one that perhaps will reinforce the technological obsession within the military for high-tech toys over low-tech and demanding skills.

---

[5] Available at: http://armypubs.army.mil/doctrine/DR_pubs/dr_a/pdf/ attp3_37x31.pdf (accessed July 1, 2014).

[6] Greg McNeal, "Army Publishes New 'Manual' on Preventing Harm to Civilians," *Forbes* (July 19, 2012). Available at: www.forbes.com/sites/ gregorymcneal/2012/07/19/army-publishes-new-manual-on-preventing-harm-to-civilians/ (accessed July 1, 2014).

The elusive and enchanting cost-free war

Within the corridors of power, it is not clear if there is a desire to rethink attitudes toward the use of force. Instead it seems that many politicians and policy-makers seem to remain enchanted with the use of force to achieve political objectives. Under the Administration of President Obama the allocation of force is shifting away from the massive, ground invasions used in Iraq, and to a lesser extent in Afghanistan, toward a more "intervention light" model. This was recently evident in the case of Libya, where politicians in Europe and the United States (in particular the interventionist wing of the Obama Administration comprised of individuals such as Anne-Marie Slaughter, Susan Rice and Samantha Power) pushed for military intervention to prevent potential human rights abuses by the Kaddafi regime during that country's civil war. The politicians sold the case for a no-fly zone and the regime change on the premise that it would be easy, but the logic of their argument was far from sound given that studies illustrate that effecting strategic change only with air power is rarely effective. Politicians on both sides of the Atlantic also undersold the difficulties in implementing a no-fly zone.[7] Compared to Afghanistan and Iraq, the model for this intervention was more dependent on air power and "smart weapons" than it was on troops on the ground. And although the conflict dragged on longer than anticipated and many of the problems predicted by critics of the plan came to pass, the overall intervention "succeeded" in ousting Kaddafi.

Importantly, the belief that a strategic solution to the Libyan crisis could be found in a limited bombing campaign is reflective of the continued desire for easy solutions promised by modernity. But, once again in line with the rather astrategic approach favored by the Americans, overall strategic and political success remains elusive. Instability in North Africa after Kaddafi's ousting continues, and concern over the ability of a post-Kaddafi Libya to develop its security and governance institutions – essential for stability – remains. The storming of US diplomatic facilities and the murder of US Ambassador to Libya, Christopher Stevens, highlight the lingering dangers of what was

---

[7] Michael Williams, "The Fatally Flawed Logic of a No-Fly Zone," *Guardian*: Comment is Free (March 17, 2011). Available at: www.theguardian.com/commentisfree/cifamerica/2011/mar/17/libya-unitednations (accessed August 2, 2012).

supposedly a "successful" intervention. Worse still, Tuareg fighters, long sponsored by the Kaddafi regime, returned to Mali after his ousting, contributing to an uprising in early 2012 that eventually saw half of the country taken over by Islamist extremists. It was not until a limited French invasion, with assistance from the United States and other European countries, in December 2012 that the Islamist forces were removed from power. Mali, however, remains unstable and the fighters remain a significant threat to regional security.

Can we expect this attitude within the American government to continue? The distinct lack of enthusiasm for Western, specifically American, engagement in Syria in the early fall of 2013 to punish the regime of President Bashar al-Assad for its use of chemical weapons is indicative that the American people, and members of Congress, may be tiring of wars overseas – even "clean" ones – that seem removed from their direct interests. After nearly fifteen years of constant "war," even "intervention light" may be too much for an American public skeptical about the true benefit of US military efforts overseas since 9/11. While the prospect of limited and cost-free interventions may continue to "enchant" those who believe that Western military might can and should be used to achieve broadly defined American interests overseas, an increasingly doubtful public, willing to challenge the true costs of "easy war," may place a damper on any interventionist ambitions of future administrations if they are not able to sell their case. Perhaps the hesitation over Syria is just one example that will not be repeated – whether or not it is a long-term trend away from the use of force is far from certain.

Post-human warfare: the next logical step?

Although the US military has worked to develop a better inherent ability to fight wars beyond its cultural comfort zone since General Petraeus' "Surge" in Iraq, warfare continues to evolve in a rather different direction. The story of the Western way of warfare is the continued dehumanization of war. For the Greeks, war, although bloody and brutal, was a very humanistic experience that placed the individual at the center of battle. Essentially, there was an integral existential aspect to the conflict and the place of the warrior in it. But over the centuries as war has become more instrumental and technology applied to make it more effective, humans have been and continue to be slowly written out of the equation.

Interestingly, there is dissent regarding these developments from within the very armed forces that are undergoing this transformation. For example, some members of the Air Force are concerned that such technological developments are increasingly taking trained pilots, who have long seen themselves as moral agents in warfare within a "fighter mystique," and reducing them to a cog in a weapons machine:

Although the prestige occupation of the Air Force remains the single-seat fighter pilot, increasingly it is not the pilots who select or even aim their weapons. Instead, weapons are programmed to strike specific coordinates by weaponeers on the ground. Targets are selected and collateral damage modeled by the targeteers, also on the ground. Increasingly, in other words, the pilot and aircraft are a delivery system for weapons that, once released in the vicinity of their targets, are largely autonomous.[8]

Yet, the two great world wars of the twentieth century destroyed much of the Western belief in the glory and valor of war, particularly in Europe. Wilfred Owen's poem penned near the end of the Great War, "Dulce et decorum Est," is indicative of the death of the warrior mentality in Europe that began in the early twentieth century. In the United States the ideal of military valor retains some appeal, but not much. Most American families would rather not see their children join the military, and increasingly those that do join, especially at the enlisted level, do so as a tool of social mobility as evidenced in the demography of the US armed forces.[9]

Although much has been written about the RMA over the last twenty years, most, if not all, of the literature overlooks the social component of change in the Western world that utilizes technological advancement. After all, RMAs historically occur to overcome a problem, and the RMA that we are living through is one driven by the problem that, increasingly, Western societies do not want to fight wars (even if politicians do).[10]

---

[8] Martin Cook, "Teaching Military Ethics in the United States Air Force: Challenges Posed by Service Culture," in Don Carrick, James Connelly and Paul Robinson (eds.), *Ethics Education for Irregular Warfare* (Farnham: Ashgate, 2009), pp. 107–111, p. 110.

[9] Sabrina Tavernise, "As Fewer Americans Serve, Gap is Growing between Civilians and Military," *New York Times*, March 24, 2011. Available at: www.nytimes.com/2011/11/25/us/civilian-military-gap-grows-as-fewer-americans-serve.html?_r=0 (accessed August 2, 2012).

[10] M. J. Williams, "The Coming Revolution in Foreign Affairs: Rethinking American National Security," *International Affairs*, Vol. 84, No. 6 (2008), 1112–1113.

Today the challenge is not a military one, it is a social one. Social drivers are pushing away from an engaged approach toward threats and security problems to a more disengaged approach centered on risk management where society expects technology, not people, to manage the risks.

The real RMA is the move away from human-centric warfare to post-human warfare. Technological innovation is making the idea of post-human warfare a reality, as is the post-modern nature of the West, where the idea that one should risk death for one's country is increasingly questioned. This is the argument made by Martin van Creveld and Christopher Coker, who observe that societies talk about soldiers not simply being killed, but "wasted" in war.[11] As noted above, families, particularly those that only have one or two children, do not want to lose one in a conflict. This marks a change from a century ago where it was common to have large families as an economic unit to sustain the family, and it was normal for children to die at an early age. Today, with smaller families and the expectation of a long life span, the loss of a child is seemingly much more tragic.

The result of this social change when coupled with technology is a move toward unmanned warfare. Far removed from the Greek citizen-soldier, or even the "Surge" that was used in Iraq, humans are seemingly destined to become only a processor in a much larger network, if not removed from the system all together. As Alvin and Heidi Toffler write in *War and Anti-War*, "Put simply, weapons or equipment in harm's way should, to the extent possible, be unmanned," the objective being "the reduction or total elimination of human risk."[12]

The result of applied science in Western warfare is that warfare today, when waged in the Western model, can be statistically safer for soldiers than staying home on base.[13] New technologies, such as unmanned aerial systems, make it relatively costless for Washington to use force when and where it wants. Because few, if any, US soldiers are placed in harm's way, the public often fails to engage with the matter. Therefore the inherent

---

[11] Christopher Coker, *Waging War without Warriors* (Boulder, CO: Lynne Rienner, 2002), p. 59; Martin van Creveld, "War," in Robert Cowley and Geoffrey Parker (eds.), *The Osprey Companion to Military History* (London: Osprey, 1996), pp. 497–498.

[12] Alvin and Heidi Toffler, *War and Anti-War* (New York: Grand Central Publishing, 1995), p. 134.

[13] Christopher Coker, *Humane Warfare* (London: Routledge, 2001), p. 12.

pressures of a democratic polity that influence politicians when they make policy decisions are greatly reduced.

The danger in this situation is that it lays the possible foundations for endless war, or, at least, endless security "exercises." If the population of the United States becomes further removed from conflict it may be increasingly possible for Western policy-makers and military leaders to conduct military operations beyond the scope of the population. As the adage goes, "out of sight, out of mind." This is evidenced in places like the Balkans and Afghanistan where, as the US force commitment draws down, the population becomes more tolerant of remaining operations, as they are simply less visible. This is also the case with the current use of drones in the War on Terror. Since the risk to US forces is minimal, few – if any – average Americans are worried about the possible blow-back of drone operations, the moral hazards of the American drone program or whether the program is even truly effective.

Will this mean that in the future the US government will be able to apply force with fewer restrictions on action from the public? Given the lack of one serious geographic, state-based threat confronting the United States today, the endemic insecurity of world politics means that the United States may feel free to use military force here, there and everywhere as a way to manage insecurity and risk. When coupled with the relatively astrategic approach of the United States in many of these conflicts, this promises to be a series of lessons in disaster. As in Iraq and Afghanistan, the danger is that the military and American politicians will see technology as a panacea for all the insecurity risks that plague the United States, rather than investing in the long hard diplomacy and economic development of areas with stubborn insecurity problems. Force cannot fix the many challenges facing the United States from the Middle East to Asia, but the danger of future warfare is that as it becomes further re-enchanted the United States will use it more frequently and with less oversight then ever in its history.

We are not alone in our concern over the seeming militarization of US foreign relations and a tendency within American society to resort too often to the use of force to solve problems overseas. Robert Gates, the twenty-second US Secretary of Defense, who served for the last two years of the George W. Bush Administration and the first three and a half years of the Obama Administration, also sounded a clarion call about the bipartisan militarization of American foreign policy.

Wars are a lot easier to get into than out of. Those who ask about exit strategies or question what will happen if assumptions prove wrong are rarely welcome at the conference table when the fire-breathers are demanding that we strike – as they did when advocating invading Iraq, intervening in Libya and Syria, or bombing Iran's nuclear sites. But in recent decades, presidents confronted with tough problems abroad have too often been too quick to reach for a gun. Our foreign and national security policy has become too militarized, the use of force too easy for presidents.

Today, too many ideologues call for U.S. force as the first option rather than a last resort. On the left, we hear about the "responsibility to protect" civilians to justify military intervention in Libya, Syria, Sudan and elsewhere. On the right, the failure to strike Syria or Iran is deemed an abdication of U.S. leadership. And so the rest of the world sees the U.S. as a militaristic country quick to launch planes, cruise missiles and drones deep into sovereign countries or ungoverned spaces. There are limits to what even the strongest and greatest nation on Earth can do – and not every outrage, act of aggression, oppression or crisis should elicit a U.S. military response.

This is particularly worth remembering as technology changes the face of war. A button is pushed in Nevada, and seconds later a pickup truck explodes in Mosul. A bomb destroys the targeted house on the right and leaves the one on the left intact. For too many people – including defense "experts," members of Congress, executive branch officials and ordinary citizens – war has become a kind of videogame or action movie: bloodless, painless and odorless. But my years at the Pentagon left me even more skeptical of systems analysis, computer models, game theories or doctrines that suggest that war is anything other than tragic, inefficient and uncertain.[14]

Gates' warning does not sound so different from that of a predecessor, Robert McNamara. McNamara wrote that the United States was possessed by an "ineradicable tendency to think of our security problem as being exclusively a military problem ... We are haunted by this concept of military hardware."[15] Decades later this problem still plagues the United States, and technology, as Gates notes, will change war further. By the time this book is published, new developments in warfare will undoubtedly have taken place and American leaders will continue to be

---

[14] Robert M. Gates, "The Quiet Fury of Robert Gates," *The Wall Street Journal* (January 7, 2014). Available at: http://online.wsj.com/news/articles/SB10001424052702304617404579306851526222552 (accessed July 1, 2014).
[15] Fred Kaplan, *The Wizards of Armageddon* (New York: Simon & Schuster, 1984), p. 336.

enchanted by the idea of cost-free war. Without critical thought the United States will remain a slave to technology, and always believe that technology will set it free from war as a brutal act, when in the end it simply perpetuates the same mistakes over and over again. As such, we assert that the history recounted in this book provides at least ten lessons which US policy-makers, military planners and citizens should take to heart as they decide how to confront and act in the crises of the future:

1. War is and never will be "easy" or cost-free.
2. Technology may help to mitigate casualties but there are no "clean" wars.
3. Fascination with technology and the results it can produce may preclude hard thinking about larger strategic goals and how they can be achieved.
4. Diplomacy and political settlements and solutions will always be more effective than the smartest weapons.
5. Weapons will continue to play an important role in compellence and deterrence.
6. Americans have struggled and will continue to struggle to understand their unconventional enemies, even if they are able to militarily dominate them for at least the medium term.
7. For Western countries there is very rarely strategic gain from violations of the laws of war.
8. The United States will continue to wrestle with the question of how to balance "annihilation" and "restraint" for at least the medium and likely the long term.
9. A turn to post-human warfare will not solve the dilemmas posed by the dueling imperatives of "annihilation" and "restraint."
10. Answering the questions related to how the United States should balance "annihilation" and "restraint" will require more than a technological perspective, and should include the insights of political science, international relations, history, ethics and philosophy.

The US military is arguably the most powerful in the world, but, to paraphrase Lord Acton, power corrupts and absolute power corrupts absolutely. This may be problematic for the United States in the coming years as the nation faces an unstable world of rising powers coupled with non-traditional security risks, particularly those posed by the fall-out of the Arab Spring. Given the technological edge of the United States and the need for a proactive doctrine of risk management, it may come to pass that the US utilizes what Martin Shaw terms "risk transfer militarism" in a bid to maintain its own security – the waging of perpetual war to prevent the realization of security risks in the homeland, all the while subjecting foreign populations to the collateral damage of American military strikes with drones.[16] Even given the distinct reluctance among the population of the United States to intervene in Syria it remains to be seen if the liberal political norms of the United States will serve as an effective enough check on the desire to wield American power in an excessive fashion in what is perceived as an ever more globalized and ever more insecure world. This tendency to intervene may worsen given the redistribution of power in the international system, away from the United States and to other poles in the system – making it more likely that an insecure superpower will attempt to wield military power to maintain the status quo.[17] Wise leadership across the American political system – executive and legislative – can prevent this outcome, but such leadership is not a given. The danger, as John Quincy Adams warned in 1821, is that in going abroad in search of monsters to destroy, the United States will become dictatress of the world – a fate most decidedly not becoming of a great liberal nation.

---

[16] Martin Shaw, "Risk Transfer Militarism, Small Massacres and the Historical Legitimacy of War," *International Relations*, Vol. 16, No. 3 (December 2002).
[17] Charles Kupchan, *How Enemies Become Friends: The Source of Stable Peace* (Princeton, NJ: Princeton University Press, 2012); Charles Kupchan, Emmanuel Adler, Jean-Marc Coicaud and Yuen Foong Khong, *Power in Transition: The Peaceful Change of International Order* (Tokyo: United Nations University Press, 2001).

Index